Kim R

P9-BBQ-039

FEELING CLOSE—
The New Loneliness Therapy

How many of these negative thoughts do you recognize? "It's a couples world." "There's nothing really special about me." "I can't live without him/her." "It doesn't pay to be loving and trusting." If you've experienced any of these pessimistic feelings, you may be lonely, but you're not alone. Drawn from over 15,000 therapy sessions with people who shared your problem, this warm, supportive book provides a successful problem-solving approach to breaking out of loneliness—to a lifetime of joyful independence and genuine closeness to other people.

INTIMATE CONNECTIONS

"This commonsense approach to shyness earns the reader's trust. Recommended."—*Library Journal*

"Clear and Compassionate."
—*Richmond Times Dispatch*

DAVID D. BURNS, M.D., is the President of the Behavioral Sciences Research Foundation and Director of the Institute for Cognitive and Behavioral Therapies at the Presbyterian–University of Pennsylvania Medical Center in Philadelphia. Among the many awards and fellowships he has received is the A. E. Bennett Award from the Society of Biological Psychiatry for his research on the chemistry of moods. Readers wishing to contact the author may write to him at: Presbyterian–University of Pennsylvania Medical Center, 39th & Market, Philadelphia, Pa. 19104.

⊘ SIGNET   Ⓜ MENTOR

HELPFUL GUIDES

(0451)

☐ **FEELING GOOD: The New Mood Therapy by David Burns, M.D.** This one-of-a-kind integrated approach to depression introduces the principles of Cognitive Therapy, which illustrate that by changing the way we think we can alter our moods and get rid of depression. (146905—$4.95)

☐ **INTIMATE CONNECTIONS by David D. Burns, M.D.** In this breakthrough book, Dr. David Burns, author of the bestselling *Feeling Good*, applies the proven principles of Cognitive Therapy to eliminating the negative thinking and low self-esteem that cause loneliness and shyness, and shows you how to make close friends and find a loving partner.
(148452—$4.95)*

☐ **BORN TO WIN: Transactional Analysis with Gestalt Experiments by Muriel James and Dorothy Jongeward.** This landmark bestseller has convinced millions of readers that they were **Born to Win!** "Enriching, stimulating, rewarding ... for anyone interested in understanding himself, his relationships with others and his goals."—*Kansas City Times*
(141954—$4.50)*

☐ **UNDERSTANDING YOURSELF by Dr. Christopher Evans.** An interesting collection of questionnaires, tests, quizzes and games, scientifically designed by a team of psychologists to offer a greater self-awareness. Photographs and illustrations included. (134532—$4.95)

☐ **OVERCOMING PROCRASTINATION by Albert Ellis, Ph.D. and William J. Knaus, Ed.D.** The scientifically proven techniques of Rational-Motive Therapy are applied to procrastination (delaying tactics, frustration, and self-disgust). Examines the causes of procrastination, and the links between procrastination and obesity, drugs, depression, and sexual dysfunction, and other personality and health problems.
(152085—$3.95)

*Prices slightly higher in Canada

Buy them at your local bookstore or use this convenient coupon for ordering.

NEW AMERICAN LIBRARY,
P.O. Box 999, Bergenfield, New Jersey 07621

Please send me the books I have checked above. I am enclosing $_____
(please add $1.00 to this order to cover postage and handling). Send check or money order—no cash or C.O.D.'s. Prices and numbers are subject to change without notice.

Name_____

Address_____

City_____ State_____ Zip Code_____

Allow 4-6 weeks for delivery.
This offer is subject to withdrawal without notice.

INTIMATE
CONNECTIONS

David D. Burns, M.D.

A SIGNET BOOK

NEW AMERICAN LIBRARY

PUBLISHER'S NOTE

The ideas, procedures, and suggestions contained in this book are no
intended as a substitute for consulting with your physician. All matter
regarding your health require medical supervision.

NAL BOOKS ARE AVAILABLE AT QUANTITY DISCOUNTS WHEN USED
TO PROMOTE PRODUCTS OR SERVICES. FOR INFORMATION PLEASE
WRITE TO PREMIUM MARKETING DIVISION. NAL PENGUIN INC.,
1633 BROADWAY. NEW YORK. NEW YORK 10019.

Copyright © 1985 by David D. Burns, M.D.

All rights reserved. No part of this book may be reproduced or utilize
in any form or by any means, electronic or mechanical, including photocopying
recording or by any information storage and retrieval system, without permissio
in writing from the publisher. For information address William Morrow an
Company, Inc., 105 Madison Avenue, New York, New York 10016.

Published by arrangement with William Morrow and Company, Inc.

SIGNET TRADEMARK REG. U.S. PAT. OFF. AND FOREIGN COUNTRIES
REGISTERED TRADEMARK—MARCA REGISTRADA
HECHO EN CHICAGO, U.S.A.

SIGNET, SIGNET CLASSIC, MENTOR, ONYX, PLUME, MERIDIAN
and NAL BOOKS are published by NAL PENGUIN INC.,
1633 Broadway, New York, New York 10019

First Signet Printing, November, 1985

5   6   7   8   9   10   11   12

PRINTED IN THE UNITED STATES OF AMERICA

This book is dedicated to lonely, shy people.
I hope that reading it will help you love and appreciate yourself
and in the process learn to get closer to others.

Contents

Preface

In 1980 I published a book entitled *Feeling Good: The New Mood Therapy*. The book described a new approach to understanding human behavior and emotions called "cognitive behavior therapy." This therapy is based on the idea that your thoughts, or "cognitions," have a tremendous impact on the way you feel and behave. You're probably aware that when you're down in the dumps, life begins to look bleak and you start to think about things in a gloomy, pessimistic way. You may not, however, be aware that your negative thoughts can actually trigger a blue mood and create feelings of pessimism. What is even mroe remarkable is the discovery, now confirmed by independent investigators around the world, that as people learn to think about themselves in a more positive and realistic way, using cognitive therapy techniques, they can overcome painful feelings and experience greater self-esteem and intimacy—often in a remarkable short period of time.

Researchers, clinicians, and the general public have expressed a tremendous interest in the cognitive approach for the following reasons:

• It's solidly grounded in an impressive body of research at academic centers throughout the United States and Europe. Psychiatrists and psychologists at the Washington University Medical School in St. Louis, the Southwestern Medical School in Dallas, the University of Edinburgh in Scotland, and the University of Minnesota in St. Paul have all confirmed the findings of a remarkable study conducted at the University of Pennsylvania in the late 1970s which showed that cognitive therapy is as effective as the best known antidepressant drugs in the treatment of severe depression.

• The interventions are practical and based on easy-to-understand methods and common sense.

• The methods frequently work rapidly, so you don't have to resort to years and years of costly analysis on a psychiatrist's couch.

• People with milder mood problems can use cognitive techniques on their own without having to resort to the use of medications or the help of a professional therapist.

• The basic theory is straightforward, philosophically exciting, and compatible with most people's personal values and religious beliefs.

Cognitive behavior therapy's remarkable impact on the current practice of psychotherapy can best be epitomized by a recent study by Dr. Darrell Smith that appeared in the journal *American Psychologist* in July, 1982. Dr. Smith surveyed a random sample of eight hundred clinical and counseling psychologists to determine their evaluations of the current status of various schools of psychotherapy. Dr. Smith concluded that "cognitive-behavioral options represent one of the strongest, if not *the* strongest, theoretical emphasis today."

This book will illustrate the application of cognitive behavior therapy to loneliness, shyness, and sexual insecurity. In my clinical practice, I have observed that people who have trouble developing close personal relationships often have much in common with people who are depressed: They suffer from low self-esteem; they're terrified by disapproval, rejection, or being alone; they're defensive and afraid of criticism; and they're excessively self-critical and judgmental because of unrealistically high expectations for themselves and others. These problems can frequently be reversed using the same cognitive therapy techniques that have shown so much promise in the treatment of depression.

As you read about these techniques and you begin to apply them to your own life, keep in mind that every human being is unique. An idea that seems clear and obvious when you read about it may not always produce the expected result when you attempt to apply it on your own. Remember that a self-help book is never intended as a substitute for professional treatment, and if a problem in the way you feel or relate to others has persisted for more than a month in spite of your own efforts to correct it, then it might be wise to obtain a consultation with a good psychiatrist, psychologist, or counselor.

Having said that, let me emphasize how rewarding it is for me to work with people who've felt lonely, rejected, or inferior for years and who suddenly begin to blossom and experience a surge of joy and self-confidence. If you've been feeling down and have had trouble getting close to people, I hope that you, too, will experience greater self-esteem and love for others as you read this book.

Acknowledgments

I would like to set the record straight. Cognitive therapy *is not* my creation or the brainchild of any single individual. Its development has been a team effort. Hundreds of leading psychiatrists and psychologists at top academic institutions around the world have been systematically. and painstakingly researching and developing the concepts presented in this book and in *Feeling Good: The New Mood Therapy*. I feel fortunate to have had the opportunity to help develop and popularize these exciting ideas, and at times I have probably received more than my fair share of the limelight. To give appropriate credit to all the people who have made major contributions to this new approach would require a book as long as this one! However, I would like to mention the names of several illuminaries whose creativity and research simply cannot be overlooked. Certainly Dr. Albert Ellis and Dr. Aaron T. Beck are two of the earliest pioneers whose courageous leadership was crucial in establishing the credibility and enthusiasm for those revolutionary methods long before they achieved the popularity and recognition they enjoy today. Other prominent researchers include Drs. Michael Mahoney, Donald Meichenbaum, Marvin Goldfried, Martin Seligman, Arnold Lazarus, Maria Kovacs, Norman Epstein, George Murphy, Ivy Blackburn, John Teasdale, Peter Lewinsohn, Steve Hollon, Lynn Rehm, John Rush, Gary Emery, Brian Shaw, and many, many more. Individuals who have played a major role in the application of cognitive therapy techniques to the problem of loneliness include Drs. Laura Primakoff and Jeffrey Young. I also want to acknowledge the contribution of Drs. Letitia Anne Peplau and Daniel Perlman, whose recent book *Loneliness: A Sourcebook of Current Theory, Research and Therapy* (New York: John Wiley & Sons, 1982) provides a useful overview of the rapidly expanding field of loneliness research in the United States and abroad.

I would like to thank Dr. Judy Eidelson for her thoughtful reading of the manuscript, and in particular for her combination of warmth and expertise as the clinical director of our institute.

I would like to mention several of my students who have been particularly influential in shaping my thinking. In particular, Dr. Stirling Morey and Tony Bates taught me a great deal about empathy, caring, and the importance of value systems. They both live by the philosophies that they teach, and they are fine therapists and scholars. Dr. Jacqueline Persons has been instrumental in encouraging creative research and the spirit of trust and collaboration among colleagues. You have all been a joy and inspiration to me. Thank you!

Drs. Gary Zimberg, Joe Volpicelli, Hyong Un, and Charlotte Swenson have provided valuable suggestions for improving the manuscript. I am grateful for their support and their friendship.

I would like to thank Howell Herring for the many long hours he put in analyzing the data that helped to shape the ideas in this book. During the first half of 1984, Howell unselfishly gave up practically every Saturday to sit down with me at the computer creating mathematical models that have proven invaluable in understanding loneliness and personal relationship problems.

I would like to give a special acknowledgment to my editors, Maria Guarnaschelli and Arnold Dolin. Maria's incredible energy and vision were a continual source of inspiration, and Arnold's advice and support facilitated the teamwork that made this project happen.

I would especially like to thank my assistant, Mary Lovell, for long, long hours far beyond the call of duty. I would also like to thank Mary on behalf of the thousands of people from around the country who have called my office or written requesting guidance and help. Mary has responded to them warmly and unselfishly and has provided that spark of hope on so many occasions. Most of all, I want to thank Mary for believing in me and for showing me the way to success.

I would like to acknowledge the contribution of the many patients who unselfishly let me tell their stories—in disguised form—in this book. Sharing your feelings and problems with others is an intimate gift that takes considerable courage. Many readers will read about you and say, "That sounds so much like me. It's such a relief to know I'm human and I'm not alone!"—thank you!

Finally, I would like to thank my wife, Melanie, for her endless patience, brilliant editing, and moral support.

A Personal Introduction

Loneliness is a problem I personally endured for the first twenty-six years of my life. From the time I was a child I felt ugly and awkward. My nicknames were "Einstein" and "Bag-a-bones." In grammar school I was rarely invited to parties. When I did go, I never participated in the really *fun* games—such as spin the bottle—because I was brought up in a very conservative religious family and my mother told me that kissing girls was wrong. When the kissing games began, I would excuse myself as politely as possible and stand on the sidelines feeling pretty left out.

In high school it seemed as if the girls I was interested in rarely had any interest in me. I went out with a few "nice" girls who admired me, but they weren't the girls I thought were really exciting. One problem was that I didn't have a good physique—my shoulders were round and my chest wasn't muscular. I tried out for football and basketball teams my freshman year, but I wasn't very talented athletically, so I was cut from both teams and gave up on sports. To make matters worse, my voice didn't change and my beard didn't start to grow until my junior year. I thought I'd never develop and contented myself that I just wasn't meant to be one of the "in people."

In all fairness, I must say I wasn't a complete outcast. Some people seemed to admire me from a distance. I received many honors and awards for my scholastic achievements, and I was often elected to student body offices—

probably because I always made a point of being nice to my teachers and classmates and because people respected me for my seriousness and intelligence—but I was lonely and didn't feel close to very many people. The idea of "scoring" with an attractive girl seemed remote at best.

My social life at Amherst College was equally meager. It was still a men's college in the 1960s, and I wasn't accepted by any of the more socially oriented fraternities, so it wasn't easy to meet women. Medical school was my final hope for a better social life. I thought a Stanford medical student might be in high demand, and California seemed as if it would be teeming with available women. However, my situation didn't improve very dramatically, and it wasn't for want of trying. I would often walk around the campus and into the nearby town of Palo Alto, trying to meet girls. Occasionally I'd sit for hours in the student union trying to strike up conversations with women. Whenever I saw an attractive woman I would greet her with lame comments such as: "Oh, what's your name? Do you go to school here? I'm a medical student," and so on. Within a minute or two she would inevitably excuse herself by saying, "I'm just waiting here for my boyfriend, who will be along any minute." This was discouraging, but I'd nevertheless try again. And again. And again. I probably became one of the most rejected men in Northern California, since I accumulated as many as fifty to sixty rejections per week. Despite a success rate of approximately zero, I continued to pursue the opposite sex, figuring that maybe *somehow* I might soon learn the ropes. All around me other people were flirting and having fun together, and I'd think, "How do they do that? Why can't I do that?"

Finally, I decided I needed a tutor to show me what I was doing wrong. I had heard about a young man named William who had a reputation as Palo Alto's Don Juan. He was a part-time junior college student who lived with his mother and drove around Palo Alto on an old motor scooter. He supported himself with various part-time jobs, one of them as a salesman in a fashionable men's clothing store. He didn't have any special status or career. But William did have one area of undeniable, incredible genius—

attracting women. They simply found him irresistible. While I was collecting an astounding string of rejections, he was being pursued by every woman in town. Though I don't mean to advocate his womanizing as a way of life, it seemed clear that if I was to get anyplace in dating, I needed to learn the secrets of a great master.

After I got to know William, I explained my problem and asked him if he'd be willing to help me. He taught me the attitudes and techniques that made him so successful and soon I discovered that I could make these principles work for me as well. This triggered one of the happiest periods of my life. My social life went from rags to riches practically overnight.

I learned that my insecurities were the result of erroneous assumptions I'd had about myself and the world since I was a child. And with a little determination and guidance, a touch of youthful creativity, and William's friendship, I discovered that those patterns could be changed. I learned that it was okay to be more sensual and direct with women, and I found the courage to conquer the fears and feelings of inferiority that had been holding me back. Then one day, when the glitter of my wild-oats sowing was beginning to lose its luster, I met a wonderful girl and we decided to spend our lives together and to raise a family.

Although what I learned has since been complemented by years of research and clinical work, my personal experience in conquering loneliness has given me the insight and ideas that have been very helpful to the many lonely people I have treated. One of them, a twenty-six-year-old single woman, told me she had been large, clumsy, and awkward as a child. She was often teased and ostracized by her playmates and had difficulty making friends. As an adolescent she felt hopeless about ever dating or developing a meaningful relationship with a boy. Her terrible self-image functioned as a self-fulfilling prophecy and she ballooned to nearly 300 pounds by the time she entered college. After losing more than 150 pounds through incredible determination, she found she still felt inadequate and depressed and had difficulty getting close to people. During the course of therapy she realized that her loneliness had more to do with her negative self-image than with her actual appearance. As she learned how to think of herself as an attractive, desirable woman and to develop greater self-esteem, her chronic feelings of loneliness and depression faded away and her relationships with men began to blossom.

Another patient I've recently treated is a thirty-five-year-old single man who's just now beginning to have his first taste of self-confidence and success with women, recently told me, "Dr. Burns, you're finally teaching me what I need to know. I've gone to psychiatrists for the past ten years because I felt lonely and inadequate. They just said, 'Go out and get some dates,' but they never taught me how to do it the way you do, and it was just a waste of time. Why didn't they use these same techniques and teach me the same things you're teaching me?" The reason is that psychiatrists and psychologists are only now beginning to understand the causes of loneliness and to develop a systematic, effective approach for treating it. If you've longed to develop new approaches to meeting the opposite sex, and to overcome the shyness and insecurity that have plagued you, then I hope this will be your textbook. Instead of feeling undesirable and left out, I want you to discover the beauty within yourself so you can then reach out to others and learn what a wonderful adventure life can be.

PART ONE

THE GOOD NEWS ABOUT LONELINESS

1

Are You Lonely?

Do you ever feel lonely and wish you had better relationships with people? If so, you're not as alone as you might think. As you can see in Table 1-1, in one recent national study by *Psychology Today* magazine, more than 50 percent of the 40,000 people surveyed reported they sometimes or often felt lonely. This suggests that loneliness afflicts more than 100 million Americans. While these figures may sound discouraging, the good news is that scientists are beginning to understand the causes of loneliness and to develop effective techniques that can boost your self-esteem and enhance your relationships with others.

The following self-assessment test will help you determine how lonely you are. This scale measures positive and negative feelings people sometimes have about themselves and others. After you read each statement, circle the dot that indicates how much it describes the way you feel

TABLE 1-1
Percentage of People in Different Age Groups Who Said They Felt Lonely "Sometimes" or "Often"*

Under 18	18–24	25–34	35–44	45–54	Over 54
79%	71%	69%	60%	53%	37%

*Adapted from M. B. Parlee, "The Friendship Bond: PT's Survey Report on Friendship in America," *Psychology Today* (October 1979).

3

between "Not at all" and "Nearly always." Read each statement carefully. Some of them are worded in such a way that a positive, happy feeling is indicated by "Nearly always," and others are so worded that an unhappy, negative feeling is indicated by "Nearly always." There are no "correct" or "incorrect" answers, so try to answer all the items according to the way you have been feeling recently.

The Loneliness Scale

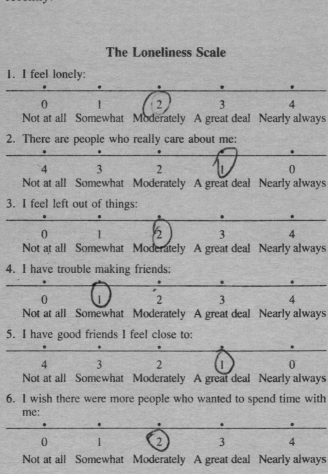

1. I feel lonely:

0	1	(2)	3	4
Not at all	Somewhat	Moderately	A great deal	Nearly always

2. There are people who really care about me:

4	3	2	(1)	0
Not at all	Somewhat	Moderately	A great deal	Nearly always

3. I feel left out of things:

0	1	(2)	3	4
Not at all	Somewhat	Moderately	A great deal	Nearly always

4. I have trouble making friends:

0	(1)	2	3	4
Not at all	Somewhat	Moderately	A great deal	Nearly always

5. I have good friends I feel close to:

4	3	2	(1)	0
Not at all	Somewhat	Moderately	A great deal	Nearly always

6. I wish there were more people who wanted to spend time with me:

0	1	(2)	3	4
Not at all	Somewhat	Moderately	A great deal	Nearly always

7. There are people I can talk to and share my feelings with:

4	3	2	①	0
Not at all	Somewhat	Moderately	A great deal	Nearly always

8. I feel empty and unfulfilled:

0	1	②	3	4
Not at all	Somewhat	Moderately	A great deal	Nearly always

Scoring the Loneliness Scale: To score the scale, simply add up the numbers of the answers you circled on each item. Since your score on each question can range between 0 and 4, your total score can range between a minimum of 0 (if your answer on every item was a 0) and a maximum of 32 (if your answer on every item was a 4). Add up your score for all ten items on the loneliness scale and put the total here: _____

Interpreting your score: The higher your score, the more lonely you feel. The following chart indicates the degree of loneliness.

Total Score	Degree of Loneliness	Percent of People Scoring in this Range
0–4	Minimal or no loneliness	20%
5–9	Mildly lonely	30%
10–14	Moderately lonely	30%
15 or more	Very lonely	20%
		Total 100%

My research using the Loneliness Scale has confirmed that loneliness is surprisingly common. I recently gave the scale to 272 married and single men and women of all ages from Dayton, Ohio. Their average score on the test was 10, indicating that most people are in fact mildly to moderately lonely. The study showed that loneliness affects both men and women of all ages and income brackets. Younger people and men tend to feel somewhat lonelier whereas highly educated people tend to feel somewhat less lonely. One surprising finding from my research is that being married does not in any way protect you from feeling lonely. This was unexpected since we often think of loneliness as an affliction of people who are single, separated, or divorced. But in point of fact, married people experience just as much loneliness and sometimes more.

What does this really mean? If being alone does not cause loneliness, and if having someone to love is not the cure, then what is the difference between people who feel lonely and people who don't? The crucial difference is self-esteem. If there's one message this book contains, this is it: Finding someone to love is not the solution to loneliness. The solution is learning to love yourself. Once you love and appreciate yourself, you'll discover that other people will love you too, and your loneliness will only be a memory.

This is not a new message, but what is new is the development of a systematic program that can help you turn this insight into an emotional reality. This book describes an effective, patient-tested program that has helped hundreds of men and women of all ages get over feelings

Table 1-2
Average Loneliness Scores
According to Marital Status*

Marital Status	Loneliness Scale Score* (Mean ± St. Dev.)	Number
Single	10.3 ± 4.8	39
Married	9.7 ± 5.5	147
Separated or Divorced	9.2 ± 5.8	56
Widowed	13.2 ± 5.7	19

*Note to Researchers: There were no significant differences in the mean loneliness scores in people who were single, married, or separated/divorced. Only the widows were significantly lonelier (the T-stat for married vs. widowed = 2.59, $p < 0.005$). The lack of a relationship between loneliness and marital status was confirmed using multiple regression techniques in which age, sex, marital status, educational level, and income were entered into the equation simultaneously.

of loneliness, shyness, inferiority, and sexual insecurity. It is based on cognitive and behavioral techniques pioneered at the University of Pennsylvania and now in use at medical centers, clinics, and universities throughout the world. These methods have been tested and found to be helpful for people with a wide variety of mood and personal relationship problems. If you're willing to work at them, you can make them work for you.

2

Understanding Loneliness

Many people who are often alone rarely feel lonely. This is because they feel good about themselves and their lives. In contrast, many other people who are usually surrounded by people who care about them—a loving partner, family, and friends—are desperately lonely and unhappy. One reason for their unhappiness is the negative way they think about themselves and other people. For example, if you feel lonely and inferior you're probably telling yourself you're second-rate. You may think you don't deserve to be loved because you don't measure up to some standard of attractiveness, intelligence, or success. A lonely thirty-two-year-old man recently lamented, "Dr. Burns, why should any woman be interested in me? Let's face the truth. They're looking for guys who are handsome and wealthy and talented. I'm not sexy or charming; I'm just ordinary. My job isn't exciting or impressive. There's really nothing very special about me."

Some lonely people feel frightened and desperate. They believe that it's terrible to be alone and they worry about growing old without a family or someone to love. For others, loneliness is an experience of bitterness. They resent their life and blame their problems on other people. Some lonely people feel hopeless because they tell themselves they'll never find happiness or have the chance to get close to others. They feel empty and unfulfilled because they think that all the satisfaction in life comes from meaningful relationships with other people.

If you've ever felt lonely or discouraged you're probably quite aware of how negative life can seem. What you may not know is that those negative thoughts actually make you feel bad. This is of tremendous importance because if you're willing to learn to think about yourself and your problems in a more positive way, you can overcome feelings of loneliness and develop better relationships with others.

You may also be unaware that all those negative thoughts that make you feel so bad are often quite illogical and unrealistic, even though they seem absolutely valid to you. Although it is a controversial idea that loneliness and depression can result from distorted negative thoughts, there is a considerable body of evidence that supports this concept. During the past several years I have been collaborating with Dr. Brian Shaw, the director of the Clark Institute in Toronto, Canada, in a study of how our thinking affects the way we feel about what happens to us. I have developed a "vignette test," which describes positive and negative events such as getting a date with someone you like, receiving a "Dear John" letter from someone you've been going with, receiving a promotion, or losing your job. We administered the test to women who did not have any serious mood problems as well as to women who were hospitalized for depression. Each woman was instructed to write down how she would be *feeling* and *thinking* if she were confronted with each situation described in the test.

The study showed that the depressed women were more likely to interpret both positive and negative events in an illogically pessimistic way, and that their feelings about each situation depended on the way they thought about it. In response to a vignette describing the breakup of a romantic relationship, a nondepressed woman wrote: "I would feel sad. My thoughts: I'd miss the relationship I've shared but look forward to meeting new people." This response is appropriate and realistic. Although she feels disappointed, she does not condemn herself or experience any loss of self-esteem. This attitude will put her in the best possible position to develop better relationships with others. In contrast, a depressed woman wrote: "I would feel sad, unhappy, hurt. My thoughts: What did I do wrong to have caused this to happen? I will never have any close relationships because of me being me.'' Her response illustrates a thinking pattern that is common in lonely people: She arbitrarily blames herself entirely and tells herself that she's no good; she assumes her problems are insoluble and that her future will be hopeless. This attitude will make her despise herself. Instead of pinpointing the problems in her relationships so she can deal with them and grow, she'll give up on life and get trapped by loneliness and low self-esteem.

Although scientists don't know why some people think about themselves in such a self-defeating way, we're beginning to develop effective methods that can help people reverse these thinking patterns so that they can feel more positive and loving and experience greater self-esteem and joy. The following self-assessment test will help you pinpoint certain thoughts and feelings that may make it hard for you to get close to others.

The Intimacy Inventory

The Intimacy Inventory lists a number of feelings that people sometimes have about themselves and their relationships with other people. Put a check (√) in the box to the right of each statement that indicates how much it describes the way you feel. If you aren't completely certain, take your best guess. There are no ''right'' or ''wrong'' answers so try to answer according to the way you usually think and feel.

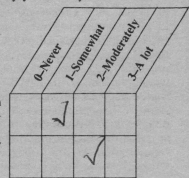

	0-Never	1-Somewhat	2-Moderately	3-A lot
1. I sometimes feel as if I'm not a very attractive or desirable person.		√		
2. I'm unhappy doing so many things alone.			√	

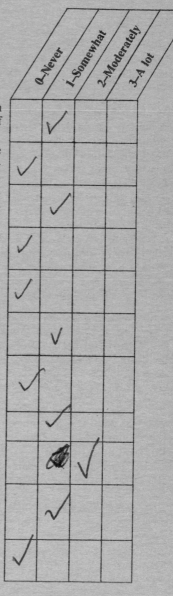

	0–Never	1–Somewhat	2–Moderately	3–A lot
3. In social situations I often feel awkward and unsure of myself.		✓		
4. It would be difficult for me to tell a friend that I was feeling lonely or upset.	✓			
5. If someone rejects me, I usually feel there's something basically wrong with me.		✓		
6. It's difficult for me to be alone.	✓			
7. I sometimes feel that intimate relationships don't give me enough personal freedom.	✓			
8. It would be very hard for me to criticize a friend or lover or tell them I felt angry with them.	✓			
9. I feel you need good looks, personality, intelligence, success, or status to be accepted and loved by others.	✓			
10. I usually try to avoid people if I'm feeling nervous or insecure.		✓		
11. Sometimes I think there's something basically wrong with me.		✓		
12. It would be hard for me to love someone who wasn't as attractive, exciting, or intelligent as I'd like my ideal partner to be.		✓		
13. I often feel abandoned when I'm alone.	✓			

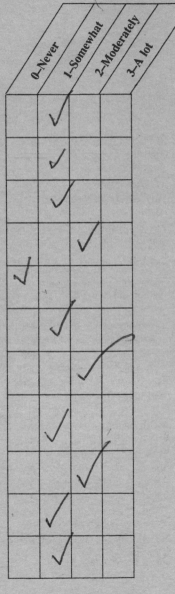

	0—Never	1—Somewhat	2—Moderately	3—A lot
14. I sometimes tell myself I'll never have a good relationship with someone I care about.		✓		
15. I usually feel I have to say yes to people, even when it might be better to say no.		✓		
16. I don't have much interest in life.		✓		
17. I think it's unfair that I don't have anyone to be close to.			✓	
18. There aren't any groups that I'd really enjoy belonging to.	✓			
19. I often feel defensive when people criticize me.		✓		
20. If people know you're feeling shy or nervous, they will usually think less of you.			✓	
21. When someone rejects me, I usually feel as if I'm not a very lovable or desirable person.		✓		
22. It seems as if the people I'm attracted to are never interested in me.			✓	
23. I feel it's abnormal to be alone.		✓		
24. I don't like to tell anyone about my weaknesses, inadequacies, or shortcomings.		✓		

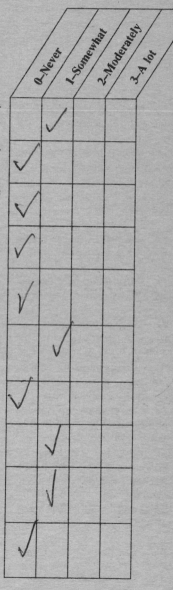

	0–Never	1–Somewhat	2–Moderately	3–A lot
25. I tend to be overly sensitive to disapproval or criticism.		✓		
26. I feel helpless and vulnerable when I'm alone.	✓			
27. It's hard for me to share my feelings with people.	✓			
28. I feel I don't have much in common with other people.	✓			
29. I think that angry feelings between friends or lovers nearly always indicate a lack of love and respect.	✓			
30. When people criticize me, I frequently get frustrated because they won't admit that what I'm saying is right.		✓		
31. I don't see how anyone could ever love me.	✓			
32. When someone rejects me, it seems like everyone's going to reject me sooner or later.		✓		
33. At times I feel that anything I do to try to improve my relationships with people just won't work.		✓		
34. I usually feel I should try to make everybody else happy, even if I make myself miserable in the process.	✓			

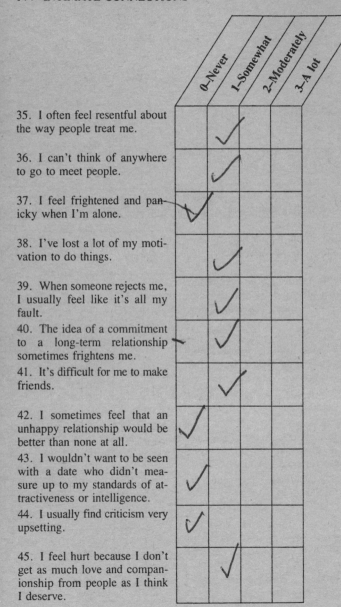

	0-Never	1-Somewhat	2-Moderately	3-A lot
35. I often feel resentful about the way people treat me.		✓		
36. I can't think of anywhere to go to meet people.		✓		
37. I feel frightened and panicky when I'm alone.	✓			
38. I've lost a lot of my motivation to do things.		✓		
39. When someone rejects me, I usually feel like it's all my fault.		✓		
40. The idea of a commitment to a long-term relationship sometimes frightens me.		✓		
41. It's difficult for me to make friends.		✓		
42. I sometimes feel that an unhappy relationship would be better than none at all.	✓			
43. I wouldn't want to be seen with a date who didn't measure up to my standards of attractiveness or intelligence.	✓			
44. I usually find criticism very upsetting.	✓			
45. I feel hurt because I don't get as much love and companionship from people as I think I deserve.		✓		

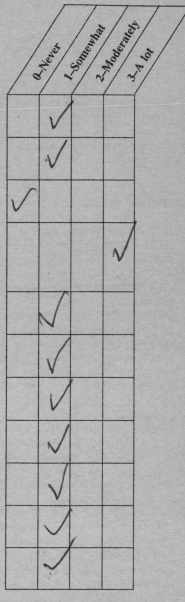

	0-Never	1-Somewhat	2-Moderately	3-A lot
46. I find it very upsetting if I don't meet all the expectations of a friend or lover.		✓		
47. I feel inferior to other people.		✓		
48. I always try to avoid conflicts or arguments with the people I care about.	✓			
49. If I don't feel a strong romantic attraction to potential dates or lovers, I tell myself there's not much point in getting involved with them.			✓	
50. I feel sad and discouraged.	✓			
51. I sometimes get so nervous I can't think of anything to say to people.		✓		
52. I sometimes feel hopeless about improving my relationships with people.		✓		
53. I find arguments or disagreements with friends or lovers very upsetting.		✓		
54. I sometimes feel trapped by intimate relationships.		✓		
55. Sometimes I feel like a failure.		✓		
56. I feel that most people wouldn't accept me once they got to know me well.		✓		

	0–Never	1–Somewhat	2–Moderately	3–A lot
57. When I'm alone I often feel empty and unfulfilled.		✓		
58. I often feel let down or disappointed once I find out what a friend or lover is really like.		✓		
59. I often think other people are to blame for most of the problems in my relationships.	✓			
60. In a conflict I'm nearly always the one who ends up giving in.			✓	

Scoring and interpreting the Intimacy Inventory: The inventory measures fifteen attitudes that can rob you of self-esteem and make it more difficult to develop friendships and intimate relationships. Each attitude is represented by four statements on the inventory which are listed in the middle column of Table 2-1. Each of these four statements can be scored between 0 (if you "never" feel this way) and 3 (if you feel this way "a lot"). Your total score for each of the fifteen attitudes can range between 0 (indicating you answered "never" on all four statements that measure that attitude) and 12 (indicating you answered "a lot" on all four statements).

Add up your score on each of the fifteen attitudes, and fill in your scores in Table 2-1. A score between 0 and 2 indicates a particular attitude is probably not a problem for you. A score between 3 and 5 indicates this attitude may be causing you mild problems. A score between 6 and 8 on an attitude indicates a moderate problem area, while a score between 9 and 12 indicates that an attitude could be a significant problem for you.

1. Low self-esteem: Many people who are shy and lonely

suffer from feelings of inferiority because they constantly compare themselves with other people who seem more intelligent, charming, and attractive. They may give themselves negative messages, like "I'm such a loser. I'm not as smart as she (or he) is. I'm not as good looking as she (or he) is. There's really nothing very interesting or exciting about me. Why would anyone care about me?" This makes them feel inadequate and they conclude that they really aren't very worthwhile or lovable.

TABLE 2-1
Your Intimacy Profile

Attitude	Statements on the Intimacy Inventory That Measure This Attitude	Put Your Total Scores for This Attitude Here*
1. Low self-esteem	1, 11, 31, 47	4
2. Romantic perfectionism	9, 12, 43, 58	2
3. Emotional perfectionism	29, 48, 49, 53	4
4. Shyness and social anxiety	3, 10, 20, 51	5
5. Hopelessness	14, 22, 33, 52	5
6. Alienation and isolation	18, 28, 36, 41	2
7. Rejection sensitivity	5, 21, 32, 39	4
8. Fear of being alone	2, 6, 23, 57	4
9. Desperation	13, 26, 37, 42	0
10. Disclosure phobia	4, 24, 27, 56	2
11. Inassertiveness	8, 15, 34, 60	4
12. Resentment and bitterness	17, 35, 45, 59	4
13. Defensiveness and fear of criticism	19, 25, 30, 44	3
14. Depression	16, 38, 50, 55	4
15. The trapped factor	7, 40, 46, 54	3

*To determine your total score for each attitude, simply add up your score for the four statements in the middle column.

2. Romantic perfectionism: Unrealistic expectations about yourself and the people you date can lead to loneliness:

• *Partner perfectionism:* You feel your partner has to be the dreamboat you always fantasized about. When someone starts to develop an interest in you, you get disappointed because that person isn't just the way you want him or her to be. You may find that you become easily annoyed and ruminate about aspects of their personality or appearance that turn you off. He or she might not be as physically appealing or intelligent as you think your ideal mate should be. The more you dwell on these things, the unhappier you become. Then you conclude that the person really wasn't good enough.

• *Personal perfectionism:* Because of our culture's emphasis on charm, intelligence, attractiveness, popularity, and success, many lonely people assume that these qualities are prerequisite to any friendship or loving relationship. They may base their self-esteem primarily on their personality or looks, worry endlessly about being too short or too tall, having a blemish or being overweight. If they feel they can't measure up to society's standards of beauty and attractiveness—and who really can?—they assume that they're undesirable and doomed to loneliness.

Romantic perfectionism can be a way of avoiding the anxiety involved in getting close to someone. Since no relationship or lover can ever be perfect, excessively high standards can be a convenient way of rejecting everybody. I saw a young woman named Allison in my office the other day who recently began dating a young man after two years of feeling shy and lonely. She told me how disappointed she felt because she didn't like the way they embraced. Apparently he was also inexperienced and didn't move his mouth properly, so that she kept bumping into his teeth every time they kissed. Instead of talking it over with him and teaching him the way she liked to be kissed—which was terribly anxiety-provoking—Allison had fantasies of breaking up with him and waiting until someone "better" came along. After we talked about her fears and inhibitions, she got up the courage to raise the issue with him in a gentle way. This led to greater openness and experimentation and soon she began to feel more intimate and excited again.

3. Emotional perfectionism: Many people feel that they should have strong romantic feelings of excitement and infatuation or there's no point in getting involved with someone. When the romantic feelings begin to fade and the initial excitement of a relationship loses its intensity, they conclude that they love each other less. They often feel that loving couples should never argue, bicker, or fight. They may be afraid of conflicts because they think that any differences or disagreements are dangerous for a relationship. They may feel that people who care for each other should always have positive, loving feelings and never feel bored, angry, or indifferent.

4. Shyness and social anxiety: Many lonely people feel awkward in groups or very nervous when they're around someone they're attracted to. They often believe that feeling tense and insecure is shameful, so they try to hide these feelings; they're afraid they'll appear weak or inferior to other people who seem more poised and self-confident. Trying to control their nervousness often backfires, because they become more and more absorbed in how embarrassed and uncomfortable they feel and this makes them even more uncomfortable. They may get so self-critical and absorbed in themselves that it becomes difficult to express any real interest in people or to concentrate on what others are saying. Then they conclude that feeling shy and nervous really is a barrier to getting close to people. What they don't comprehend is that their lack of self-acceptance, and *not* their shyness, causes most of their problems.

5. Hopelessness: Many lonely people feel hopeless about ever developing a circle of friends or finding a partner they could care about. They may believe they just don't have what it takes to get close to people or that they're too old and all the good people are already taken. The belief that they'll never get close to people tends to act as a self-fulfilling prophecy, because once a person gives up, things generally don't improve much. This makes it seem like the problem really is hopeless.

6. Alienation and isolation: Lonely people have trouble making friends and finding groups or organizations they'd feel comfortable joining. They don't know where to go to meet people or how to develop friendships with the people they do meet. Sometimes they're convinced they're basically "different" and don't have much in common with others. They think that people wouldn't be interested in them or wouldn't accept them once they got to know them well.

7. *Rejection sensitivity:* Lonely people are frequently so afraid of rejection that they avoid taking the risks that are necessary to date and get close to people. The fear of rejection results from several types of distorted thinking:

• Overgeneralization: You tell yourself that any rejection will be the beginning of a never-ending string of rejections because there's something inherently defective about you. In my office recently, a twenty-two-year-old woman named Lisa told me how hopeless and discouraged she felt about the breakup of an intense three-week love affair she'd had with a young man she'd met during the summer. She was absolutely convinced he left her because she was missing some "essential ingredient" she needed to have a man love her and she felt certain that she'd end up being alone forever. When I asked her what this "essential ingredient" was, she was unable to come up with anything specific. She just felt that he had scrutinized her and found her undesirable and now she was branded as a reject for time eternal. It took a number of therapy sessions and the blossoming of a new relationship to convince her just how off-base her earlier assessment had been.

• Self-blame: Lonely people are likely to blame themselves for problems in their relationships and tend to assume that any romantic conflict or rejection is entirely their fault. Their friends may reassure them that it takes two people to make or break any relationship, but in their heart of hearts they "know" it isn't true and that their own inadequacy or badness was entirely responsible for the breakup.

• All-or-nothing thinking: When you break up with someone, you conclude that the relationship was "a total failure" or that you're "a total failure" instead of pinpointing the relative strengths and weaknesses of the relationship so you can learn from the experience and grow. You may also idealize the person who rejected you and tell yourself he or she was "perfect" for you. You dwell on all the person's good points, ignore any deficiencies, and conclude that life without that one person is bound to be barren and meaningless.

• Mind reading: People with low self-esteem are quick to assume that others are having negative thoughts and feelings about them, and as a result they frequently misinterpret what's really going on. Some lonely people even assume that perfectly neutral events are rejections. A woman I treated became despondent when she asked a man who worked in her office, "Where's the Kleenex?" He answered, "The Kleenex is on the desk." She felt crushed because she'd been having fantasies about him and concluded from his comment that he wasn't interested in her. Later in her therapy, when she learned to be more assertive and got to know him better, she was surprised to discover that he'd also been having romantic fantasies about her. They ended up developing an intimate relationship!

8. *Fear of being alone:* Lonely people nearly always have a difficult time feeling happy and contented when they're alone. If you believe you can't feel truly secure or fulfilled unless you have someone to be close to, you may mope and treat yourself in an uncaring, insensitive way whenever you're alone instead of getting involved in activity that would be more challenging and productive. Then you feel bored and conclude that it's not much fun to be alone. Your lack of self-respect may alienate others because they sense how needy and desperate you are. They may avoid you, and this makes you feel even more lonely and inadequate—a vicious cycle.

9. *Desperation:* Some people not only feel that being alone is bound to be boring and unrewarding, they also feel panicky and frightened whenever they're alone. One of their major motivations in forming relationships is to avoid the sense of helplessness, desperation, and abandonment they feel whenever they have to be by themselves for any extended period of time.

If you're not afraid of being alone, missing someone you care about can be a positive experience that reflects the love you feel for them. If you're single and unattached, the desire to enhance your life with a loving relationship is healthy and the longing you feel can motivate you to develop meaningful relationships. These feelings are quite different from the emptiness, desperation, and self-pity that so many lonely people experience. They want someone to love them primarily because they're afraid of being alone, and the search for love becomes more of an act of selfishness than the desire to share one's life with another person one genuinely cares about.

10. Disclosure phobia: You may have difficulty sharing your thoughts and feelings with people because you're afraid they might think less of you. You may think that feeling depressed, lonely, or inadequate is a sign of weakness, so you don't want to let anyone know that you feel this way. You may also feel that your ideas and interests are stupid and think that other people just wouldn't be interested in what you have to say.

11. Inassertiveness: Many lonely people are inassertive and find it difficult to express angry feelings or to criticize anyone. You may find it hard to tell people what you want because you think you'd appear overly selfish or crass. You may also find it tough to say no when other people ask you for things that aren't in your best self-interest, because it makes you feel so guilty to disappoint anyone. This often stems from the idea that it's always your responsibility to please others and the belief that if you don't live up to everybody's expectations something bad will happen.

12. Resentment and bitterness: Although lonely people will usually say they want nothing more than to find someone to be close to, they are often quite bitter and critical of others. They sometimes project the impression that they really don't like people very much and they have a difficult time understanding the connection between their own negative attitudes and the problems they experience with others. They blame people for not being friendlier and more interested in them and they seem unwilling to take a look at how they're alienating others and how their resentment drives people away. Developing a greater sense of self-esteem and self-acceptance can often be the first step in solving this difficult dilemma.

13. Defensiveness and fear of criticism: Many lonely

people are overly self-blaming and sensitive to any disapproval or criticism. They become so upset when confronted by any personal shortcoming that they lash out defensively instead of owning up to their faults or evaluating the criticism objectively. They may get argumentative and insist that they are "right" and the other person is "wrong." This frustrates other people, who either avoid them or become more critical and judgmental. Things get very unpleasant and this reinforces the idea that it really is terrible to be criticized—another vicious cycle.

14. Depression: Loneliness researchers have consistently documented that people who feel lonely are quite likely to be suffering from depression and low self-esteem. The symptoms of depression include, among others, feelings of sadness and discouragement, a loss of motivation, an excessive tendency to criticize and blame yourself, and a loss of interest in life. When people overcome these feelings of depression, and experience greater self-esteem, they nearly always find it much easier to develop satisfying relationships with others.

15. The trapped factor: Many people are afraid of getting close to others. They may find intimate relationships constricting and feel trapped and confined once they make a long-term or exclusive commitment to someone. They experience love not as an exciting adventure, but as a burden or a duty that robs them of personal freedom.

Did you recognize yourself or someone you know in any of the descriptions of these fifteen attitudes? These attitudes can make you feel bad about yourself and other people. Keep them in mind as you read the following chapters. I will describe a step-by-step program that has helped many people build a more positive personal value system, enjoy greater self-confidence, and develop more satisfying relationships with others.

When you begin to apply these techniques, remember that change often requires persistence and hard work over a period of time. Many of the vignettes in this book are based on therapy sessions when patients made significant breakthroughs in the way they felt and related to others. These moments can be very exciting and informative, but it's important to realize that there was usually a period of hard work that led up to them. I do not want to convey the idea that these methods work like magic or that they will solve all your problems overnight. They are powerful tools that can help you change your feelings, and your behavior, but this often requires systematic effort over a period of time. Sometimes trial and error and patient persistence will be required. Given this attitude, the results can be most gratifying.

I want to warn you that certain ideas and techniques I describe may be contrary to the way you ordinarily think and act. You may feel skeptical and at times resist some of these suggestions. If you feel that a particular method is silly or misguided, maintain your skepticism but have the courage to check it out with an experiment. Try the method and prove to yourself that it doesn't work. You may learn that it isn't particularly helpful for you. That information can help you move on to another method that will provide the important breakthrough. You may also be surprised to learn that a method or an idea that at first seemed so foolish and counterintuitive turns out to be the first step on the path to better self-esteem.

PART TWO

SELF-LOVE
COMES FIRST

3

The First Step:
Learning to Like and
Love Yourself

"There's really no one I can feel close to."

"Being alone means I'm a misfit."

"It's a couples' world."

"I feel inferior to other people."

"I've always been rejected in the past, and the future will all be the same."

"I feel like I'm too old. Life has passed me by. All the men my age want younger women. What if I wind up a lonely old maid?"

Do these thoughts sound familiar to you? Do you ever think you really aren't very special or lovable? Are you afraid you'll never have a rewarding relationship with someone you care about? If so, this chapter could be an important turning point in your life.

Shy, lonely people often feel inadequate and believe they aren't *good enough*. A lonely thirty-year-old woman told me, "Dr. Burns, every night for years I've cried myself to sleep. I feel so lonely. Every morning when I walk to work I see all the 'beautiful people.' The men are wearing pin-striped suits and the woman look like models. They look so poised and charming. I don't have a glamorous career and I'm not gorgeous or particularly clever. Why should anyone care about me?"

There's some truth in these comments. People who are terrific-looking and have outgoing personalities may find it easier to attract others. But this in no way guarantees that they'll be able to form loving, lasting relationships. I've treated many "beautiful people"—men and women who were exceptionally attractive, personable, and successful—yet they, too, felt lonely and had difficulties getting close to others. A stunning blonde told me in tears that she hadn't had a date in more than two years. A handsome politician from New York told me he could somehow never get beyond the dating stage to form the kind of intimate, close relationship he'd been yearning for. He told me, "I'm forty-four years old, and all I want is a wife, a family, and a home in the suburbs. But I just can't seem to make it happen. Time seems to be running out on me. I feel lonely and afraid. What's wrong with me?"

If good looks, personality, and a fancy career aren't the keys to intimacy, then what is? Shy and lonely people nearly always suffer from two problems. The first, and probably the most important, is the inability to like and love themselves. The problem is usually not that lonely people are really any less lovable or desirable than anyone else but that they often *think* they are. Learning how to love and appreciate yourself is a necessary prerequisite to getting close to others.

The second problem that plagues lonely people is the inability to like and appreciate others. The loneliest people are often the quickest to find faults and flaws in other people. They often seem to dislike people of the opposite sex. Their bitterness may come from being rejected in the past, but it also leads to more rejections—a vicious cycle.

Lonely people often are unaware of their lack of self-esteem, and they may deny the hostility they project toward others. They don't notice the brutal way they constantly put themselves down, and they think they feel bad because *other* people don't like them. They usually don't recognize that their unhappiness comes from within and that their real enemy is their lack of positive feelings for themselves. They feel lonely and isolated because they don't know how to love themselves—and this is what ultimately drives people away.

You may agree that self-esteem is important, but you may wonder, "How can I develop positive feelings about myself when I feel so alone and lonely? How can I project

joy and self-confidence when I feel inferior and rejected?''
There are four crucial steps:

• Stop abusing and neglecting yourself and start treating
yourself in a more loving and responsible way. Make a
commitment to get creatively and productively involved in
life.

• Give up the habit of putting yourself down and learn
to think about yourself in a more realistic and compassionate manner.

• Get rid of certain self-defeating attitudes and develop
a healthier and more positive personal value system.

• Confront and conquer your fear of being alone.

The effectiveness of every technique in this book depends on achieving these goals. If you learn how to develop a loving relationship with yourself when you're
alone, there's little chance of failure when you attempt to
form relationships with others. But if you continue to
believe that only someone else will make you truly happy,
there's little chance of success.

In the past ten years I've conducted over fifteen thousand individual therapy sessions with people who felt depressed, lonely, and shy. Nearly every one of them has
made the same mistake. They believe that all they need is
that exciting man or that gorgeous woman to save them
from boredom and desperation and to make their lives
fulfilled. *Nothing could be further from the truth.* The
belief that you need a loving partner before you can feel
happy and secure is one of the major causes of loneliness.
This attitude will make you feel inadequate and will actually drive people away. That special person you're searching for is looking for someone to excite him or her and to
enhance his or her life, not for a needy person who can't
make it alone. Learning to like and love yourself is the key
to intimacy.

The very moment you begin to feel good about yourself,
you will start to project positive feelings to other people.
They will suddenly sense the love and positivity within
you, and they'll be attracted to you. I've seen this happen
over and over again! The more needy and desperate you
are, the more likely you are to get rejected. In contrast,
when you give up that need for other people and begin to

appreciate yourself, you suddenly find yourself in hot demand! This is a paradox: People will avoid you as long as they sense you're desperate. But when you feel contented and you no longer need them, they'll chase after you and need you. It sounds crazy, but it's true!

Let's face the facts: People who feel grim and down on themselves are about as marketable as lepers, whereas people who like themselves and feel happy about life give off an irresistible energy that makes them attractive. Once you experience self-esteem, you'll begin to realize that you *are* sexy and desirable. Instead of desperately chasing people and ending up empty-handed, you'll notice that people are chasing you. And like many of my patients, you may become *so* successful that you'll have to start beating them away with sticks! Then you can select the one special person you want to form a meaningful relationship with.

The Importance of Being Alone

One of the best ways to overcome loneliness and develop self-esteem is to decide to *avoid* dating for a while. Better yet, you might want to avoid relationships with everyone, if you have the courage! This might seem like an unusual approach to social success. In your heart of hearts you "know" that one good friend or lover would be the solution to your problems. You may feel convinced that life would be empty without someone you can trust who really cares about you.

In fact, you're absolutely right. All you need is one person you can really count on to comfort and support you, someone who will always be tender and caring. But that person is *you*. You must develop a loving relationship with yourself before you can relate successfully to others. When—and *only* when—you learn how to like and love yourself, and to be as happy as a clam when you are alone, can you benefit from the dynamite "social rags to riches" program in the following chapters.

People who cannot appreciate themselves feel unhappy when they're alone and just can't seem to form intimate, rewarding relationships with others. They lose either way.

But people with self-esteem are quite happy when they're alone, and that joy is only enriched by their relationships with others. They win both ways.

If you are tempted to turn to Part Three to learn the secrets of flirting and connecting with other people, DON'T! You'll simply defeat yourself. You've got to learn to be alone and happy *before* you're ready for relationships with other people.

Get Creatively Involved in Life. One of the biggest mistakes that lonely people make is to wait around for a friend or lover before they get creatively and productively involved in life. You may live in a messy, undecorated apartment because you feel there's no point in creating a pleasant living environment for yourself unless you have someone to share it with. You may eat fast food on the run because you think it's abnormal to eat alone. On evenings or weekends you may sit around and watch TV or drink or overeat because you pine for a companion and you think, "I'm all alone tonight. There's no point in doing anything because I feel so lonely. Why put out the effort?" This attitude will only make you miserable and rob you of self-esteem, and that will make it harder for you to develop a loving relationship with someone else.

Dr. Laura Primakoff, a colleague who's done pioneering work in cognitive group therapy for loneliness, asks lonely people this question:

> How long would you live with someone when all you had were bad meals, for example, tuna from out of the can [or] T.V. dinners and the place was always a mess; most of your spare time was spent watching T.V. and listening to the radio; when you hardly ever went out or did anything at home that was interesting? (One group member "jokingly" answered, "Would you believe ten years?")*

---

*L. Primakoff, "One's Company; Two's a Crowd. Skills in Living Alone Groups," in *Cognitive Therapy with Couples and Groups*, A. Freeman, ed. (New York: Plenum Press, 1983), pp. 261–301.

Of course, you won't enjoy your own company if you treat yourself so shabbily. Many people think that self-esteem is a magical elusive feeling that you either have or don't have, but this is not the way it works. Self-esteem is the commitment to treat yourself in a kindly, loving manner when you're alone. This is an *active* process that requires effort and energy.

Think of it this way. Suppose that special person you've been longing for suddenly came into your life. How would you treat him—or her? What would you do together? What would you serve him? How would you decorate your apartment or home for him? I suspect you'd wear your nicest clothes, cook your favorite foods and do the things that you love the most to show him how much you cared for him and to make him feel special. Well, that's exactly the same way to create self-esteem—you treat yourself as if *you* were that special person. After you've begun to treat yourself well for a period of time, you'll begin to like yourself more and to feel good about yourself. But if you insist on doing nothing because you feel lonely and discouraged, you'll just continue to feel bad.

Many single people draw a blank when I suggest they substitute creative, rewarding activities for their usual dreary lifestyle. They claim they can't think of anything to do, or they argue that there's no point in doing anything if they're alone. The following list may be helpful to you. Although most of the suggestions might sound obvious, it's just these kinds of ordinary activities that can make an enormous difference in how you feel about yourself and your life.

• Think of things you *used* to enjoy in the past and do them now, even though you feel absolutely convinced you wouldn't enjoy them anymore because you're lonely. You might have played a musical instrument in high school. Perhaps you still have your old guitar in the closet. Get it out or borrow one and start practicing. Take lessons. Join a musical group. You may be surprised at how rewarding it can still be for you.

• Think of things you'd enjoy doing with someone else, such as going to a play, shopping, or hiking. Try doing these things by yourself, even though you think they'd be a lot more fun with someone else.

• Do something you've been putting off, such as balancing your checkbook, writing letters, or straightening up your files. You can often get a tremendous boost of energy if you stop procrastinating and do these things. Here's an important tip: Don't wait until you "feel" like it. Make the decision to *do* something whether or not you "feel" like it. Once you've started, *then* you'll "feel" like doing it. Action comes *before* the motivation, and not vice versa!

• Do something for self-improvement, such as dieting, jogging, or exercising. You might want to work on overcoming a bad habit, perhaps smoking, drinking excessively, or abusing drugs or tranquilizers.

• Develop a talent or skill—take karate, dancing, or art lessons; get a personal computer and learn to program it; go back to school or take a night school class.

• Start a hobby: photography, coin or stamp collecting, gardening, gourmet cooking, or skydiving.

• Seek personal and spiritual growth—get involved in activities at your church or synagogue, study yoga, or join an assertiveness training class.

• Get involved in sports, such as bowling, skiing, tennis, bicycling, skating; and attend sporting events.

• Find entertainment—go to a library or bookstore and get something interesting to read; go to movies or plays; try shopping or visiting local museums.

• Do something for others: Get involved in charitable activities or volunteer work; spend one day a month with a boy or girl with no parents; think of people you know who are lonely, ill, or troubled and do something for them. This will help you break out of your preoccupation with yourself so you can begin to think of others. It can help you shift your thinking from what you *need from* others to what you have to *offer* and *give to* others. Reaching out to others in an active, loving way will help you break out of your feelings of desperation, isolation, and helplessness.

When you are doing these things, try to plan ahead and organize your time. Make an hour-by-hour schedule of activities and stick to it. This will give you things to look forward to and counteract the tendency to sit around for hours and hours feeling sorry for yourself.

It can also be helpful to make a list of the advantages of

living alone so you won't be constantly ruminating about how wonderful life would be if only you were involved in a romantic relationship. It's crucial to view your time with yourself not as a deprivation, but as a unique opportunity to explore and experience life in a full, intense manner. This commitment to yourself will prepare you to make a commitment to a partner later on. Your list of advantages might include:

• You have more time and emotional energy for yourself.

• You can be free to feel and express your emotions.

• You can get involved in interests and pleasures that are meaningful to you.

• You can be involved with many people in many different ways.

• You can discover your own values, beliefs, and interests.

• You can increase your frustration tolerance for not always getting what you want—namely, love.

• You can decorate and create the kind of living environment that is most personally appealing to you.

• You can be free to be creative and to be an individual without fear of judgment or criticism. You can eat what you want when you want to. You can be totally private and do what you please without the constraints and distractions of living with someone else. You can be as bizarre and outrageous as you choose; listen to the music you like the most; sing and dance; wear what you want or run around the house naked if you choose!*

Many lonely people resist these suggestions. They refuse to adopt a productive, creative attitude because of the assumption that they're bound to feel bad when they're alone. They have a tendency to give up on life because they believe that the only "real" happiness comes from being with others. They may recall many wonderful times when they felt close to their friends and family and countless other times when they were lonely and unhappy and conclude that this is the way things have to be.

If you subscribe to the notion that you're bound to be

---

*Adapted from Dr. Laura Primakoff's "One's Company; Two's a Crowd," op. cit.

miserable when you're alone, you may turn it into a self-fulfilling prophecy because you will mistreat yourself when you are alone. Instead of making yourself a lovely meal or taking yourself out to dinner at some pleasant place, you sit at home eating a peanut butter sandwich, staring at the wall, and telling yourself what a loser you are. Then at the end of the evening you conclude that being alone *really is* no fun! But aren't you fooling yourself? Suppose you invited someone special over to dinner and you treated that person the same way. Imagine serving your date a peanut butter sandwich and telling each other what losers you are. How enjoyable would that be?

Being alone will never make you unhappy, but treating yourself in an unloving manner certainly will. It's your self-abuse, and not the fact that you're alone, that makes you feel lonely. One way to prove this to yourself is to perform an experiment to test your belief that you're bound to feel miserable whenever you're alone. Turn to the Pleasure Predicting Sheet on page 37 and write this across the top: "Hypothesis—I can't feel happy and fulfilled when I'm alone." Or you might write: "Hypothesis—it's more rewarding to be with people I care about than to do things alone." To test your hypothesis, make a list of activities that have the potential for pleasure, personal growth, or learning in the "Activity" column of the sheet, as illustrated in Figure 3-1, p. 37. It's important to schedule creative, worthwhile activities that you can do by yourself just as you would if you were with someone you cared about a great deal. For example, if you decide to cook dinner for yourself, start by going to the store and picking out your favorite foods. Then bring them home and prepare them carefully. Set a nice table for yourself and put on some music, just as you would if you were having company.

In the second column of the Pleasure Predicting Sheet, which is marked "Companion," record who you do each activity with. Put the word "Self," rather than the word "Alone," next to those activities you do by yourself. This will remind you that you are never really alone. Try to schedule some activities by yourself, some with friends of your own sex, and some with members of the opposite sex. That will allow you to compare how rewarding and enjoyable these three categories of activities can be.

In the third column, which is the "Predicted Satisfaction," estimate how satisfying or rewarding each activity will be between 0% (not at all satisfying) to 99% (the greatest possible satisfaction).* Record your predictions *before* you do each activity. Finally, after you have completed each activity, record how satisfying it actually turned out to be in the last column, "Actual Satisfaction," using the same 0% to 99% rating system.

Fred, the man whose Pleasure Predicting Sheet is illustrated in Figure 3-1, fell into a depression shortly before Christmas of 1983 because his wife, Pat, unexpectedly walked out on him to live with another man. Fred was firmly convinced that he needed Pat's love to feel happy and fulfilled. He told me, "Dr. Burns, I'm a *people* person. I *need* Pat's love. There's just no way I could ever feel good again without her." I suggested he test this belief with the Pleasure Predicting Sheet. As you can see, he scheduled a number of activities: jogging, straightening up his desk, cooking a gourmet meal for himself, talking to Pat on the telephone, and taking out a woman he had met. Fred had very low expectations for most of these activities, since he was convinced that life without Pat was meaningless. You can see his low predictions for any activities that didn't involve his wife in the third column of his Pleasure Predicting Sheet in Figure 3-1.

Fred walked into his next session glowing. He had enjoyed many of the activities far more than he had imagined. His date with Lynn, the woman he'd met, was quite rewarding, and he gave it a 95% rating (he had predicted 25%). This wasn't consistent with his belief that he needed his wife's love to feel good. His telephone conversation with his wife was actually the *least* enjoyable activity. This forced him to question his belief that she was the source of his happiness, and he began to think about his marriage in a more realistic light. He admitted that while

---

*It's best *not* to estimate your satisfaction as 100% because you can always imagine that things could be a little bit better!

Figure 3-1

Hypothesis: There's no way I could feel happy without Pat's love.

PLEASURE PREDICTING SHEET

ACTIVITY Schedule Activities with a Potential for Pleasure or Personal Growth	COMPANION (If Alone, Specify Self)	SATISFACTION	
		Predicted (0–100) (Record This *Before* Each Activity)	Actual (0–100) (Record This *After* Each Activity)
Jogging	Self	50%	80%
Straighten up my desk	Self	50%	75%
Cook and eat a nice meal	Self	50%	80%
Call wife	Pat	90%	5%
Date	Lynn	25%	95%

Copyright © David D. Burns, M.D.

their relationship had a number of positive aspects, there were a number of serious deficiencies. Most important, Fred discovered that many of the things he did by himself were just as satisfying as, and often *more* satisfying than, the things he did with other people. This helped him discover that in the final analysis only one person in this world could ever make Fred happy—and that person was Fred! Liberation!

This is one of the greatest discoveries a person can make. During the first week in January, Fred told me, "Dr. Burns, I was alone on Christmas, and I was alone again on New Year's Eve, and you know what? These were the happiest holidays of my life! I actually *enjoyed* being with myself. It was a delicious experience. If you had told me this was possible the first time you saw me in early December, when I felt so miserable, I would have said you were crazy!"

What do you think? Do you still think you need some-one else's love and companionship to feel good about yourself? Do you believe that if you're alone you're bound to feel empty and lonely? If so, do an experiment with the Pleasure Predicting Sheet. Schedule a series of creative activities by yourself as well as with other people. Predict how enjoyable each one will be. Then do each activity and rate your actual enjoyment. You could be surprised by how it turns out!

One woman who used the Pleasure Predicting Sheet after years of loneliness and low self-esteem described how it affected her:

"I just started concentrating on things outside of me and I began to take an interest in the universe: to really enjoy the beauty of everything, the sensual experience, the intel-lectual experience, everything life has to offer. I began to tell myself, 'This is the only life I have, and I'm going to enjoy every minute of it. Enjoy the moments as they pass.' I discovered that I could just enjoy looking at the river, looking out my window. Every second I try to find some-thing to enjoy. Especially I try to enjoy people. Fascinat-ing. And things just happened. I started to do this as an academic exercise at first. You know, just to get away from my own feelings of disappointment and emptiness.

And then I found that the exercises were starting to transform me. I started getting good vibrations from people, and this reinforced the good feelings I was beginning to develop about myself because I discovered I could really enjoy being by myself when I was alone.

"I used to believe that there was something about me that made me ultimately and essentially unattractive. I felt this emanated from my very core and was unchangeable. I believed this 100 percent. But I don't believe it anymore. I think that the process of giving pleasure to myself, finding satisfaction in so many things in life, is a very fulfilling experience. It made me feel good about myself. It made me value myself more.

"I got rid of the idea that I had all through childhood that because I was large and ugly and unattractive I could only measure myself by my achievements. I discovered that I was a good person in and for myself, of myself. I didn't need to measure up to any invisible standards anymore. I became happy just with myself. Then I started getting lots of positive feedback from other people, and so all of this reinforced the positive self-image I was building within myself as a result of learning to be happy alone.

"I remember the first day I really started to work at this. I came out of a therapy session where I had learned about the Pleasure Predicting Sheet, and I started to predict how satisfying various experiences would be. I remember walking into a coffee shop and sitting at a lunch counter eating soup and some man started to talk to me. It turned out that he had been an author—he was an author and went on the lecture circuit. He was in the White House in the State Department and was a speech writer for the President. It was just a fascinating experience.

"I started to tune in—not just to people with unusual experiences—but to everyone. First it was just an experiment to see if I could get outside of myself and make any of these techniques work. And I was surprised to learn that I could take so much pleasure in things, that I could focus on living for the moment instead of waiting for the future to be better than today.

"I've also met with some very pleasant experiences with men in varying degrees of closeness. This has been a very psychologically and emotionally expanding experience for me, but I don't feel that I *need* a man in my life, and I haven't felt that for some time. I *want* a man sometimes. But I don't need a man to feel productive or happy. It's the same with many other things in my life. I can have many fulfilling experiences doing a variety of things, but I think that I could live without them if I had to. I don't need a man to reassure me that I am an attractive human being or that I am desirable. I think that I'm developing that assurance in myself."

Once you start using the Pleasure Predicting Sheet, you may realize you can be happy for *brief* periods of time when you're alone and involved in something interesting, but you may still believe that if you're alone for a long time you will ultimately feel depressed and lonely. You may argue, "Sooner or later if I had no friends to be close to, I'd just go bananas." While it's true that we are social creatures and that there can be many benefits to having intimate friends, it still doesn't follow that you will have to feel miserable if you're alone for a long period of time. There are two ways to prove this.

One way to find out if you can be happy for a long time by yourself is to test it with an experiment. Spend longer and longer periods of time alone. Start with an hour, then a day, then a weekend, and maybe even an entire week or a month or more. You may not have the luxury of spending an entire month alone, since you have to go to work and earn a living. However, you could choose to spend all of your evenings and weekends alone, or you could spend several weeks entirely alone during a vacation. It's crucial that you continue using the Pleasure Predicting Sheet and that you schedule creative and enjoyable activities for yourself. Continue to treat yourself with love and compassion and see how your capacity for satisfaction changes when you're alone for longer periods of time.

I have performed this experiment myself on a number of occasions, and many of my patients have done the same. I've discovered, much to my surprise, that my capacity to enjoy myself *increases* the longer I'm alone. In order to be happy when you're totally alone, you'll have to learn how to develop a good relationship with yourself, and that can take time. But once you catch on, you will discover that you get better and better at befriending yourself. It can be very reassuring to find out that you can accept and enjoy yourself indefinitely, if necessary. Then you will know that you *never* have to feel lonely.

Another way to prove this to yourself is with the "Deserted Island Fantasy."* Imagine that you're the sole survivor on a desert island after a shipwreck. Assume that the island has a reasonable climate as well as an adequate supply of berries, fish, and other foods and that a box of supplies, such as cooking utensils, has washed up on shore. Now, how would you feel and what would you do? Your first impulse might be to sit on the beach and feel sorry for yourself. That would probably be very upsetting. After you got tired of moping you might make a shelter for yourself for the evening. Can you imagine doing that? Can you see yourself constructing a little hut out of palm leaves and sticks? How satisfying was it, between 0% and 99%, to construct this hut? Can you see that this was more rewarding than weeping piteously on the beach?

What are you going to do next? It's dinnertime, and you're hungry. You might want to look for some berries to pick. As you go exploring, you discover a crystal-clear pond with a waterfall and you can see some fish swimming. Can you see the pond and the fish? Get a stick and make a spear. Now the stick is in your hands. Visualize this as vividly as you can. Now see if you can spear a fish . . . oops? You missed! Try again. You missed! This will take some practice and concentration—there's a fat fish moving slowly. Do you see him? There! You got him! He's out of the water, wiggling on your stick. Now you can clean him for dinner! How satisfying was this between 0% and 99%?

Now you bring your fish and berries back to camp so

---

*The use of a Deserted Island Fantasy as a projective psychotherapy technique was originally developed by Dr. Arnold A. Lazarus. Readers interested in learning more about other uses of the Deserted Island Fantasy can consult: A. A. Lazarus, *The Practice of Multi-Modal Therapy* (New York: McGraw-Hill Book Company, 1981), pp. 103–127.

you can prepare dinner. First you'll have to build a fire. Gather some sticks and arrange them. Can you see the sticks? Are they arranged? Now light the fire . . . it's burning nicely. Now put the fish in the pan. Can you see it frying? After it's cooked you can eat it, along with the berries. Can you imagine how good they taste? Ask yourself how satisfying this has been between 0% and 99%. I suspect you might find these activities quite challenging and enjoyable.

Here's the rub. Most people will admit they could enjoy building their campsite and gathering food and cooking, but they insist that after a period of time they would eventually feel bored and lonely. This might occur after one day or after ten days. When this happens, you will have a new challenge, another problem to solve. And how would you solve the problem of boredom and loneliness if you were on the desert island? Well, if you were bored you could find something interesting to do. You might want to get involved in walking or jogging. Start with a mile a day and see how long it would take to work yourself up to marathon distances. You might also want to explore the island. You could make a map or study the wildlife there. You could go for a swim in the pond with the waterfall. Perhaps there's a dormant volcano you could climb and explore. Or you could get involved in yoga or meditation. Or you could gather rocks and spell "HELP" in giant letters on the beach.

So what's the point? Boredom and loneliness have little or nothing to do with being alone. If you want to mope and feel unhappy, you can. This is just as easy when you're surrounded by friends and family as when you're alone. But if you want to feel fulfilled, that potential also exists within you. Virtually any pleasure or experience you can enjoy sharing with another person you can enjoy sharing with yourself. The real problem is, not being alone, but the belief that being alone is bound to be a miserable, empty, or terrifying experience. I suspect you'll discover that being alone can often be as enjoyable as being with other people who are dear to you.

4

Think Your Way
to Self-esteem

If you're home alone on a Saturday night you may punish yourself with a steady barrage of self-downing thoughts, such as "I'm such a loser. I have no one to be with tonight." If you're at a restaurant or a theater, the parade of self-abuse continues: "I'm out of place. All of these people are having fun and I'm all alone. They probably think I'm peculiar. What's wrong with me?" You're probably unaware how hard you're being on yourself because these thoughts are so habitual and they seem so realistic. If you want to overcome loneliness, you'll have to learn to talk to yourself in a more positive and supportive way.

But how can you do this? Remember the Deserted Island Fantasy? One of the most famous of all castaways was Robinson Crusoe.* After the shipwreck he thought of himself as a "solitaire, one banished from human society," hopeless and living on an "island of despair." He felt absolutely miserable, abandoned, and entirely depressed. But he found that by writing down the negative, "evil" thoughts that were upsetting him and substituting more positive, "good" thoughts, he began to feel much better. His double-column technique is illustrated in the following examples, which are quoted from the text:

---

*Daniel Defoe, *Robinson Crusoe* (New York: Signet, 1960).

Evil	*Good*
I am singled out and separated, as it were, from all the world to be miserable.	But I am singled out too from all the ship's crew to be spared from death; and he that miraculously saved me from death can deliver me from this condition.
I am divided from mankind, a solitaire, one banished from human society.	But I am not starving and perishing on a barren place, affording no substance.
I have no soul to speak to, or relieve me.	But God wonderfully sent the ship in near enough to the shore, that I have gotten out so many necessary things as will either supply my wants, or enable me to supply myself even as long as I live.

Although you might view this as quaint, during the past decade a similar method, illustrated in Figure 4-1, has been used by psychiatrists and psychologists around the world and found to be remarkably effective in the treatment of problems such as depression, loneliness, and low self-esteem. At the top of the Daily Mood Log, you describe the situation that's upsetting you in the space marked "Upsetting Event." You might feel bad because a friend criticized you or because you're home alone without a date on a Saturday night. Ben, the twenty-nine-year-old man whose Daily Mood Log is illustrated, became despondent when Kathy, the woman he'd been dating for several months, turned down his marriage proposal. Kathy said she loved him but didn't feel ready to settle down yet. In the space marked "Feelings," Ben indicated that he felt crushed, hurt, and hopeless. Proposing had taken enormous courage, since he was afraid of commitment because of fears of getting "trapped" in an unsatisfactory relationship. In the past, Ben had always been the one who was "hard to get," and now that the tables were turned he found himself confronting a situation he wasn't prepared to handle.

Once you've described the upsetting event and recorded your feelings, write down your negative thoughts in the left-hand column that's labeled "Automatic Thoughts." They're called "automatic thoughts" because they flow through your mind automatically without any conscious decision or effort on your part to put them there. You can see that Ben was being extremely self-critical. He was telling himself, "I can't bear life without her. Something must be seriously wrong with me because all of my relationships end up in the toilet. I'll probably lose her to some creepy guy," etc.

FIGURE 4-1
The Daily Mood Log*

DESCRIBE THE UPSETTING EVENT—Kathy declined to marry me "for now," so I broke off the relationship.

NEGATIVE FEELINGS—Record your emotions and rate each one on a scale from 0 (the least) to 100 (the most). Include feelings such as sad, anxious, angry, guilty, lonely, hopeless, frustrated, etc.

Emotion	Rating (0–100)	Emotion	Rating (0–100)	Emotion	Rating (0–100)
1. Hurt	95%	3. Inadequate	95%	5. Crushed	99%
2. Frustrated	95%	4. Hopeless	99%	6.	

AUTOMATIC THOUGHTS	DISTORTIONS	RATIONAL RESPONSES
Write down your negative thoughts and number them consecutively.	Identify the distortions in each "Automatic Thought."	Substitute more realistic and positive thoughts.
1. I can't bear life without her.	1. Magnification.	1. It's disappointing to be turned down and it's natural to feel hurt, but it's silly to say I can't bear life without her!

AUTOMATIC THOUGHTS	DISTORTIONS	RATIONAL RESPONSES
2. Something must be seriously wrong with me because all of my relationships end up in the toilet.	2. Personalization; all-or-nothing thinking.	2. Kathy may be afraid of commitment or she may not be right for me. Either way, it doesn't mean there's something wrong with me, and it's certainly not true that all my relationships end up "in the toilet." I deserve credit for proposing and taking a risk!
3. I'll probably lose her to some creepy guy.	3. Fortune-telling.	3. There's no definite proof I'll "lose" her—she simply isn't ready to consider marriage at this time. If I do lose her, she'll hopefully find a guy who's good for her.

AUTOMATIC THOUGHTS	DISTORTIONS	RATIONAL RESPONSES
4. I can't stand the pain and I won't be able to function.	4. Magnification; all-or-nothing thinking.	4. I can bear the pain, even though it's not very comfortable. I *can* function if I choose to.
5. She never really loved me but used me selfishly.	5. Mind reading; all-or-nothing thinking.	5. She is attracted to me, even though she may not love me enough to get married. She's exploring our relationship, not "using me." I can't be "used" unless I let myself. No one is forcing me to pursue this relationship.
6. I'm a total failure at life.	6. All-or-nothing thinking.	6. That's nonsense! I'm quite successful at many things.
7. I'm a fool. A sucker. I gave my best and got the shaft.	7. Labeling.	7. I'm not "a fool" but a human being. Getting rejected at times is all part of the game.

AUTOMATIC THOUGHTS	DISTORTIONS	RATIONAL RESPONSES
8. That bitch knew all along that she was going to dump me, but she strung me along anyway.	8. Mind reading; labeling.	8. If she was "stringing me along" it might be due to certain fears and insecurities of hers. Possibly she was attracted to me and wanted to see if her feelings would become stronger.
9. Now I'm humiliated in front of my parents. She liked them a lot, but I wasn't good enough for her and now they know it, too.	9. Mind reading.	9. My parents will probably give me extra support. I have no reason to feel humiliated. I did nothing shameful, and being turned down doesn't mean I'm not "good enough."
10. It doesn't pay to be loving and trusting to women. You can't trust them anyway.	10. Overgeneralization.	10. Am I saying that *no* relationship will work just because this one didn't? That's ridiculous.

AUTOMATIC THOUGHTS	DISTORTIONS	RATIONAL RESPONSES
11. If I was a real man I'd kill myself and end the charade of my existence. I have no guts. I'm just a rich kid, a pussy-whipped wimp. God forbid if Kathy knew what I was really like!	11. Labeling.	11. There's no such thing as a "real man" or a "pussy-whipped wimp." I've had a real disappointment and I deserve support, not condemnation.

OUTCOME—Review your "Rational Responses" and put a check in the box that describes how you now feel:
☐ not at all better; ☐ somewhat better; ☑ quite a bit better; ☐ a lot better.

*Copyright © 1984, David D. Burns, M.D., from *Intimate Connections* (New York: William Morrow & Company).

It's important to realize the enormous impact that these negative thoughts can have on the way you feel. What's even more important is that these gloomy thoughts—which can seem so totally valid and convincing when you feel bad—are frequently quite distorted and illogical. The ten types of twisted thinking that lead to negative feelings such as depression, anger, and anxiety are listed on Table 4-1. It's a good idea to become familiar with these distortions because understanding them is the key to understanding your loneliness and low self-esteem. Even more important, you can overcome these negative feelings by learning to think about yourself and your life more realistically.

Ben's fifth negative thought, "She never really loved

me but used me selfishly," would be an example of "jumping to conclusions," the fifth distortion listed in Table 4-1, since he's assuming that he knows Kathy's motives. There are many other reasons why she might have turned him down—maybe she feels insecure and isn't sure that she loves him enough to make a major commitment. Ben's thought would also be an example of "all-or-nothing thinking," since he's assuming that Kathy loves him either totally or not at all. This is quite unrealistic, because people can have a wide range of feelings for each other, both positive and negative, that can be relatively stronger or weaker at different times. Love is not like a light switch that's either on or off.

Once you've pinpointed the distortions in your thoughts, substitute others that are more positive and realistic in the right-hand column. You can see how this helped Ben put the experience in its proper perspective so he could think about the problem in a more objective and compassionate manner instead of ruthlessly ripping himself to shreds. This is the *essence* of self-esteem. Anyone can feel good when things go his way, but when the chips are down, you have your greatest opportunity to love and support yourself.

Ten Ways to Untwist Your Thinking

After you've written down the negative thoughts that are bothering you, sometimes you'll immediately feel better because you can see how negative they are. However, it isn't always so easy because sometimes the negative thoughts can seem awfully realistic. Many of my patients tell me that when they're stuck, if they write down their negative thoughts and then wait a few days and review them again, it suddenly dawns on them how unreasonable these thoughts are, and they begin to feel better.

One of my associates at the Institute for Cognitive and Behavioral Therapies at the Presbyterian-University of Pennsylvania Medical Center recently described a problem with a twenty-seven-year-old woman named Virginia, whom he was treating for depression. Virginia felt lonely and was having difficulties with her boyfriend, Nick. One day around noon, Virginia called Nick's office on impulse. Nick's

TABLE 4-1
The Ten Forms of Twisted Thinking

1. All-or-nothing thinking: You look at things in absolute, black-and-white categories.

2. Overgeneralization: You view a single negative event as a never-ending pattern of defeat.

3. Mental filter: You dwell on one negative detail, so your vision of the entire situation becomes dark and cloudy, like the drop of ink that discolors the entire beaker of water.

4. Discounting the positive: You insist that your positive qualities or accomplishments "don't count."

5. Jumping to conclusions: (A) Mind reading—you assume that people are reacting negatively to you when there's no definite evidence for this; (B) fortune-telling—you arbitrarily predict that things can't change or will turn out badly.

6. Magnification or minimization: You blow things up out of proportion or shrink their importance inappropriately. This is also called "catastrophizing."

7. Emotional reasoning: You reason from how you feel: "I feel like a failure; therefore I must really be one."

8. "Should" statements: You criticize yourself or other people with "shoulds" or "shouldn'ts." You tell yourself you "should have" done this or you "shouldn't have" done that. "Musts," "oughts," and "have tos" are similar offenders.

9. Labeling: You identify with your shortcomings and mistakes and label yourself as a "fool" or a "loser," or a "jerk" instead of pinpointing the cause of the problem so you can learn from it or try to correct it.

10. Personalization and blame. You blame yourself for something you weren't entirely responsible for (such as getting an illness or getting divorced). Conversely, you may blame other people, external events, or fate and overlook the ways your own attitudes and behavior may have contributed to a problem.

This table was adapted from D. D. Burns, *Feeling Good: The New Mood Therapy* (New York: William Morrow, 1980; Signet, 1981). For further information, see Chapter 3, "You Feel The Way You Think."

secretary told Virginia that Nick was away from his desk for about an hour. Virginia felt hurt because of her thought, "He's probably avoiding me. I'll never get a man." This thought was typical of many upsetting thoughts Virginia had each day. When you've felt insecure and lonely, you, too, may have felt convinced that you were doomed to be alone forever. Virginia and her therapist couldn't come up with a "Rational Response" that was convincing and helpful to her, so they asked me for a consultation.

When you feel trapped by a negative thought like this, it can be very helpful to write it down and circle it, as in Figure 4-2. Each arrow represents a separate strategy to help you refute your negative thought. Having many approaches available will increase your chances to turn things around so you feel better again.

The first technique is to identify the distortion(s) in your thought, using Table 4-1 as a guide. Once you see how illogical a thought is, it's usually much easier to combat it. Virginia's thought involves "mind reading" because she's jumping to the conclusion, without any real evidence, that her boyfriend is avoiding her. A second distortion is "fortune-telling" because Virginia predicts she'll be alone forever. She has no way of knowing that this relationship will break up, and she has no crystal ball that can forecast the future. A third distortion is "labeling," since she upsets herself by wondering if she'll ever "get" a man. This label makes a love affair seem like a competition or a poker game and creates feelings of desperation and possessiveness. Most men are more interested in being "loved" than in being "gotten." A fourth distortion is "emotional reasoning," since Virginia reasons from how she feels. She feels worried and insecure, so she thinks there must be real problems in her relationship. She feels rejected, jealous, and hurt, so she assumes she's been betrayed. This way of thinking can be extremely misleading because your thoughts, not external reality, create your feelings. When your thoughts are distorted and unrealistic, your feelings won't reflect what's really happening. Some forms of psychotherapy are based on the idea that "getting in touch with your feelings" is the key to mental health and emotional maturity, but this isn't always the case. It's certainly important to be aware of how you feel, but it's also important to realize that your feelings aren't always a reliable guide to the way things really are.

After you've identified the distortion(s) in a negative thought, try to think about the situation in a more realistic and compassionate way. One useful technique is called the "Double-Standard Technique." Ask yourself what you'd say to a dear friend who was in a similar situation. Would you say, "Gee, your boyfriend is probably avoiding you.

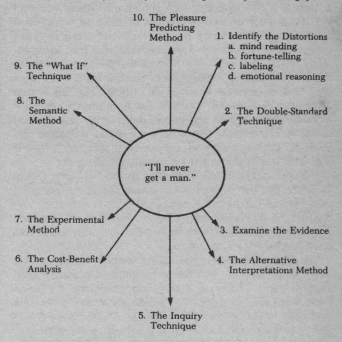

10. The Pleasure Predicting Method

1. Identify the Distortions
   a. mind reading
   b. fortune-telling
   c. labeling
   d. emotional reasoning

9. The "What If" Technique

8. The Semantic Method

2. The Double-Standard Technique

"I'll never get a man."

7. The Experimental Method

3. Examine the Evidence

6. The Cost-Benefit Analysis

4. The Alternative Interpretations Method

5. The Inquiry Technique

FIGURE 4-2
Ten Ways of Combating Negative Thoughts

When you're upset by a negative thought, it can be helpful to use a variety of strategies to put the lie to it, because you never know which approach will be the most helpful to you. Once it dawns on you how self-defeating and unrealistic your negative thought is, you'll generally feel much better about yourself.

You'll never get a man''? I suspect you'd never talk to a friend like that because it would be cruel and illogical. But then why do you talk to yourself like that? Will treating yourself in a cruel and illogical manner help you? The essence of self-esteem is to treat yourself with the same objectivity and compassion you would extend to a friend.

The third technique in Figure 4-2 involves asking yourself, ''What is the evidence for this particular thought?'' Certainly, when a real problem exists you should confront it honestly and directly, but sometimes when you feel insecure your fears will come out of the blue when there isn't any solid evidence to support them. Your negative thoughts will only *seem* valid because you feel so upset. Virginia needs to ask herself whether there's any reason to think that Nick is avoiding her. Has he been upset with her? Has he seemed annoyed or critical? Has his sexual drive been diminished? Does he fail to return phone calls? Does he show up late and cancel dates at the last minute? If so, it could mean that there are some problems and conflicts that Nick and Virginia need to deal with. But if not, then it's unlikely that he's really avoiding her.

Virginia can also ask herself if there's any convincing evidence that she'll ''never get a man.'' Has she gone out with men in the past? Certainly she has. Is she going out with a man in the present? Clearly she is. If so, it hardly seems likely that this will be her last and only chance to develop a loving relationship.

The ''Alternative Interpretations Method'' in Figure 4-2 can also be helpful. Instead of jumping to upsetting conclusions about why something is happening, make a list of various possible explanations. While it's remotely possible that Nick might be avoiding Virginia, it's far more likely that Nick is at lunch, that he's involved in a conference, or that he's away from his desk to do an errand.

A fifth approach is called the ''Inquiry Technique.'' If Virginia has concerns about Nick's feelings about the relationship, she should probably just ask him how he feels. Although that might seem like obvious or trivial advice, you'd be surprised how many people go around trying to read other people's minds. They assume how people feel instead of simply asking them. Virginia can ask Nick what he likes most about her and their relationship. She can also ask him about the things that turn him off. When you ask people for specific negative *and* positive reactions to you, it makes it much easier for them to be honest and to open up. Virginia may discover that Nick's very happy with how things are going. If she finds out that there are some problems, she can deal with them constructively instead of constantly worrying about and becoming obsessed with how terrible things are. In my experience, dealing with real problems is generally less stressful than dealing with the imaginary problems we create in our minds.

The sixth technique, illustrated in Figure 4-3, is the "Cost-Benefit Analysis." Ask yourself how a particular thought or attitude will help you and how it will hurt you. Sometimes we worry and get obsessed with things because we believe our fears are like magic charms that will protect us. You've probably known straight-A students who constantly complain about how badly they're doing. They predict the next exam will be the disaster that will end their career, even though there's not one shred of evidence for this. Usually they end up doing great on the test, only to become obsessed with how awful the next examination will be. Do you know why they do this? They often believe that if it weren't for all their constant worrying, things actually would fall apart. They feel that being in a constant state of stress and turmoil is the price they must pay for success, and they believe that if they develop a positive, optimistic outlook, the world will fall apart.

People in love affairs sometimes fall into the same trap. Virginia may have the attitude that if she assumes that Nick is on the verge of leaving her, she'll be protected and assured of his love. In point of fact, the opposite is more likely to occur. People who don't trust that others can love them often alienate people with their insecurity, jealousy, and suspiciousness. This fuels the fire and makes them feel even more insecure. In contrast, if you assume that you are lovable and that others do respect you, this is likely to be a self-fulfilling prophecy because your positive feelings about others will make them feel good and they'll find you even more attractive and desirable.

Figure 4-3
Cost-Benefit Analysis

My Upsetting Thought: He's probably avoiding me. I'll never get a man.

Advantages of Believing This	Disadvantages of Believing This
1. I won't get complacent and then get hurt later on.	1. I'll feel depressed and desperate.
	2. I'll feel insecure and jealous.
	3. I don't really have any evidence that he's avoiding me, so I may just upset myself over nothing.
(35)	(65)

The seventh technique is the "Experimental Method." Sometimes a scientific test of your negative attitudes can be a powerful way of putting the lie to them. One way Virginia could test her belief that she'll "never get a man" would be to flirt with twenty interesting men in the next two weeks. It's quite likely that a number of them will respond positively. This could boost Virginia's self-confidence and put the lie to her fears that Nick represents her one and only chance for love. It would show her just how unrealistic her pessimistic expectations about her future really are.

The eighth approach is the "Semantic Method." Sometimes just changing the language you use can put things into a different perspective. Trying to "get" a man is likely to be a pretty frustrating way for Virginia to approach her relationships. She needs to think more about "loving" Nick than "getting" him. What are his needs and feelings? How can she make him feel special? Caring about others is far more productive than worrying about losing them. Sometimes the loneliest people project so much insecurity and self-centeredness that they drive people away and end up making things worse for themselves.

The ninth approach is the " 'What If' Technique." Instead of trying to disprove your negative thought, you use the opposite strategy and ask yourself, "What if this negative thought were really true? What would that mean to me? Why would it be upsetting to me?" Write down the negative thoughts and fantasies that come to mind, because they will give you important hints about the deeper fears and the irrational attitudes that make it hard for you to get close to others. Virginia had the thought, "If he really is avoiding me, it means he'll reject me. That would mean I was unlovable and I'd be alone forever. Then I'd be miserable and life wouldn't be worth living."

These thoughts reveal several self-defeating beliefs about love and marriage that may be creating problems for Virginia:

1. Conflicts and disagreements with people I care about are dangerous. If there's a problem in a relationship, it means I'll probably be rejected.

2. If Nick rejects me, it's necessarily my fault and it proves that I'm basically unlovable.

3. If one man rejects me, it means that I'll be alone forever.

4. If I'm alone, then life is not worth living.

Modifying these attitudes can help you conquer the deeper fears that rob you of self-esteem and make it hard to develop meaningful relationships. Sometimes it helps to list the advantages and disadvantages of these attitudes. Virginia can ask herself how it will help her to believe that her whole existence and future and potential for happiness depend on Nick. And how will it hurt her to believe this? Does Virginia want to give Nick so much power over her self-esteem? Sometimes you can sabotage a relationship by making someone overly important to you. In contrast, if you make them a little less important by deciding you can live without them, you will often feel more relaxed, and this can improve your relationship.

The tenth technique—the "Pleasure Predicting Method" —involves the use of the "Pleasure Predicting Sheet" described earlier. Instead of ruminating about how awful life would be without Nick, Virginia needs to take control of her life and get involved in some productive activities on her own. This will remind her that he really isn't her only source of happiness and satisfaction. If Virginia feels empty and miserable whenever she's alone, it's unlikely that a relationship with Nick could ever make her feel very secure or happy in the long run. But once she discovers that she can make her life satisfying and meaningful when she's alone, she'll feel better about herself and she'll have more to offer Nick.

Many single people have trouble being alone because they feel self-conscious and awkward whenever they go out by themselves. You may be reluctant to schedule creative, enjoyable activities for yourself, such as going to good restaurants or movies or operas, because you feel that other people might think less of you if they see you there alone. This attitude puts you at the mercy of other people and restricts your freedom. Suppose you go to a restaurant by yourself and you feel uncomfortable. You may be telling yourself, "I'm out of place here. I'm making everyone uncomfortable." You can use your Daily Mood Log right on the spot. Borrow a pen from the waiter and jot down these negative thoughts on a paper napkin. Then substitute more positive, rational thoughts: "It's my right to be here, just like anyone else. It's unlikely that the other people are terribly concerned with whether I'm eating here or not." You may resist using the Daily Mood Log in a restaurant because of your thought, "Someone might wonder what I was writing down and think I was peculiar!" If so, write *that* negative thought down, identify the distortions in it, and substitute a rational response. Your thought involves mind reading, since you're assuming you know what other people think. It also involves fortune-telling, since you anticipate that something bad will happen if someone has a negative thought about you. You might fantasize that rumors will spread like wildfire if someone sees you alone in a restaurant and that soon everyone in town will ostracize you. How would you talk back to these negative thoughts?

How to Conquer Your Fears of Being Alone

The Feared Fantasy Technique is another powerful method that can help you get over the fear of doing something alone. Write out an imaginary dialogue in which a stranger approaches you and actually says all the unpleasant things that you think other people might be thinking about you. Although no one would ever really say such insulting things to you, writing the criticisms down and talking back to them can help you see just how illogical and ridiculous they really are.

The following is an excerpt from a therapy session with a woman named Sarah who went to a movie by herself but felt out of place when she noticed all the couples together. In the following dialogue she pretended to be a nasty stranger who was berating her for being alone, and I played her role to show her how to handle the criticisms:

SARAH (IN THE ROLE OF THE NASTY STRANGER): You're all alone here. That must mean that nobody wants to be with you.

DAVID (IN THE ROLE OF SARAH): I chose to come here by myself. I enjoy being by myself.

SARAH (AS THE NASTY STRANGER): But everyone else is paired off in couples. Don't you feel strange? After all, this is a couples' world!

DAVID (AS SARAH): Why should I feel strange? It's true that there are a lot of couples and families here, but I also see several single people. I like to think of it more as a "humans' world" than as a "couples' world."

SARAH (AS THE NASTY STRANGER): But other people might think that nobody cares about you.

DAVID (AS SARAH): As a matter of fact, I don't have an intimate relationship just now. Should that be upsetting?

SARAH (AS THE NASTY STRANGER): That means you have no real friends and you're probably alone all the time.

DAVID (AS SARAH): Well, what's so terrible about being alone?

SARAH (AS THE NASTY STRANGER): Well, maybe you're a loony who can enjoy being alone, but you should realize you're making all these people uncomfortable. I mean, they take one look at you and they think, "What's she doing here all alone. She must be *weird!*"

DAVID (AS SARAH): Well, if they get too uncomfortable they might have to try to find a theater that only admits couples. But if they want to go to a public theater like this one, they'll just have to learn to tolerate seeing occasional single people. But I don't understand why seeing me sitting alone would make anyone uncomfortable. Are you afraid my singleness might be infectious? Are you afraid of being alone?

This dialogue helped Sarah see how unnecessary it was to be overly concerned about what other people might think of her when she was alone. I want to emphasize the importance of actually writing out this type of dialogue if you want to change the way you think and feel. Committing your fears and self-criticisms to paper can help you see how cruel and absurd they are. This can help you develop more realistic and self-accepting attitudes.

Developing Healthier Attitudes

Overcoming your fear of being alone may involve a change in your personal value system. Many people tell themselves, "I can't feel truly happy and fulfilled unless I have a loving relationship with someone who cares about me." Bret, a divorced man, felt desperately lonely and unhappy. He visited singles bars and chased women every night of the week because he was absolutely convinced he couldn't be happy until he developed a relationship with a woman. This approach wasn't very successful because women sensed how needy and desperate he was, and they gave him the brush-off or avoided him. I tried to persuade Bret to give up his desperate woman chasing and use the Pleasure Predicting Sheet to see if he could learn to be happy doing things on his own. Bret stubbornly refused and insisted he needed a woman before he could feel worthwhile and find happiness. He said it made him more human and lovable to believe this and told me he wasn't about to stop chasing women, no matter how miserable he felt.

One of the best ways to modify a self-defeating attitude is to do a Cost-Benefit Analysis, as indicated in Figure 4-4. Ask yourself how a particular belief will help you and how it will hurt you. If you feel convinced that you can't be happy until you have a partner, make a list of the advantages and disadvantages of believing this. This list may help you see that the costs outweigh the benefits of this particular way of thinking. Then you can revise your belief and substitute a more constructive attitude in its place.

FIGURE 4-4
Cost-Benefit Analysis

Belief: I can't feel truly happy and fulfilled unless I have a loving relationship with a partner who cares about me.

Advantages of Believing This	Disadvantages of Believing This
1. This attitude will make me work very hard at finding someone to love.	1. When I don't have a partner I'll feel empty and depressed.
2. When I find someone to love I'll feel happy and worthwhile.	2. I'll be putting my self-esteem in the hands of others. Women will be able to manipulate me because I'll be so afraid of being rejected.
	3. I may drive women away because I'll be so needy and dependent. They'll realize I don't have any real self-respect.
(40)	(60)

Revised Belief: It can be desirable to have a loving relationship with a woman I care about, but it's not a "need" like oxygen. In the meantime, I can survive happily on my own.

When you do this exercise, don't make the mistake of listing the advantages and disadvantages of *having* someone to love. List the advantages of believing you can't feel happy or worthwhile until you have someone to love. No one would deny that loving relationships with others can enhance your life. But if you're pursuing a partner to fill a void because you feel desperate and empty whenever you're alone, then you've fallen into the trap of basing your self-esteem on other people.

After he completed his list, Bret was surprised that the disadvantages of needing love far outweighed the advantages. The disadvantage that made the strongest impact on him was the realization that he was so afraid of rejection that women could easily manipulate him. He had given his ex-wife extensive financial concessions, and often bought expensive gifts for the women he went out with. Instead of appreciating his generosity, they just got more and more demanding. Eventually he would end up getting rejected anyway.

He decided to modify his attitude and to think about a loving relationship with a woman as an important personal goal but not as a "need" like oxygen. He then gave up his bar hopping and developed activities with several male friends—volleyball and hunting and fishing on weekends—which he found far more rewarding than carousing in single bars.

You may still resist the idea that being alone can be fulfilling. You're probably thinking, "But isn't it basically true that people *need* love? Isn't it selfish and sick to think that people can make themselves happy? Isn't it basically abnormal to be alone?" Another patient of mine, a lonely thirty-four-year-old single man named George who was making himself miserable chasing after women he met at discos and singles bars, began using the Pleasure Predicting Sheet and was surprised to notice that when he was visiting the Philadelphia Museum of Art by himself he actually began enjoying himself. When I suggested that this wasn't consistent with his belief that he "needed" love and was bound to be miserable whenever he was alone, he became annoyed and insisted that "it's abnormal to be alone." I suggested that George list the advantages and disadvantages of believing this, as illustrated in Figure 4-5. Balancing the costs against the benefits of this attitude helped him see just how irrational and destructive it was, even though it had seemed to him like a wonderfully idealistic and helpful notion. His "Revised Belief," which is listed at the bottom of Figure 4-5, emphasized the healthy aspects of time spent alone as well as time with others, and helped him make a greater commitment to his life.

Some people are afraid to discover they really don't need a partner to feel happy and worthwhile. They think that they'll lose all their motivation to get close to people and that they'll turn into "loners." This concern is unrealistic because you can want something in a healthy way without having the neurotic "need" for it. Very few people would argue that playing tennis is a human "need." If tennis courts suddenly disappeared from the surface of the earth, most tennis players would get involved in other equally enjoyable sports and continue to lead happy and productive lives. This shows that playing tennis is not a human need, yet people still love to play the game.

Figure 4-5
Cost-Benefit Analysis

Belief: It's abnormal to be alone.

Advantages of Believing This	Disadvantages of Believing This
1. I'll try hard to meet women.	1. I'll feel bad whenever I'm alone.
2. When I have someone to date I'll feel relieved.	2. I'll be desperate and insecure when I try to approach women. This will turn them off.
	3. I'll think of myself as a second-rate loser.
	4. I won't take a positive attitude toward my life until I find someone. I won't try new things and experiment when I'm alone. I'll just pity myself and feel trapped in my loneliness.
	5. When I'm dating someone I'll be so worried about rejection that I'll be afraid to express my feelings and to be myself. This lack of self-confidence may turn people off.
(20)	(80)

Revised Belief: Relationships with others can be a source of growth and sharing, but being by myself can also be a healthy and positive experience.

This same reasoning applies to relationships. Once you discover that you don't really "need" other people because you have the capacity to feel happy and fulfilled when you're alone, you will still find that relationships can be a tremendous source of joy and satisfaction. Finding someone to share your life with can give you a unique opportunity to grow. Once you learn to love and like yourself and to be happy when you're alone, I predict you'll have more, not fewer, opportunities for sharing genuine love with people you care about.

Some people do enjoy and cherish their time alone, but they feel ashamed of this because our culture promotes the joys of love and togetherness so much that we begin to feel as if anyone who enjoys being alone is somehow defective. Several years ago I treated a young woman named Paula who was troubled because what she loved more than anything else was art. Paula could get completely absorbed in painting, and she often spent many hours as happy as a lark wandering through art museums and galleries studying the works of the great masters. Although Paula was dating actively and had many good friends, she sometimes preferred to spend time alone, even though she felt guilty about enjoying it.

Paula was troubled because her friends seemed excessively preoccupied with men, and they didn't seem to understand why she wanted to spend so much of her time alone. One girl friend had even told her it was abnormal to enjoy being alone and she was in danger of becoming a recluse. Paula sought therapy to see if there was, in fact, something dreadfully wrong with her.

To help Paula overcome this fear, I suggested she write a little essay entitled, "The Importance of Being Alone." You may be interested to know that within weeks of writing this memo Paula became engaged to an exciting man she'd been dating and was married shortly thereafter.

The Importance of Being Alone
(which is not to say being lonely)

I'll only feel lonely if I don't know how to be alone. Being alone is getting in touch with myself, becoming acquainted with my likes and dislikes, learning who I am, and loving myself.

These things are important to learn because they are what make me happy. I cannot get along with others unless I know and enjoy myself. When I feel happy with myself, then being myself comes naturally in any situation.

I used to be concerned about what I thought I should do and whether a given situation was going well; I rarely had any time to enjoy myself. I was trying to be several different people at once: my "should" self (what I "should" be); X's and Y's ideal (what I second-guessed they would like me to be); and my ideal (what I wanted to be). Rather than pleasing half of these people half of the time, I was confusing everyone most of the time. And I was depressing myself; I felt like a hermit crab, living in someone else's old shell to protect my thin skin. I was always worried: what if people discovered the real me, and didn't like her?

Even at that time, I spent time alone, but hardly ever enjoyed it. I would tell myself, "It's egotistical to be alone and enjoy it. It's wrong and you should feel guilty." It is selfish to want to be alone, but there's nothing wrong with being selfish when my actions don't harm anyone. They cannot—I am alone. I can indulge myself. I can go to a museum and stand in front of a painting for 15 minutes or skip a room entirely. Or stay at home and read a book, take a long bath and clip my toenails, or even do nothing at all. All the while, I am learning what I enjoy, who I am, and what a nice person I can be to spend time with. Three pats on the back.

This is not to say that being alone is superior or that other people are unimportant. I can value their opinions, appreciate time spent with them, and recognize what's unique and special about them. But in doing something with someone I still create my own pleasure. The satisfaction of knowing I can please someone else is never more than the satisfaction of knowing that I can please myself. I do things with other people not to increase my pleasure but because being with them gives us both a different and broader range of enjoyment.

I have an ability to please myself, which can never be lost but only misplaced occasionally. I am my likes, dislikes, code of ethics, and morals: I am self-compatible.

Paula's statement shows the beginning of her belief in her own self-sufficiency. If her growth stopped at this point, she would risk becoming too narcissistic and self-centered. But your belief in yourself is simply the first step in learning to trust and reach out to others. Liking and accepting yourself need not be a symptom of sickness but the sign of health, and the joy that comes from within can make you more, not less, open to love and intimacy.

Serious lay readers and professionals who are interested in learning more about how cognitive therapy techniques can be used to overcome loneliness and low self-esteem may want to consult Appendix C: "How to Overcome an Inferiority Complex."

PART THREE

MAKING CONNECTIONS

5

How to Radiate
an Irresistible Glow

Most lonely people want nothing more than to learn the secrets of how to connect with other people. You may feel that all you need to be happy and fulfilled is a loving relationship with someone who cares about you. Nothing could be further from the truth. If you still believe that someone else is going to make you happy, you may have a tough time when you try to apply the powerful techniques described in the next few chapters. Once you've learned how to love yourself, then you'll find it much easier to connect with others.

Look Attractive. The first thing to do if you want to date more is to make yourself *look* terrific. Many shy and lonely people dress in a drab, unexciting way. This is a real mistake because it projects insecurity and a lack of self-esteem. If you dress in appealing clothes, you'll be projecting the message: "I'm desirable. I'm sexual. I like myself. You'll like me, too." That's half the battle.

In the introduction I described how a friend of mine from medical school days helped me overcome my loneliness and social awkwardness. One of the first principles William emphasized was the importance of dressing attractively and looking your best. He politely pointed out that my wrinkled white dress shirt, sloppy jeans, scuffed black dress shoes, white socks, and two-dollar haircut weren't exactly a turn-on for women. He took me to a fashionable men's clothing store and showed me just what to buy. He helped me select some expensive slacks and a matching silk shirt. Then he had me buy some slinky Italian shoes, with a belt and socks of just the right color, along with Hollywood-type wrap-around dark glasses. The whole outfit seemed outrageous, but William insisted that women loved men who were dressed to the teeth and it was critical to wear superb, perfectly integrated clothing. Finally, he urged me to go to a hair boutique, where I had a fifteen-dollar hair styling, which was expensive in the 1960s!

Well, I can tell you that the first time I went outside wearing my "hustling uniform" I really felt ridiculous! I felt about as conspicuous as if I were in a Donald Duck costume. But then a funny thing happened. As I was walking around a shopping mall I thought I noticed an attractive woman looking at *me* for the first time in my life—and I thought I even saw some desire in her eyes! I felt as if I'd been hit by a jolt of lightning!

If you're having trouble getting people of the opposite sex to notice you, maybe you should also take a long, hard look at the way you usually dress. It may be that you've given up on yourself, and this is reflected in your clothing. A change in your image can have profound effects on how people perceive you and how you feel about yourself.

Men can get ideas about the kinds of clothes that turn women on from a magazine such as *Gentleman's Quarterly*. Although the clothes such magazines illustrate are often quite expensive, the pictures will give you an idea of the ultimate in men's fashions. You can get similar but far less expensive outfits if you shop around. You should observe men you see in restaurants, in movies, on planes, or in other places who look great and who seem to be surrounded by admiring women. How are they dressed? If you dress in a similar way, you'll find out just how much excitement your attractive clothing—and you—can generate.

I do not mean to imply that there is a certain way everyone must dress in order to appear attractive to others. Attractiveness in clothing can be very subjective and individual. For example, for a woman who is high-collared, a long-sleeved dress may appear more attractive than if she were to wear a low-cut slinky gown. The important thing is to experiment with various styles and colors that emphasize your good features and bring out different appealing aspects of your personality, and to resist getting stuck in one approach because you think it is a part of your identity.

If you're not naturally clothes- and fashion-conscious, try to get as much input from other people as possible. Go into the better department stores and the fashionable men's boutiques. Look at the various styles that are popular this season. Find a salesman who's dressed in a perfectly integrated outfit and ask him to help you select something that will make you look sexy. Ask a friend what colors and styles would be flattering to you. Women *love* to give men this kind of advice, and their comments are usually right on target. I find that when I'm alone looking for clothes, I can get good suggestions from women who are shopping in the store. They almost always seem interested and happy to help out.

You men may resist these ideas because you're thinking, "I shouldn't have to lower myself by wearing ridiculous clothes." Or, "I'm not that kind of flashy person. I'm more the serious, genuine type. I'm not going to try to be a Burt Reynolds look-alike." Or, "Women should like me just the way I am. I shouldn't have to 'play the game.' "

The problem with these ideas is that they often result from insecurity, not sincerity. They sound rather unrealistic and self-centered. I'll bet that you find women who look well groomed and who obviously take good care of themselves much more sexy and appealing. Think of your ideal, fantasy lover. Picture her right now in your mind's eye. How does she look? How is she dressed? No doubt she looks terrific and is wearing a very attractive and flattering outfit. Well, women are just as attracted to color and fashion as you are, if not more so. When you look your best, women will appreciate you more. Paradoxically, being a little narcissistic can actually be a way of caring about others, because you're thinking about what appeals to them rather than selfishly and rigidly insisting on your own way of doing things.

The same applies to women. Don't be afraid to wear upbeat, sexy clothes. Go to the boutiques and look in the women's fashion magazines. Be a little outrageous. Step outside of the role or image you ordinarily have of yourself. Try to get away from the idea that you have one identity, whether it's that of a housewife, a secretary, a student, a doctor, a teacher, or an artist. Your personality has many facets, and it's a mistake to label yourself as any one thing because this will just restrict you. When you see an unusual and interesting outfit, don't say, "Oh, that's not *me*!" There is no *one* you, and this kind of defensiveness will only keep you stuck in a rut and make you less exciting to men.

Experimenting with different images and clothing can give you a broader sense of the range of your humanity and the vast, undiscovered potential that exists within you. You can have the experience of being whatever you imagine yourself as being. Allow yourself to expand your capacity as a human being by identifying with *many* roles and you can enrich the fabric of your life and the depth of your relationships.

Clothing is a uniform. It conveys a message, it allows you to play a particular role. You may be under the mistaken impression that if you don't dress or behave exactly as others expect you to but instead wear something outrageous—say, a sexy, slinky dress with a low-cut neckline—you'll look foolish or risk disapproval. In reality, by daring to explore more dimensions of yourself—allowing yourself to be wild and adventurous at times or tender and romantic at others—you'll usually get far more positive responses from others, who will be intrigued by the idea you have many interesting sides to your personality. The message this conveys is one of power. You're not a helpless victim. You're to be treated with respect and dignity. This will bolster your self-esteem. As you discover that your fears and inhibitions were just a figment of your imagination, you'll experience a high, a feeling of exhilaration. That's why mountain climbers are often people with a fear of heights: If they didn't have the fear, they wouldn't get the stimulation of acting in spite of it.

Feelings of insecurity and inferiority are based on the illusion that you're somehow less desirable and worthwhile than other people. By dressing creatively, you can bring in a new kind of illusion to replace the old one. Where the first one was negative, heavy, and destructive, the second one can be light-hearted, creative, and playful—and much healthier for you. And, I might add, a lot more fun!

There's one disclaimer. There are many people who aren't fashion- and appearance-conscious who develop wonderful, loving relationships with others. Certainly your self-esteem and capacity to care for others are infinitely more important than how you look. If you find it easy to develop positive, rewarding relationships, there's no reason whatsoever to feel you have to change your appearance. But if you are having trouble attracting people—as I did for so many years—a few changes may be indicated because you're wasting many precious opportunities for intimacy and love. Paying some attention to the way you look can be an important part of the solution because a positive, exciting self-image can be a way of respecting yourself and caring for others.

Think Attractive. In addition to looking your best by dressing in sexy, appealing clothing, it's important to think about yourself in a positive way. Much of the latest research in psychiatry and psychology shows that the messages people give themselves have an impact on the way they feel and behave. Telling yourself that you're a sexy and desirable person can have powerful effects on your self-image and the way other people respond to you.

Athletes and salespeople call this "psyching," and the technique is equally important when it comes to dating. I first learned about it from a prostitute I was treating for depression. She said that when she was depressed she wouldn't feel very attractive and this made it difficult to attract men. She said she discovered that she could overcome this if she put on a favorite record and dressed very slowly in front of a mirror. While she was dressing she would say things to herself like, "Look at those beautiful breasts. They're like ripe melons. How luscious! Look at that beautiful face and smile. You're irresistible!" At first she wouldn't believe these positive messages because she felt dumpy and fat. But she would persist, and as she was dressing she would begin to feel better about herself. By the time she went out she would be looking and feeling terrific. She described this as a "glow of sensuality" that she radiated when she walked down the street or entered a bar because she could sense that all the men's eyes were glued on her and they all desired her.

At first I was mildly shocked by her revelation, but as I thought about what she had said I realized that she had stumbled upon a fundamental truth: The messages we give ourselves have a great deal to do with how attractive we feel and the beauty we project to others. She confided to me that while she knew that many of my readers and patients wouldn't approve of her life-style, she hoped I would share this information with lonely people because she felt it might be helpful to them. It's okay to take pride in your appearance and to be proud of the way you look. Say nice things to yourself about your figure and your personality. Give up the idea that you're not good enough. Remember that loving yourself is just the first step toward loving someone else.

Some people have a deep fear of dressing attractively or looking sexy. There can be two reasons behind this. The first reason is a lack of self-esteem. If you see yourself as a loser, it may feel more natural to dress in plain, unappealing clothes. This also helps you keep your anxieties low, because if you don't come on too strong, people won't notice you and it won't seem as if you really have to compete for a mate. By maintaining a low profile, you won't have to confront your fears of rejection.

A second reason for dressing poorly is the fear of sexuality. Many people were raised to believe that sex is dirty or bad. Because they think that having a healthy pride in their own bodies and appearance is the same as being promiscuous, they become overly conservative and repress their own sensuality and creativity.

One way to overcome these inhibitions is to write down your negative thoughts about looking sexy and attractive, like the young woman whose Daily Mood Log is illustrated in Figure 5-1. Her lack of self-esteem, fears of disapproval, and shame about her shapely body are quite apparent. Talking back to her negative thoughts helped her take a greater sense of pride in her looks so she could give herself permission to dress more attractively. While this was just one aspect of developing greater self-esteem, it was an important step; before long she was dating a young man regularly and was subsequently married.

These suggestions, like others in this book, must be applied with common sense. You'll notice in Figure 5-1 that one of her inhibitions had to do with leaving her blouse unbuttoned at the top. Obviously, leaving one or two buttons open can project a more relaxed and friendly style, whereas leaving three or four buttons undone may attract more attention than you really want! Again, friends whose appearance you admire can provide valuable advice about what looks best on you.

Other people have the opposite problem. They're not ashamed of their good looks; they just feel convinced they aren't attractive enough to develop a satisfying relationship with someone they'd care about. They say, "I'm so plain-looking," or, "I'm just ordinary. Nobody desirable would be interested in me." It's true that people who are exceptionally attractive frequently do have an easier time getting dates, and if you're only average- or plain-looking, you may have to work harder at first to make contacts with people. But it's important to realize that good looks don't guarantee a successful relationship. I've treated numerous "beautiful people"—both men and women—who not only *looked* attractive but were intelligent and successful, and yet were terribly lonely and had difficulties getting close to anyone because they didn't feel good about themselves. By the same token, I've known and treated numerous people who were not at all attractive by normal standards but had a positive self-image and had no difficulty whatsoever forming intimate relationships.

If you don't believe me, you can do some research by conducting a little survey of your own today. Look at a dozen couples of various ages you see walking along the street, going to movies, eating in restaurants, and so on. Rate how attractive each partner is on a 0 to 10 scale. Keep a list of the ratings for the men and the women in each relationship. I think you'll discover that people who are only "average-looking" are just as likely to be with partners as people who are exceptionally handsome or beautiful. You'll also notice that sometimes both partners will be very attractive and sometimes there will be a

FIGURE 5-1
The Daily Mood Log

DESCRIBE THE UPSETTING EVENT—Fears about dressing in a more sexy, appealing way

NEGATIVE FEELINGS—Record your emotions and rate each one on a scale from 0 (the least) to 100 (the most). Include feelings such as sad, anxious, angry, guilty, lonely, hopeless, frustrated, etc.

Emotion	Rating (0–100)	Emotion	Rating (0–100)	Emotion	Rating (0–100)
1. Anxiety	90%	3. Embarrassed	90%	5.	
2. Guilt	90%	4.		6.	

AUTOMATIC THOUGHTS Write down your negative thoughts and number them consecutively.	DISTORTIONS Identify the distortions in each "Automatic Thought."	RATIONAL RESPONSES Substitute more realistic and positive thoughts.
1. I can't appear to be a sexual person. People might look down on me or try to force themselves on me.	1. Fortune-telling; emotional reasoning.	1. Aren't all people "sexual" people?
2. I shouldn't leave the top button of my blouse open and I should wear loose-fitting clothes.	2. "Should" statement.	2. Why shouldn't I? I like it that way. It looks better. Why should I hide my body?

AUTOMATIC THOUGHTS	DISTORTIONS	RATIONAL RESPONSES
3. I think my body is too attractive.	3. Disqualifying the positive.	3. My body is well-developed and I can be proud of it. How attractive is "too" attractive, anyway?
4. I think my body looks a lot nicer than the kind of person I am inside.	4. Emotional reasoning.	4. What kind of person is that? I have many nice parts to my personality. I'm friendly and caring and I deserve to like myself.
5. I'm a rotten person.	5. Labeling	5. That's nonsense. My inner core is not rotting away. I wouldn't say such a cruel thing to someone else I cared about, and I don't need to be cruel to myself.
6. But I have sexual fantasies about people, and yet I don't have a boyfriend.	6. "Should" statement.	6. It's perfectly okay to have sexual fantasies about anyone I want to. My thoughts are private and I'm free to have any fantasies I want. After all, people can't read my mind!

AUTOMATIC THOUGHTS	DISTORTIONS	RATIONAL RESPONSES
7. Maybe people will like me because of my fantasies or because of the wrong reasons.	7. Mind reading.	7. Physical attractiveness is just one part of liking someone, but it's a legitimate part.
8. I'm afraid I can't find a boyfriend because they won't like me and then I'll feel rejected.	8. Fortune-telling.	8. Certainly everybody won't like me but I am attractive and intelligent and I have a nice personality so I probably will be able to find a boyfriend.

OUTCOME—Review your "Rational Responses" and put a check in the box that describes how you now feel:
☐ not at all better; ☐ somewhat better; ☐ quite a bit better; ☑ a lot better.

*Copyright © 1984, David D. Burns, M.D., from *Intimate Connections* (New York: William Morrow & Company).

substantial difference between how attractive the man is and how attractive the woman is. A handsome hunk of a man whom you rate as 9 out of 10 on your attractiveness scale might be paired with a woman whom you would only rate as a 6, and vice versa. This will make you aware of two very old but important concepts: Beauty is in the eye of the beholder, and there is more to forming a relationship than just appearance.

So what would it really take to get people interested in you? I've found that many shy, lonely people really don't have an accurate idea of what members of the opposite sex are really looking for. A twenty-seven-year-old single man named Brad was convinced that women were looking for men with these characteristics: popular, a "breadwinner," charismatic, dominant, very macho, and a "football player type." Since none of these characteristics fit him, Brad believed that he'd never have much success with women.

I suggested that he ask a number of women to list the five most desirable and the least desirable characteristics they were looking for in a man. The results of Brad's survey are listed in Figure 5-2. As you can see, several of the attributes he had considered absolutely essential for sex appeal, such as being a muscle-bound, macho, egocentric superstud, actually appeared on the undesirable list. In contrast, many of his strengths, including reliability, considerateness, the ability to have fun, a sense of humor, and sensitivity, appeared on the list of the most desirable characteristics. Brad's findings were not unusual. Take your own survey if you don't believe me. You can ask friends of yours and you can also approach strangers on the street. Tell them you're involved in a psychological study. I believe you'll discover that most of the qualities women are looking for are ones that any man with a sense of caring, commitment, and self-esteem could easily fulfill.

Some shy and lonely people are very insecure about their physical appearance. You may have a preoccupation with some aspect of your body—perhaps you have a blemish, a crooked nose, small breasts, or heavy thighs—and conclude that you are hopelessly flawed and undesirable. Often this obsession can simply be a cover-up for your fears of dating or getting close.

I recently treated a shy college student named Ray who was afraid to talk to women because of his preoccupation with his "crooked teeth." He was convinced his teeth were the first thing that women noticed about him. He did have buck teeth that had been straightened out when he was a child, but he felt they still didn't look completely normal. I couldn't detect any problem and tried to reassure Ray that he was good-looking and that his teeth and smile looked great, but he simply discounted my comments and insisted I was just trying to be nice to him.

I suggested that Ray test this belief by asking several

FIGURE 5-2

	Five Most Desirable Male Characteristics	Five Most Undesirable Male Characteristics
Annie	1. Reliability 2. Considerate and warm 3. Fun 4. Good-looking; attractive 5. Honest	1. Using a girl (all the time) 2. Sarcasm 3. Unmannerly beginning 4. Mauler (sexually aggressive) 5. Superstud; egocentric
Allison (on street)	1. Sensitive 2. Sense of humor 3. Integrity 4. Being themselves 5. Not overambitious	1. "Macho" 2. Inconsiderate
Sandy	1. Eyes, hands 2. Honesty 3. Open-mindedness 4. Sensitivity 5. Warmth	1. Stereotyped expectations about women 2. Muscle-bound 3. Egocentric
Pat	1. Warm 2. Sensitive 3. Sense of humor 4. Self-esteem 5. Intelligent	1. Dishonest 2. Egocentric

friends of both sexes to name several things about his appearance that they specifically disliked and several things about his appearance that they specifically liked. He agreed to write down what everybody said. Asking for both negative and positive comments guaranteed that if his teeth *were* noticeably crooked someone would mention it. He was amazed that not a single person commented on his teeth. Some of them suggested that he needed a more stylish haircut and should get some spiffier outfits. The positive comments focused on the fact that he was tall and muscular and had an attractive face and a warm, appealing smile. These comments put the lie to his belief that the first thing people noticed about him was his crooked teeth. We were then able to work on the real problem: his lack of self-esteem and his fear of rejection.

You may object because you feel there's something about your appearance that genuinely makes you less attractive and desirable. Just last week a young man named Terry told me that he was short and that this made him a less worthwhile person to know and to date. It's certainly true that tallness is one of the traits that society values, but the real question is whether or not you're obligated to buy into this standard. If you have self-esteem, your glow will make you attractive regardless of your physical stature, and if you don't, no amount of physical attractiveness can make you feel very good about yourself. Believe me: *Plenty* of tall, attractive men and women feel very inadequate and insecure because they lack self-esteem.

I suggested that Terry do a Cost-Benefit Analysis of telling himself that his short stature made him less worthwhile and desirable. How would it help him to believe this? Were there some payoffs? And how would it hurt him to believe this? What was the price he was paying for his poor self-image? His Cost-Benefit Analysis is illustrated in Figure 5-3. Once he listed the advantages and disadvantages of his negative self-image, he was much more willing to give it up. He decided to substitute this new attitude in place of the old one: "I'm a worthwhile person to know regardless of my height!" Looking at it from this perspective gave him greater self-confidence, and over a period of time he became more assertive and successful in his dating.

You can do a similar Cost-Benefit Analysis. Ask yourself how it will help and hurt you to think less of yourself because of any bothersome imperfections. As you begin to accept and value yourself, I suspect you'll discover that others will begin to perceive you more positively as well!

In summary, here are some concrete suggestions about how you can develop greater sex appeal:

1. Dress your best. If you look terrific, you'll feel terrific. Ask friends for help and work at it. Don't be afraid to be a little outrageous and sexy. If you feel a particular look doesn't suit your personality or your image

Figure 5-3
Cost-Benefit Analysis

Belief: If I were taller I'd be a more worthwhile person to know.

Advantages of Believing This	Disadvantages of Believing This
1. I can avoid the discomfort of approaching people I'd like to get to know.	1. I'll have low self-esteem and feel undesirable.
2. I'll have something to blame for my loneliness.	2. I'll feel frustrated and defeated.
	3. I'll be wasting energy thinking about a situation I can't change.
(40)	(60)

Revised Belief: I'm a worthwhile person to know regardless of my height!

of yourself, so much the better. Your "image" of yourself is just an illusion, a trap. There are more "yous" inside of you than you ever dreamed of. Shedding your skin and getting in touch with these other "selves" can make life more of an adventure and help unleash your sex appeal.

2. Pick out your good features and capitalize on them. They may be your smile, your eyes, your sense of humor. Tell yourself what a personable, desirable creature you are, even if you don't believe it at first. Imagine people admiring you and wanting to be with you. Give yourself positive messages like, "Oh, what a hunk of a man [or luscious woman] I am. I'm really going to turn people on today. The people I talk to will feel great, and I'll feel great, too." This will help you project a glow of sensuality, and you'll begin to notice that people really will respond to you more positively.

3. Your self-esteem is more important than how handsome or beautiful you "really" are. If you like yourself and project those positive feelings toward others instead of putting yourself down and telling yourself what an inferior, miserable creature you are, others will begin to like you, too.

4. Remember that physical attractiveness will not guarantee a long-term satisfying relationship. Ask people of the opposite sex about the qualities they desire most and least in a partner. This will help you develop a more realistic idea of what people are really looking for, and you'll discover that having people love and desire you is not an impossible dream but a very accessible goal.

6

Your Rags-to-Riches
Social Program

"Where can I find someone to love? It seems like all the good people are taken."

"Whenever I meet someone interesting, it turns out they're married."

"The people I'm attracted to never seem interested in me, and vice versa."

I frequently hear these complaints. But they're based on a misconception. There is, in fact, a RIVER of single, available, desirable people out there. Where you go to meet them will depend in part on where you live. Social customs vary from place to place. When I was living on the San Francisco peninsula it was quite easy. There were numerous activities such as neighborhood parties, night school classes, rock concerts, and "happenings" in public parks where single people would congregate evenings and weekends. Some metropolitan centers such as Philadelphia or Chicago may not have quite the same open, warm, and freewheeling atmosphere that the West Coast offers, but if you have the right attitude, you can talk to people at street corners, bus stops, elevators, cafés—virtually anywhere. The following step-by-step program will show you precisely how to make contact and establish meaningful relationships with people you're attracted to.

Step One—Smile Practice. The first step involves smiling at strangers. During the next week I want you to smile at a minimum of five strangers every day. You may resist this suggestion because you think you'd look ridiculous or you feel insecure about your ability to smile on command. I had this problem myself. Following a television appearance on the "Bob Braun Show" in Cincinnati, a friend who was watching the show commented that it was an excellent interview but that I had made one error, and that was forgetting to smile. She emphasized that selling books involves a certain amount of sex appeal, and that if I would smile and project a warm, friendly image to the camera I could enhance my effectiveness.

I realized that what she was saying was absolutely true, but this was a *tremendous* problem for me because I had frozen in front of every camera since childhood. I was often teased because I squinted and had a crooked smile, and this made me so anxious I felt I simply *couldn't* smile when I was under pressure.

I made the decision on the spot to conquer this problem with a technique I called "smile practice." I began by smiling at inanimate objects. I started smiling at door handles, plants, chairs, and other objects in the hotel where I was staying—I smiled at over one hundred objects within ten or fifteen minutes. I had no idea if the smiles were any good or not, but at least I was forcing the corners of my lips upward. Next I began to smile at myself when I walked past mirrors. I looked a little silly but not as terrible as I thought. Then I went outside and started smiling at animals. Dogs were extremely receptive because they seemed hungry for friendship and wagged their tails enthusiastically.

Finally I was ready for human beings. This felt like my first jump off the high dive of a swimming pool. I felt certain that my smile would look awkward and that people would think I was an A-1 jerk. Nevertheless, I forced out a few smiles at strangers in the hotel. I was surprised that they nearly always smiled back. My smile would then become genuine and spontaneous because I was so tickled to see other people respond positively. Over the next several weeks I made it my practice to smile at practically every person I met—my patients, my family, store clerks, and so on. I had never been able to smile at will before, and it seemed like a fabulous new toy.

As the last stage in my smile practice, I asked my children and their friends who were playing at our house to come up to me unexpectedly anytime they wanted and command me to smile. I told them to rate each smile between 1 and 10 for spontaneity and warmth. I felt this would put me in the most awkward possible situation and it would be good training for television. I was surprised that my ratings were consistently between 7 and 10. This did a lot to boost my self-confidence, and now I find that I can smile whenever I want to, even in front of a television camera, and I *love* to have my picture taken—something I used to *dread!* I've also found that my relationships with people have become warmer and friendlier. I think that if you begin your smile practice today and apply this technique with persistence, you will get results similar to mine within a few weeks.

Step Two—Hello Practice. Once you're comfortable with smiling at strangers, start saying hello to them. Begin by smiling and saying hello to five strangers every day for the first week. This may sound like a tall order, but you can actually accomplish it in one minute on any busy sidewalk. If you're afraid you'll look foolish, start by saying hello to people you would not consider to be potential dates. Try people of the same sex, older people, or children. This can bolster your self-confidence. Once you get rolling, it will begin to feel more natural and comfortable. Then you can say hello to attractive people of the opposite sex.

When you're doing this, be sure to look people directly in the eyes and say hello before they're past you, so they'll have a chance to respond. Many people will be pleased and return your smile and hello, but some people may ignore you or scowl. It's important to understand why they might react like this. Some people aren't used to being treated in a positive, friendly way and they may think you're talking to someone else. If you live in a large metropolitan area such as New York City, some people may be frightened because they'll think you're a mugger or a dangerous person. However, I think that in the majority of cases you'll get good responses from people, and this will elevate your mood. (As with any technique, you must apply this one with common sense. If you're walking down a dark alley in a questionable neighborhood at two A.M., it's obviously best to stare straight ahead and walk as quickly as you can.)

It can be useful to predict how many positive responses you'll get out of every ten attempts. Then you can smile and say hello to ten people and calculate your batting average by counting the number of people who say hello. If you have a very negative self-image, you might anticipate that virtually no one would smile or say hello. In contrast, if you're a perfectionist you may expect that everybody should respond to you in a warm and positive way. Both extremes tend to be unrealistic. Most people find they get friendly responses between 25 and 75 percent of the time. You may find that when you're in a positive, outgoing mood your response rate will tend to be a little higher than on those days when you feel you're under a dark cloud.

Stop saying "I can't." Some readers will resist saying hello or approaching strangers in a friendly, positive way. You may tell yourself, "I can't" or "I just *couldn't* do that." But this isn't true. What you really mean is "I don't *feel* like it" or "I don't *want* to because I'm not used to doing something like that and it seems scary." The problem with saying "I can't" is that you may begin to take this language seriously and believe that you really are paralyzed and hopeless when in fact you really aren't.

A thirty-two-year-old divorced man named Jack felt shy and lonely. He hadn't met any new women since separating from his wife and felt fated for bachelorhood. I suggested that one way to meet women was to smile at them and say hello and start a conversation. Jack reacted violently and insisted he "absolutely couldn't" do something like that and argued that it was an "impossibility." I suggested that we break the task down into its smallest component parts to see how realistic his objections were. He listed these steps:

- Locate an attractive woman.
- Walk up to her.
- Move the corners of my mouth up to form a smile.
- Open my mouth and say "hello."

Jack acknowledged that he could easily *locate* an attractive woman, since he taught on a university campus, but he stuck to his guns and insisted that it would be a physical impossibility to get his body to walk up to her to say hello. We then broke this down into its smallest component parts. These included:

- Lift my left foot off the ground.
- Move it forward.
- Relax my muscles so that gravity will pull my leg to the earth.
- Repeat this with my right foot.
- Continue alternating my right and left legs until my body is close enough to the woman to smile and say hello.

Jack wasn't about to give up so easily and insisted that he "couldn't" get his left foot off the ground. Our conversation evolved like this:

DAVID: When you say you couldn't get your foot off the ground, what do you mean?

JACK: It would be stuck. If there was an attractive woman, I couldn't possibly take even a single step in her direction.

DAVID: Suppose you reached down and grabbed your ankle with both hands and started pulling with all your might. Do you think you could move your foot then?

JACK: No, it would be like it weighed four hundred pounds and I couldn't budge it.

DAVID: Well, that's an interesting theory. Would you be willing to test it with an experiment? Walk across the campus and locate an attractive woman, and then see if your left foot gets stuck on the ground. Try, try with all your might to move it, and then you can see whether or not it really will budge. Would you agree to perform this experiment as homework between sessions?

Jack was furious and insisted I just "didn't understand" him because I was asking him to do something he "couldn't" possibly do. I stuck to my guns and repeated my request that he do the experiment and find out. I even offered to go outside with him and observe him to see if his foot really was stuck and suggested he could even call me for assistance in the event his leg became paralyzed and he couldn't drag it off the ground.

Jack left the session with fantasies of terminating his treatment so he could find a more "realistic," sensitive, and understanding therapist. He went home and lay down on his bed and ruminated about how wrong it was of me to ask him to do something he "really couldn't" do. Then, he said, a light bulb suddenly went off in his head and it dawned on him that in fact he probably *could* actually do it if he wanted to. He jumped out of bed and ran out of his room, quickly spotted and approached a coed, and said hello to her. Then he did it again. And again. He wasn't especially successful in getting the women to respond positively to him—that would come later. But he had literally taken "the first step." He came back to the next session feeling elated.

Step Three—Secrets of Flirting. What is flirting? Flirting can be defined as kidding around in a slightly outrageous, light-hearted, affectionate way with sexual and/or romantic insinuations that aren't necessarily serious. Flirting can be nonverbal or verbal. Nonverbal flirting includes dressing well, walking and moving your body in a sexy way, and projecting friendly facial expressions such as a smile, a wink, or a twinkle of your eyes. It also includes touching. You might hug a friend or touch his or her hand or shoulder during an animated conversation.

Verbal flirting involves making complimentary comments that will turn the other person on. As an exercise, give out ten compliments to people this week. Start out with people who seem "safe"—relatives or friends—and build up to people who seem more "dangerous"—strangers or people you admire and want to know better. You can compliment people on their warm smiles or on something they're wearing, such as an attractive tie or a piece of jewelry, or on something they say. *Any* compliment will do. You'll be amazed at how effective this can be. People are hungry for approval, and a compliment will nearly always generate a warm response. This in turn will make you feel good.

You'll have to decide whether to give sincere, genuine compliments or phony, insincere ones. Most people feel more comfortable giving out the sincere variety, but sometimes a little insincerity will work even better! Flattering people can set them more at ease than acting deadly serious all the time. After all, why would you flatter someone if you weren't sincerely interested? If you genuinely like someone, there's really no such thing as a phony compliment. If you're talking to an attractive man you'd like to date, you might say, "You're really cute! Women must find you irresistible!" If he has a nice build, you could say, "Gee, you must be an athlete. Do you lift weights a lot?" If he responds in the affirmative, you might ask if he gives private showings. Other flirtatious comments would be "Do you know that you're the foxiest lady in this office complex?" or "You know that you're the cutest man in the building? When are you going to let me seduce you?"

Many readers will find this approach ridiculous or absurd. It is. That's the whole point. It's often better to have a smile on your face and to be a little red with embarrassment because you're acting slightly outrageous than to come across in a dull, serious way. If you're too sincere, people will get nervous because they simply won't know where you're coming from. When you're being blatantly flirtatious, it seems to set people at their ease. Even if you sound a little foolish, most people tend to be enormously forgiving. Your awkwardness and vulnerability can often make you even more appealing than if you're too polished and slick.

This principle, like any other, can easily be abused. If you have no real concern for people and you're flattering them so you can manipulate them or take advantage of them, then what you're doing is hostile. But if you're interested in someone, go ahead and make that person feel like the greatest. Romance is, after all, a kind of benign illusion that helps people get close!

Face the facts: Being too serious and heavy is a *sure* turnoff to virtually every human being on the surface of the earth! One way to lighten up is to gaze into their eyes in a serious, romantic way while you're flirting with them and simultaneously fantasize something humorous or erotic. If you're trying to strike up a conversation with a young doctor, imagine him on rounds in the hospital wearing diapers. Or you could imagine him in your favorite sexual fantasy while you talk to him. This will put a smile on your lips and a twinkle in your eye, and that's the essence of flirting.

Try to remember that the main purpose of flirting is to

have fun. Ignore your ego and remind yourself what you like about the people you're flirting with. You can tease them or flatter them and get them to talk about themselves. Try to pick up energy from the sights and sounds of the environment rather than dwelling on how nervous and uncomfortable you feel. Remember that flirting doesn't have to lead to serious relationships but can simply be a way of being playful and friendly.

At first, for practice, flirt with people who don't make you overly anxious. A lonely graduate student began by flirting with people she wasn't seriously interested in. Their enthusiastic responses gave her morale a boost, and then she began to flirt with classmates who did interest her. She offered this advice to other lonely women: "Remember to wear something that you feel sexy in. Flatter the man because it's fun and show him that you enjoy his company. People will react positively, and this will help you overcome your feelings of insecurity and self-doubt. Don't forget that you can also *touch* the other person. You might want to touch his arm and say, 'Oh, what a nice shirt you're wearing.' This can do a great deal to set people at ease and generate warm responses."

Remember, too, to respond positively when other people compliment you. Make an upbeat, appreciative comment instead of downgrading yourself in a self-effacing manner. Your appreciation will project a more positive self-image, which will enhance the effect of your compliments.

Many people feel inhibited about flirting in spite of how much fun and how effective it can be. If you feel that way, write down the negative thoughts that come to mind when you think about it, as illustrated in Figure 6-1. Lisa is the shy young woman mentioned in Chapter Two who became upset when a three-week love affair fell apart. She felt quite nervous and insecure around men and believed she was destined to be lonely forever because she was missing some "essential ingredient" that would make men love her. When I suggested that she start flirting with attractive men, she was flabbergasted. Talking back to her negative thoughts helped her overcome her inhibitions enough to begin to smile and flirt with a few men. Once she got some positive responses, her self-confidence jumped and soon she was dating one of them.

FIGURE 6-1
The Daily Mood Log*

DESCRIBE THE UPSETTING EVENT—I feel inhibited about flirting with Tom at the swimming pool.

NEGATIVE FEELINGS—Record your emotions and rate each one on a scale from 0 (the least) to 100 (the most). Include feelings such as sad, anxious, angry, guilty, lonely, hopeless, frustrated, etc.

Emotion	Rating (0–100)	Emotion	Rating (0–100)	Emotion	Rating (0–100)
1. Anxious	99%	3.		5.	
2.		4.		6.	

AUTOMATIC THOUGHTS Write down your negative thoughts and number them consecutively.	DISTORTIONS Identify the distortions in each "Automatic Thought."	RATIONAL RESPONSES Substitute more realistic and positive thoughts.
1. What if I carry it too far or say something stupid?	1. Fortune-telling.	1. I can only learn through practice. Eventually I'll get better at it.
2. What kind of impression will he get of me? He might think I'm "a flirt."	2. Mind reading; labeling.	2. He might be attracted to me. There's no such thing as "a flirt," but it might be a good thing if I was a little more flirtatious.
3. What are the other guys at the pool going to think of me?	3. Mind reading.	3. They may feel jealous and wish I was flirting with them!

AUTOMATIC THOUGHTS	DISTORTIONS	RATIONAL RESPONSES
4. They may have a low opinion of me.	4. Mind reading.	4. That's always possible, but it wouldn't be the end of the world. I'm pretty lonely as it is, so what do I really have to lose?
5. If I make a fool of myself it would mean there was something wrong with me and I'd never learn.	5. All-or-nothing thinking.	5. No, it would just show I wasn't very good at flirting yet. If I work at it, I'll get better at it.

OUTCOME—Review your "Rational Responses" and put a check in the box that describes how you now feel:
☐ not at all better; ☐ somewhat better; ☐ quite a bit better; ☑ a lot better.

*Copyright © 1984, David D. Burns, M.D., from *Intimate Connections* (New York: William Morrow & Company).

When you study Figure 6-1, you'll see that Lisa was afraid that if she tried to flirt she'd make a fool of herself or people would look down on her and think she was "a flirt." These concerns seem almost universal among shy, lonely men and women. A wonderful way to overcome these fears involves the Feared-Fantasy Technique. Simply imagine that a group of people see you trying to flirt with someone and they're all looking down on you. Write out an imaginary dialogue in which they say the worst possible things to you. You can pretend that they're all snickering, pointing their fingers at you, and trying their hardest to humiliate you. Then see how you would talk back to their put-downs. This can be fun and help you get over your inhibitions.

The following dialogue illustrates your possible responses to the most insulting critic. Imagine that you have unsuccessfully approached a young woman in an attempt to flirt with her. The critic tries to make you feel embarrassed.

CRITIC: Gee, I saw you trying to flirt with that attractive woman in the elevator.

YOU: Oh, did you? I was hoping to get to know her. She seemed very attractive.

CRITIC: Well, you sure made a fool of yourself. You must be a real jerk trying to pick up strange women like that.

YOU: How does that make me a jerk?

CRITIC: Only a jerk would go around flirting with women he doesn't even know. Furthermore, you were really clutzy. With corny lines like that, you'll never get to first base.

YOU: Can you give me any suggestions about some better lines so I can get to first base? I'll be happy to listen to any tips that you've got. I'm always eager to learn.

CRITIC: I refuse to give you any tips about flirting. All I want you to know is that a lot of us were watching you and we think you're a real fool. You should feel terrible! We all despise you and we're laughing at you and looking down on you.

YOU: Well, you can certainly laugh as much as you want to. Should I feel terrible about that? I really would like to meet some women, and this seems to be a good way to do it. Sometimes women respond in a friendly way and sometimes they don't. Why are you looking down on me? Is it because I'm lonely, or is it because I'm not real self-confident and good at flirting yet, or what?

CRITIC: Anyone your age who's single must be a real reject. What's wrong with you?

YOU: Is there a maximum acceptable age for being single these days? Do you think that being single means there's something wrong with me? Please explain this. I seem to be having trouble understanding your point.

I hope you can see from this dialogue how unnecessary it is to be overly afraid that someone would look down on you when you flirt. If you're very outgoing, there probably *will* be times when you make a fool of yourself and get put down. So what? While it's natural to feel nervous when you approach an attractive stranger and embarrassed when it doesn't go so well, it's important not to let these feelings hold you back. You have only one life to live and there are a lot of fabulous people out there who you can get to know if you will confront your fears instead of always having to play it safe.

Many single men I treat ask me, "What if the woman I'm trying to flirt with shoots me down and makes a rude, sarcastic remark?" Remember that people who act nasty often feel insecure. Their insensitivity reflects on them, not you. It's usually best to respond in a matter-of-fact way without getting defensive or sarcastic or thinking you have to be terribly clever. Suppose an attractive woman is standing in line with two of her friends at a cafeteria. You decide to smile at her and say hello. What's the worst that could happen? Suppose she gives you a hard time. She ignores you and turns to her friends and says, "Oh, isn't he being cute today?" What do you do?

Instead of insulting her or moping about it, go ahead and strike up a conversation with someone else in the vicinity. People will generally notice how hostile she was and be supportive toward you. This will often make her feel jealous, and it will show that you didn't let her get under your skin. She acted childish, but you kept your cool. You won because you didn't accept her invitation to feel put down.

When I was an insecure young man, I once asked an older friend who seemed exceptionally self-confident what to do when someone is giving you a hard time. He said, "That's easy. Just turn around, click your heels, and walk off in the opposite direction. Pretty soon, she'll be chasing you." It doesn't *always* work that way—but you'd be surprised at how often it does! At the very least you'll avoid getting dragged down by someone else's unpleasantness.

How to Motivate Yourself to Flirt

Many lonely people are extremely reluctant to flirt and approach attractive strangers. Let's face it, dating can involve a lot of stress and hard work. It can be very uncomfortable at times, especially when you get rejected. It may seem a lot easier just to daydream and fantasize until that special someone comes into your life. But it might be a long wait!

One of the attitudes that can get in the way of flirting is the "spontaneity belief." Many lonely people believe that friendships or loving relationships should just develop spontaneously, so they shouldn't have to work on developing them. Some people think that deliberately looking for companionship is shameful and embarrassing. Others, who acknowledge the need for actively looking for a partner, will nevertheless regard perfectly legitimate ways of meeting people—such as flirting or saying hello to strangers—as cheap and degrading or "not nice." Dr. Laura Primakoff has pointed out how irrational this is when you consider that most people would never think they should be able to get a job, an education, or a new home without working at it, and yet they believe they shouldn't have to work hard at developing friendships and love relationships. Perhaps the fear of rejection explains this self-defeating attitude. As long as you insist that relationships should just happen spontaneously, you won't have to be assertive or take risks with people. But you may not get very close to people, either!

One way to motivate yourself to be more outgoing is to make a list of the advantages and disadvantages of taking the initiative and actively trying to meet new people, and a second list of the advantages and disadvantages of settling for the status quo and leaving things in the hands of fate. Then balance the advantages and disadvantages of each option against each other. The architect whose lists are illustrated in Figure 6-2 found that the advantages of flirting and dating many attractive women outweighed the disadvantages by a 70:30 margin. In contrast, the disadvantages of the status quo were greater than the advantages by a 80:20 margin. This cost-benefit analysis gave him the determination to get the ball rolling, and within several

Figure 6-2
Cost-Benefit Analysis

Option A: Flirt with many attractive women

Advantages of Option A	Disadvantages of Option A
1. I'll get over my fears and inhibitions.	1. I'll get shot down a lot.
2. I'll meet people to start relationships with.	2. I'll feel nervous and awkward.
3. I'll feel better about myself.	3. It will take determination, time, and effort.
(70)	(30)

Option B: Settle for the status quo

Advantages of Option B	Disadvantages of Option B
1. I can avoid anxiety.	1. I'll be unhappy and frustrated.
2. I won't get shot down.	2. Nothing will ever change.
3. I won't look foolish in public.	3. I won't have much of a chance to meet someone who really interests me.
(20)	(80)

weeks he was going out with a number of interesting women he had met.

When you're flirting and approaching people, it can be important to realize that when you're hot, you're hot, and when you're not, you're not. Recent research by Dr. Frederick K. Goodwin and his associates at the National Institute of Mental Health has indicated that many people go through distinct cycles in which their moods, outlook, self-confidence, and energy levels appear to oscillate. These cycles appear to originate in the hypothalamus, a part of the brain that controls our circadian (or "twenty-four-hour") rhythms. While the importance of these cycles in our mood swings is not fully understood, it's important to be patient with yourself during those periods when you sense you're low on self-confidence, because you may be in that part of your cycle when you're having difficulties being productive or feeling sexy and positive. It seems for a while as if everybody dumps on you and you can't connect with anyone. Even if you aren't terribly successful, keep trying, because you can learn from these experiences. Suddenly your fate will begin to change and you'll discover that you're in the opposite phase of your cycle. You'll feel much better about yourself, and other people will find you sexier and more appealing as well.

Where to Meet People

When you are thinking about ways of meeting people, find activities that turn you on. Decide what interests you and get involved in a group of people with similar interests. When I was living in Palo Alto a late friend of mine, Robb, formed a group called the Mid-Peninsula Free University. This was a school that involved no credits, grades, fees, or qualifications and you could either attend or teach classes, depending on your mood. The classes, which met in people's homes, were on subjects like yoga, hiking, Zen, political activism, poetry readings, psychodrama, encounter marathons, and nude weekends. There might be night schools or programs of this type in your area that offer speakers, seminars, or personal growth experiences. If you like singing, join a choral group. You could investigate the programs offered by your local "Y"; these could include diverse activities ranging from karate classes to weekly dances and field trips. Your church or synagogue probably has numerous social programs. You could consider joining a theater group or a political organization. The list of possible ways and places to meet people is limited only by your creativity and persistence.

It will help you to develop "pro-social" skills and interests that can help you meet other people. Nightclubs and singles bars can be high-pressure, competitive situations that make you feel awfully insecure. Instead, get involved in activities where you can rub shoulders with people naturally and spontaneously. For example, if you join a racquetball club, you'll be developing a new skill and you'll have the chance to meet people in a relaxed atmosphere. Then when you meet someone who interests you, you can invite him or her to play racquetball some afternoon instead of going out on a more formal date. This lets your companion know that you're an interesting person with something to offer rather than just someone who feels desperate or is on the make.

Don't be afraid to be imaginative and creative when you're trying to think of ways to meet people. Once when I was feeling lonely and bored I went to an art store and purchased a drawing tablet and charcoal and went around town drawing pictures. I was surprised at how easy it became to meet people because everyone seemed to be interested in what I was drawing and it was easy to strike up conversations with people. Although I didn't have much artistic talent it seemed that most people really weren't concerned about that—or they couldn't tell the difference. When I saw an attractive woman I wanted to meet I would ask if she wanted me do her portrait. This required considerable courage, given my feeble level of artistic skill! But most people seemed immensely flattered and immediately accepted. Most people love to be the center of attention. Apparently it's very romantic to have an "artist" ask you to model. I found that a particular coffeehouse near the campus turned out to be an excellent spot, and whenever I wanted a date I'd just go there with my drawing pad and pretty soon I'd meet somebody.

A *"Mutual Admiration Society."* Friends can be very helpful in getting you dates. Develop a "mutual admiration society" that involves several single friends who are also looking for dates. Tell them that you'll fix them up with several interesting men each month if they'll do the same for you. A woman who capitalized on this technique said that she and two of her best friends found it much easier to promote and rave about each other than to promote themselves. When she saw an attractive man at a night school class or at work she would tell him that she had a special friend that she knew he'd like and she'd be glad to fix him up. She was quite uninhibited about approaching men like this because her own ego wasn't on the line and she didn't have to worry about getting rejected.

She could easily arrange several dates for her friends each month. They would reciprocate, so she would get an equal numbers of dates with interesting men. This mutual admiration society gave them all a never-ending supply of exciting men.

Of course, this means making close friendships with people of your own sex. You may be hesitant to do this because you're fixated on finding a partner or because you're caught up in feelings of jealousy and resentment toward potential friends of the same sex. This can be a real mistake. Other single people can be an asset because you'll have a social support network and you won't feel so isolated.

The Rags-to-Riches Method. There's an incredibly effective method for meeting people that was first suggested by a thirty-two-year-old divorced woman I was treating who'd felt lonely and isolated for most of her adult life. Trish had only had one humble date in two years and couldn't think of any way to meet men until she came up with a bright idea. I was skeptical about Trish's idea, so I asked a colleague about whether or not it was wise. He said she would probably meet any number of eligible men using her method, so I suggested she should go ahead and give it a try. I could not have predicted what an incredible transformation her social life was about to undergo. You might also have many serious doubts about her method, but you may discover that your doubts are based on some irrational assumptions that you have.

What Trish did was to put an ad in the *Philadelphia Magazine* personal section. Sounds absurd, right? Her first ad, which was worded somewhat conservatively, actually stimulated over thirty responses (via the magazine's post office box). What was surprising was that approximately half of the letters she received actually seemed very interesting, so she called these fifteen men to see how they sounded. Trish used only her first name and didn't give out her phone number. Nearly every one of them sounded okay, so she set up a luncheon date with each. (This is only the *beginning*! It gets wilder!) When she met them, she was surprised that the majority of these men appealed to her and asked her out.

She was sufficiently encouraged to place a second ad, which was worded in a more creative manner. This one generated more than ninety responses. (To see her ads, turn to the Appendix at the end of this chapter, on page 103.) Once again, about half the respondents seemed to be the kinds of men she was looking for. Pretty soon she was meeting one new man every weekday for lunch, and every evening she had a date with a man she liked from a previous luncheon. This meant she was having as many as ten to twelve dates each week. Whenever things slowed down a bit, she just placed another ad and got a new crop of candidates. I helped her with the wording of her third ad, and she got more than three hundred responses to it. In addition, being in such demand made her feel so good about herself that men she met in her daily life also became attracted to her and started asking her out, too. For a lovely, lonely lady whose social life had been a zero, these sudden changes were mind-boggling.

I was curious about whether this technique would help other women I was treating who were having trouble meeting men. Over a dozen of my patients have subsequently tried it, and they were nearly always pleased with the results. What was amazing was their discovery that they could specify *precisely* the kinds of men they were looking for, stipulating age, intelligence, and looks, and whatever they asked for, they got! One woman had always had the fantasy of having a boyfriend with a yacht, so she included "must have yacht" as one of the stipulations in her ad. Twenty-five men with yachts wrote to her, and she went out on moonlight cruises with eight of them (sounds fantastic, but it's true). One of them sent a chauffeur-driven Rolls-Royce to pick her up! Three of the yachtsmen proposed to her! She didn't marry any of them, but she had a heck of a good time and promptly placed a second ad.

If you decide to place an ad in a publication such as the *Philadelphia Magazine*, I have found that certain principles can be important in the wording. It seems that ads that are warm, upbeat, and a little bit sensual are more effective than ads that sound overly serious. On the other hand, you don't want to be too far out or blatantly sexual, either.

It's really a matter of balance. Describe yourself in a positive, intriguing way, using words that stimulate the imagination and create a lighthearted, fun-loving impression. Don't be afraid to come on strong in a somewhat slick, self-assured style, using a Madison Avenue approach, because you may actually get more responses from the sincere men you're looking for than you will if your ad sounds defensive and insecure. Negative wording such as "no oddballs please" or "no married men" may generate hostility in readers and a number of oddballs or married men will be sure to write to you.

Here are two appealing ads from a recent *Philadelphia Magazine:*

> SOMEWHAT NEW TO AREA, certainly new at this and slightly apprehensive, 36, SWF, successful professional, attractive, loyal, romantic, enjoying wit, outdoors. The Ritz seeks a gentle man of character and charm for potential relationship. Box ——, PHILADELPHIA Magazine, 1500 Walnut, Phila., 19102.

> QUIRKY INTELLIGENT WOMAN desired by Center City SWJM, 31. Enjoys funny movies, adventurous music, the arts, new wave dancing, racquetball, ethnic dining, 76ers, snuggling near my fireplace with two terrific cats. Box ——, PHILADELPHIA Magazine, 1500 Walnut, Phila., 19102.

If you're placing an ad, be thoughtful about which publication you decide to use. If you place an ad in an underground newspaper, you may not get the same kinds of responses as you would in a more respected publication. Also remember to use your common sense to ensure your personal safety. It seems unwise to publish your name, address, or phone number. Having the respondent write to you in care of the magazine will protect your anonymity. Once you've decided to meet someone because you like his letter and he sounds interesting on the phone, you can arrange to meet him for lunch in a public spot that will be safe for you. This will give you a chance to get to know him and check him out before you accept a date.

Remember that you will probably get pretty much what

you advertise for, and this may not be pleasing to you. One extremely shy woman who suffered from social anxiety insisted on writing an excessively conservative ad appealing to uptight, hardworking men who were "honest, sincere, and dedicated." She got responses from twenty-eight men who were, in fact, excessively "honest, sincere, and dedicated." The only problem was that they tended to be hideously boring, rigid workaholics and her dates had all the intrigue and excitement of a funeral. Ads that are upbeat and friendly are likely to generate a far more interesting group of suitors.

*Appendix**
Trish's Ads

Ad No. 1:

I'M LOOKING for a companion/friend (straight), 30 to 40, male or female, who enjoys horseback/bike riding, jazz & classical music, the theater, museums, international cuisine, cinema, the Siamese Cat Fancy (cat shows), and a very informal life-style. Want to share some wholesome leisure with an honest, down-to-earth, sensitive woman of 35, dutch treat? Write to T.W., P.O. Box 100, Phila., PA 19100—NO GIGOLOS PLEASE!

Ad No. 2:

ARE YOU an over-35, 5'9" or taller, intelligent Jewish gentleman? A slim, blond, green-eyed Jewish gentlewoman seeks you to warm her nights. Respond to P.O. Box 100, Phila., PA. 19100.

---

*These are the first two ads placed in *Philadelphia Magazine* by Trish, who was described on pages 100 to 110 of this chapter. You can see that her first ad sounded a little defensive and was probably too long. This one received about thirty replies. Her second ad, which is warmer and more lighthearted, generated over ninety replies. Approximately half of the men who answered both ads were eligible and attractive.

A Typical Reply

Dear Box 100,

In response to your ad in *Philadelphia Magazine*, I am a 40-year-old [lawyer, doctor, engineer, college professor, Ph.D.], 5'10" tall, 175 lbs., recently divorced and considered by my friends to be physically attractive. I am seeking a special person whose interests will be compatible to mine, with whom I can develop a meaningful relationship based on mutual respect. I am tired òf the bar scene, have many varied interests [stated], lead an active professional life, and travel a good deal. Please contact me at [phone number[so that we can arrange to meet over [dinner, a drink, coffee] to see if our interests coincide.

Sincerely yours,

Trish's Comments

If anyone had told me a year ago that the personal ads in *Philadelphia Magazine* would constitute an extremely efficacious way of meeting unattached, eligible bachelors, I would have laughed heartily and commented that this would have to be the last resort for the lonely, depressed, and quietly despairing! However, the two ads noted above are mine, and the composite reply below them is generally representative of the 120 responses they generated, not to mention the ads inserted in the magazine by various gentlemen which I answered and which, in most cases, elicited a prompt and enthusiastic response. So there were other lonely, discouraged people in the world, after all. It was encouraging to know I wasn't alone with my feelings.

After two divorces and a lot of miscellaneous depression, I found myself unattached at thirty-five, very rusty socially, lonely, depressed, and floundering by myself, in search of a way to acquire dates and meet people whose interests would be compatible to mine (never caring for the singles bar scene, which in my opinion is demeaning to one's self-esteem). Really compatible! I began to realize how much ground the term covered! As the responses to my ads and those I answered arrived, I realized that here was a very safe and effective manner of gauging a prospective date's general interests, appearance, personality, religious preference, and general social background, in most cases before ever arranging a first meeting. This was highly preferable to the average "blind date" and friendly "fix-up" I had been accustomed to in the past.

The responses arrived at my rented post office box. I answered those sounding interesting via telephone call or letter, qualified the respondent over the telephone, in most cases without even giving my full name or phone number, and arranged a "first meeting," usually over dinner, coffee, or a drink in a public restaurant or hotel lobby ("safe spot") where we could meet. In almost all cases, the quality of the respondents was absolutely astounding (after weeding out a very small percentage of married men looking for "side action" and a few shaky-sounding replies!).

Since placing these ads, I have enjoyed many delightful evenings of dinner and conversation with some really interesting individuals, some of whom I have never seen a second time and some whom I am still dating. As of today, I haven't found a man I consider to be completely compatible, but I've been so busy dating and answering letters, I simply can't find time to bemoan the fact that perhaps no one can expect perfect compatibility of another, and somewhere along the line a compromise can be made.* At any rate, my feelings of loneliness and isolation have dissipated a good deal, and I feel that I have done something really constructive about a very disturbing situation.

So don't be depressed if you're divorced, widowed, or just plain single and having a problem meeting eligible men or women to date. Place an ad in the magazine of your choice, sit back and wait for the responses to arrive, choose a respondent whose interests appeal to you, and who knows, you might just find that special person you're seeking. You certainly won't be lonely or depressed. You simply won't have time!

Author's Note: After a period of active dating, Trish did fall in love and got married. She's now been married for several years.

7

Overcoming Shyness and Social Anxiety

One problem that can make it awfully hard to smile and flirt is shyness. Every time you think about talking to someone attractive, you may get nervous and tell yourself:

> I'll really make a fool of myself if I try to talk to her [or him]. I'll get so nervous that I won't be able to think of anything to say. My face will get red and she [or he] will notice how embarrassed and awkward I feel. She [or he] will think I'm a real idiot.

A handsome but exquisitely shy twenty-two-year-old Cornell college student named Rod told me how nervous he felt while he was having lunch with a young lady who seemed quite interested in him. As she was talking on and on in an animated way about her summer vacation, Rod sat and worried about how tense he felt. He kept telling himself, "This is awful. I must control these feelings. I shouldn't feel like this!" He started stirring his tea furiously and concentrating on the way it swirled in the cup, hoping this would distract him from his nervousness. The more Rod tried to control his feelings, the worse they got, and he developed the fear that his face might start twitching. Although he'd never really had any noticeable facial tic, he could feel the muscles in his eyes, forehead, and mouth getting stiff, and he felt as if the muscles were on the verge of going out of control. He reasoned that everything would be okay if he could hide his emotions through tremendous willpower but that if his face twitched, she'd think he was a weirdo who was trying to seduce her and she'd get disgusted.

In an attempt to keep his face from twitching, Rod put the wooden tea stirrer in his mouth and began to move it around like a toothpick, pressing it against the edges of his lips. He reasoned that if his mouth or cheeks did begin to twitch, he could pretend it was caused by the stirrer. Then the waiter came up and began to clear the table and remove the empty teacup. Rod panicked and blurted out, "I'm not done with it yet." The waiter looked puzzled and walked away. Rod felt that he'd made a gigantic fool of himself and that all the eyes in the restaurant were glued on him. The girl he was with continued to talk on and on for another forty minutes. He sat quietly and tried desperately to maintain control of his nervousness the entire time. Finally she excused herself to go to class, and Rod went back to his dorm feeling humiliated.

Although Rod's reactions might seem extreme, you'd be surprised how many people suffer from feelings of shyness and insecurity in social situations. Almost everybody feels self-conscious part of the time. Even people who appear to be supremely confident will admit that they often feel very nervous and insecure. Many well-known show-business people—including Johnny Carson—who seem to be masters of polish and self-control have been afflicted by shyness.

Have you noticed how some people seem to be comfortable with themselves in virtually any situation? They seem interested in people and they set others at ease. They can generate stimulating conversations with anybody at the drop of a hat. They can talk to strangers almost as easily as they would talk to old friends.

Perhaps you've felt envious of them and wondered how they do it. Maybe you believe it's just not in the cards for you to be like that. You may think you're destined to feel awkward and shy forever. You're not! You can overcome this problem if you want to. It means changing some of your basic attitudes and applying a few surprisingly simple communication techniques that virtually *anyone* can master—if you're determined and willing to put in a little effort.

You might think that being around other people makes you nervous—but it really doesn't. You might believe that the problem is with your "personality"—you might think you're just not the self-confident, outgoing type of person. But this isn't the real problem, either. The real culprit is the negative thoughts you have when you're feeling shy and insecure. Do any of these self-defeating thinking patterns sound familiar to you?

Fortune-telling. You anticipate that people will dislike you or that you're going to feel uncomfortable when you talk to them. When you see an attractive woman (or man), you may tell yourself, "She probably wouldn't be interested in someone like me." In your mind's eye you may picture yourself sweating profusely and saying something stupid while everybody watches and snickers. These thoughts function as a self-fulfilling prophecy because they make you intensely uncomfortable and you may give up and not try to talk to her at all.

"Should" Statements. Once you begin to feel nervous, you add fuel to the fire by telling yourself, "I *shouldn't* feel so shy. I *should* be more relaxed." The more you try to control your feelings, the more out of control they seem to get. Then you feel helpless and ashamed and wonder how anyone could ever respect or love you.

Overgeneralization. You see any rejection or social foible as a never-ending pattern of defeat. If you forget someone's name or make a foolish comment at a cocktail party, you tell yourself, "Why am I *always* saying such stupid things? I'm such a stupid jerk!"

Mind Reading. You assume, without any real evidence, that other people don't like you. A woman who called her boyfriend and learned that he was out to lunch became very despondent because she told herself, "He's just avoiding me. I'll *never* get a man." At a dinner party or social gathering you might feel self-conscious and out of place because you think, "These people probably think I'm a real bore."

It's important to learn to think about social situations in a more positive and realistic way. Once you begin to feel more self-confident, other people will feel better about you. You'll get into a positive mood cycle because your increased self-esteem will lead to greater social success, whichin turn will lead to more self-confidence.

To make this happen, you will have to change the way you think and the way you communicate with people. Divide a sheet of paper into three columns, as in Figure 7-1. In the left-hand column, write down the upsetting thoughts that make you feel shy and insecure. These are called "Automatic Thoughts" because they automatically go through your mind whenever you feel nervous. Try to identify the kinds of distortion in these negative thoughts and record them in the middle column. Then write down more realistic and self-endorsing thoughts in the right-hand column.

Ted is a twenty-three-year-old policeman whose thoughts are illustrated in Figure 7-1. Ted had been shy around girls since his early teens. Part of the problem was that he was strikingly handsome and his mom and dad often told him that he should have lots of dates with the best-looking girls and sweep them off their feet. Although his parents were probably trying to build up his confidence, these comments had the opposite effect and made him feel pressured and insecure. There was such a gap between how inadequate he felt inside and what he thought people expected of him that he felt ashamed and began to think there was something seriously wrong with him. He believed his embarrassment and shyness were unmanly and had to be covered up. Whenever he was around an attractive woman, he'd get tongue-tied and self-critical and tell himself that he wasn't *supposed* to be reacting this way. This, of course, only made things worse.

As you study the way Ted talked back to his "Automatic Thoughts" in Figure 7-1, you will see the theme of self-acceptance. Instead of berating himself for feeling shy and self-conscious, he learned to *accept* these feelings without shame. Instead of viewing them as abnormal or shameful, he began to think of them as natural. Instead of thinking he was "unmanly," he decided to tell himself he was human and vulnerable.

Ted was surprised to discover that once he gave himself permission to feel shy and nervous, he suddenly began to feel more relaxed and in control. This is called a "para-

FIGURE 7-1
Overcoming Shyness with the "Triple-Column" Technique

AUTOMATIC THOUGHTS	DISTORTIONS	REALISTIC RESPONSES
1. I'm getting nervous and up-tight, and that's ridiculous.	1. "Should" statement.	1. It's not ridiculous to get nervous. It's natural.
2. I *shouldn't* feel so shy because I'm attractive by society's standards.	2. "Should" statement.	2. Even good-looking people can feel nervous and insecure at times.
3. Most people think I shouldn't be nervous.	3. Mind reading; "should" statement.	3. *I'm* the one who's saying that I'm not allowed to feel nervous, but I have no evidence that other people expect so much from me.
4. If I get uptight, I'll look like a fool and people will be turned off.	4. Mind reading; fortune-telling; labeling.	4. Feeling uptight makes me human, not "a fool." If someone is really interested in me, it's unlikely they'll get turned off just because I'm nervous at first.

AUTOMATIC THOUGHTS	DISTORTIONS	REALISTIC RESPONSES
5. But if someone does get turned off by me, that would show what a socially inept loser I am.	5. Overgeneralization; labeling.	5. Being shy or nervous doesn't make me a "socially inept loser." Some people will like me, and some people won't. If someone thinks less of me because I'm nervous, that will have to be their problem.

doxical technique" because you overcome a problem by surrendering to it instead of resisting it. Accepting your limitations can often be the pathway to growth, whereas putting yourself down and insisting that you should be different from the way you are will simply make you feel inadequate and make the problem worse. Shyness is really just a form of emotional perfectionism, because you're trying to measure up to some imaginary goal of how you think you *should* be instead of accepting yourself as you really are.

Ted was doubly surprised that this new philosophy seemed to enhance his sex appeal. When he told a woman he met that he had a tendency to feel shy and nervous at times, she confessed to being very attracted to him and said his openness made him seem even more appealing! She said she was tired of insensitive men who were always trying to be macho and emphasized that Ted's sensitivity was one of his greatest assets because many women might feel a little intimidated by his good looks.

I suspect some readers may be thinking, "But what if she *didn't* react that way? The fact is, some people *will* think you're weak or peculiar if you tell them you're nervous. Our society values poise and self-confidence. Women are attracted to winners. Face the facts!'' There's certainly some truth to this. Some people probably will reject you if you're nervous. But it's important to remember that no matter *what* you're like—whether you're rich or poor, insecure or outgoing, brilliant or average, attractive or plain—some people will like you and others couldn't care less about you. *Nobody* gets accepted by everyone. But if you have self-esteem and accept yourself, then far more people will be attracted to you. If you feel nervous and you're putting yourself down about it with a constant barrage of self-abuse, people will get turned off. *But it's your self-hatred, not your shyness, that's driving people away!* And by the same token, the moment you decide that your shyness doesn't make you one iota less desirable or lovable, you'll suddenly discover that most other people aren't particularly concerned about it either.

So how can you learn to accept your shyness without feeling ashamed and inferior? One thing that can help is to make a list of the advantages and disadvantages of telling yourself that shyness makes you less worthwhile. Then make a second list of the advantages and disadvantages of telling yourself that shyness only makes you more human, as illustrated in Figure 7-2. This can help you become more self-accepting.

Another way to get over your fear of shyness is with the "survey technique." Shy people nearly always have the belief that their nervousness is highly unusual and that other people are far more self-confident than they really are. Why not do a little research and find out? Ask a number of friends the following questions: (1) If you had to ask someone for a date, would you feel shy or nervous? (2) Have you ever felt uncomfortable talking to someone of the opposite sex? (3) Do you ever feel nervous in groups or in social situations? (4) Do you ever feel nervous when you have to give a talk in front of a group of people? (5) Do you think someone who feels shy or nervous is abnormal or inferior?

I suspect that you'll discover that there are far more people than you thought who feel nervous and shy at times

Figure 7-2
Cost-Benefit Analysis

Belief: My shyness and nervousness make me less worthwhile.

Advantages of Believing This	Disadvantages of Believing This
1. I'll try hard to control my feelings.	1. Trying to control these feelings usually just makes them worse.
2. I won't let on to people how insecure I feel. That way they won't have the chance to reject me.	2. When I feel shy I get self-critical, and that's like adding fuel to the fire.
	3. My self-esteem will depend on my emotions, which I can't always control.
	4. I'll feel lonely because it will be hard to share my real feelings with people.
(25)	(75)

Revised Belief: My shyness and nervousness only make me more human.

Advantages of Believing This	Disadvantages of Believing This
1. I won't hate myself for being nervous.	1. By taking more risks, I may be rejected more frequently. (But I'll also have more chances to get close to people!)
2. I'll accept myself.	
3. It will be easier to take the risk of talking to people and opening up.	
(60)	(40)

and that there's really nothing shameful or unusual about these feelings.

Another way to get over your feelings of embarrassment is to write out a dialogue with an imaginary, hostile stranger who is rejecting you because of your shyness, as described in Chapter Four. Have them attack you by saying those vicious, humiliating things that a real stranger would never actually say. It might go like this:

STRANGER: I get the feeling you're so nervous your face seems bright red.

YOU: As a matter of fact, I do feel nervous. I have a problem with shyness when I first meet someone.

STRANGER: How ridiculous! What's wrong with you? Are you some kind of a nut?

YOU: It's interesting that you'd think my shyness makes me a nut. How did you come to that conclusion?

STRANGER: Well, it seems very abnormal. I wouldn't tell anyone if I were you.

YOU: Why not? I'm not ashamed of my feelings. I think it's very natural to feel nervous at times. Don't you ever feel that way?

STRANGER: Absolutely not! I'm no loony! I can control myself.

YOU: Well, you have better self-control than I do. Does it bother you that I'm nervous?

STRANGER: Absolutely! I don't want to have anything to do with you. I don't even want to be seen with you. I think you're a *sicko*!

YOU: Why wouldn't you want to be seen with me? Are you afraid that you might start getting nervous or that my shyness is contagious? Are you concerned that people might think less of you if they saw us together?

STRANGER: To be sure! I only go around with people who are extremely self-confident and poised.

YOU: I can see that you're quite concerned about what other people think of you. I'd think it would be uncomfortable to have to be on guard all the time.

Certainly a real stranger would never say these things. The put-downs are simply projections of the fears that lurk within your own mind. The purpose of this type of dialogue is to give you the chance to examine these fears for what they are and to see how illogical and unnecessary they are. The stranger you fear is no one other than yourself, and learning to talk back to the stranger's condemnations can help you discover how to love yourself in spite of your imperfections. Self-acceptance, not perfect self-control, is the ultimate triumph.

In addition to changing your basic attitudes and thinking patterns, you can boost your self-confidence by modifying your fantasies and daydreams. Before a date or a party you might imagine yourself feeling awkward, foolish, and tongue-tied. You may visualize these painful, awkward scenes over and over again. These mental pictures can upset you just as much as your self-critical, negative thoughts. If you don't believe me, try a little experiment right now. Imagine having someone criticize your ideas in front of a group of people who are quietly snickering at you. Or imagine being on a date and being unable to think of anything to say. These are long, embarrassing silences. You feel uncomfortable and your face is getting red. Can you see the scene? Try to picture it as graphically as possible. Make it just as awful and as vivid as you can.

Now: How do you feel? Do you feel a little tense and awkward? Well, that's exactly what you may be doing to yourself when you feel shy and nervous. And the important thing to realize is that *those fantasies actually create the bad feelings.* Furthermore, since you put them there, it's within your power to get rid of them!

Why not visualize social encounters in an upbeat way instead? Before going to a party, try to picture yourself talking in a warm, animated manner and getting good responses from others. Imagine feeling positive about yourself and expressing an interest in the people you meet. Sometimes a humorous or erotic image will help you feel relaxed. If you're talking to a woman and feeling overly heavy and tense, why not look deeply and longingly into her eyes and imagine how she'd look as a burlesque dancer in sexy undies? This will lift your spirits, make *her* feel good, and serve as an antidote to your nervousness. Practice putting these positive or humorous images in your mind every night for five minutes before you go to sleep. You might find it helpful to put strong, pleasant memories in your mind, such as skiing down your favorite slope on a brisk winter day. Then imagine skiing with someone you just met who you care about. This can do a great deal to increase your confidence!

In addition to changing your fantasies and thinking patterns, it's important to learn how to communicate with people so you get into the flow of the relationship instead of being inhibited and preoccupied with how uncomfortable you feel. The following three techniques can be very helpful, especially if you practice them persistently. While you may feel uncomfortable at first, eventually you'll find that your discomfort will fade and it will be much easier to get to know people.

1. Small Talk. Many shy people tell me, "I can't ever think of anything interesting to talk about." It is a simple matter to skim the newspaper or a recent magazine so you can make a written or mental list of several current events. What's the latest sports news? What's the Dow-Jones average doing? What's happening overseas? What are the latest books and movies? A simple comment like, "Do you think the Phillies will pull out of their slump?" is usually enough to trigger a conversation. Jot down several topics on a three-by-five card and keep it in your pocket. You'll probably never need to look at it, but just having it with you can give you the assurance that you'll never be without a topic for conversation.

Remember that people also want to know about *you* as well as world affairs. What are your goals? What do you enjoy? What turns you on? And off? Some people feel inhibited about this because they say, "I'm only a cabdriver. My life isn't very special or glamorous." They think their job or personality is simply routine and wouldn't interest anyone. This will just operate as a self-fulfilling prophecy, because if you don't feel good about yourself, then other people may not think there's anything interesting about you, either. But whatever your occupation, your life is as interesting as anyone's. You just need to open your eyes to the uniqueness of your own human experience. Can you think of anyone whose life is exactly like yours? If you're a cabdriver, you can talk about that eccentric professor, celebrity, or streetwalker you gave a ride to the other day.

Sometimes people are less interested in where you're at than where you're going. What are your plans? What are your aspirations and dreams? Maybe you want to build a house or complete your degree. One cabdriver I rode with told me how he would work for six months to save up money and then he'd take off for six months to hike through Europe. His life-style amazed me. He was far poorer but, in many ways, far richer and freer than I was! Another cabdriver explained that he'd brought his family here from Jamaica to escape the poverty, but found conditions even worse in the States. He was disillusioned, lonesome and yearning to be home. He described Jamaica so vividly I felt I was visiting there.

You can also share your fantasies with people. Maybe you'd like to scuba-dive in the Caribbean . . . or be a beach bum in California . . . or ski in Switzerland. You don't need to have the assets to get there—just sharing your dreams with people can turn them on. And who knows—maybe they'll just decide to share a few of their dreams with you!

2. The Johnny Carson Technique. * Many shy people have the erroneous notion that in order to be popular you have to impress people with your poise, your looks, your charm, or your intelligence. You may believe you need to think of clever witty things to say. This is an enormous fallacy. People who come on too strong usually just turn people off. Trying to impress people will make you anxious because you'll feel as if you're in the spotlight and have to perform. This attitude has been called "spectatoring" because you become like a spectator who's constantly judging your own performance and worrying about whether it's good enough.

The Johnny Carson technique can help you break out of this trap. Instead of becoming obsessed about how much other people like or dislike you—which is, after all, pretty *self*-centered—become *other*-centered. Learn as much about other people as you can. Find out what's special and

---

*This term was created by Dr. Jeffrey E. Young, who is on the clinical faculty of the Department of Psychiatry at the University of Pennsylvania.

unique about them. They'll appreciate you and like you because of your interest in them. The key to sex appeal is not sweeping people off their feet but letting other people sweep you off your feet! Everybody has the craving to be loved and appreciated, and if you're willing to make other people feel appreciated they'll often find *you* irresistible.

The simplest way to do this is by asking people questions. You can pretend that you're a talk show host. Get people to talk about what interests them by saying, "Tell me more about that. . . . How did you get interested in it?" Johnny Carson uses this technique to excellent advantage. He appears relaxed, intelligent, and in control because he gets his guests to talk about what's important to them.

Many shy people put pressure on themselves to come up with interesting, exciting topics for conversation. This isn't necessary. What most people want is for you to pay attention to them. For the last fifty years psychiatrists and psychologists have made a handsome living just by nodding their heads knowingly and asking a few questions. If they can get away with it, so can you! Of course, once you get to know someone, you'll feel more relaxed and talking about the things that interest you will come naturally, but it's important to know that when you feel shy and you're trying to get to know someone, just asking questions and expressing a little interest in them can often be enough.

The Johnny Carson technique involves three straight-forward methods:

• *Paraphrase*. Repeat what the other person says. Restate it in your own words. If someone says, "More rain. What a miserable day!" you can say, "Yes, the weather's really been lousy. It *is* miserable."

• *Inquiry*. Following this up by asking a question. In the above example you could go on to ask the person what he or she likes best about sunny weather. Does he or she like tennis? Swimming? Summer vacations?

• *The Disarming Technique*. People will usually feel enormously rewarded if you find some little grain of truth in what they're saying and actively agree with them. If someone says they like tennis, you could say that tennis is a great sport and ask them how long they've been playing.

If they're talking about politics or philosophy, you could say, "That's an interesting idea!" or, "I like your thinking. It's quite similar to that of Gandhi" (or Mick Jagger or Ronald Reagan or whomever). Even when someone expresses a controversial and somewhat illogical point of view, make a point of finding *some* truth in it instead of arguing with them. This will make them feel special and more open to your ideas.

Perhaps you think this is too simple. It's very tempting to think that life is hard and people are terribly complex. But those can just be excuses. Most people are basically very simple. They want you to like them. That's the way I am. It *thrills* me when people express a little interest in me. You can capitalize on this if you paraphrase what people say, ask them questions about what they're doing, and find some truth in what they say. Get them to talk about themselves. If you do, I suspect you won't feel shy and lonely very long!

Let's say that I'm trying to get to know you—you could be someone I met at a party or at a professional symposium. You might tell me, "I read your book and it just seems a little bit too rational and logical." I could reply, "You're absolutely right about that. Life isn't always so logical and so easy. Can you tell me more about your ideas on this? I'd like to learn more about your thinking."

Now, how would you feel? I suspect that my disarming comment would make you feel relaxed and accepted, and you'd see me as someone who was flexible and receptive to your ideas. This could be the basis of a good discussion or even the beginning of a friendship. In contrast, if I got defensive and argumentative, I'd probably alienate you and you'd end up thinking I was an A-1 jerk.

The disarming technique will backfire if you make a sarcastic comment or if you don't do it in a genuine way. But if you're willing, you can *always* find some truth in what people say, even if you think that their ideas are absurd. Suppose that someone says, "Republicans [or Democrats] are all a bunch of jerks!" You could reply, "There *are* some jerks in the Republican Party, all right. Who are some of the people who turn you off?" Notice that you've found *some* truth in the other person's point of view without having to say anything phony or incorrect. This will give the other person a chance to ventilate, and you'll avoid a frustrating argument.

This doesn't mean that you can't ever present an alternative or contradictory idea. Many people love controversy, and a good argument can be fun. But the important thing is not to project hostile feelings toward people or to get overly dogmatic when you disagree with them. Let them know that you disagree with their ideas without trying to put them down or acting defensive or arrogant. If you view a conversation as a competition or an ego battle, you're bound to have an unpleasant experience, but if you view it as an opportunity to share ideas with someone you like and respect, it will be almost impossible for you to fail.

3. *Personal Disclosure.* When I was a student at Amherst College I decided to keep a journal recording my inner thoughts and feelings. I never planned to show it to anyone because the things I wrote down were completely private and personal. Some of them had to do with painful recollections from childhood—times I was criticized or felt hurt and cried, times when I felt confused, lonely, and insecure. I also wrote down fragments of dreams and sexual fantasies, such as wanting to be undressed with an older girl who lived across the alley from us when I was eight. I included memories of shameful urges and feelings like anger and hatred, as well as descriptions of my hobbies and the things I loved when I was growing up—visiting magic stores and coin stores and wandering through the Denver Museum of Natural History. I also jotted down scattered feelings and personal impressions about my college classmates and their parents.

One day a terrible thing happened. I went back to the dorm after dinner in Valentine Hall, and I suddenly realized I'd left my journal in the coatroom in the lobby where the students left their books and jackets while they were eating. I raced back to Valentine Hall in a panic and was dismayed to discover that my journal was gone. It had vanished! I was terribly embarrassed. Who had picked it up? I was terrified that somebody might find it and find out the truth about who I was. I looked for it desperately, but it simply couldn't be found. Days and weeks passed, and eventually I gave up on ever finding it again.

About a month later, I was hanging up my jacket in the same coatroom in Valentine Hall. As I reached up to put my books in the rack, I saw my brown, tattered journal, just where I'd left it! I grabbed it and quickly raced through the pages, feeling frightened and humiliated. I discovered this new entry, written by a stranger, where I'd left off: "God bless you, to use a phrase. I read this as it lay here in the Valentine lobby. I am a lot like you only I don't keep a diary and I'm grateful to know there are others like me. I hope things turn out well for you." I was stunned and tears came to my eyes. It had never dawned on me that anyone could know about all my inner feelings, secrets, and fantasies and still care about me or respect me. And the irony was that of all the papers I'd ever written in college to try to impress people, these warm comments in my journal were the best feedback I'd ever gotten! And what a miracle to have someone respond so warmly! To me!

I've learned this lesson over and over in my life. The times that people seem to like me the most are when I'm being myself—sharing my vulnerabilities, fears, and self-doubts, as well as my aspirations and the things that excite me the most. But this can be difficult, because we often tell ourselves that we have to measure up to some external standard of the way we think we *should* be. Accepting ourselves as we really are and sharing ourselves with others admittedly seems risky, but it can be the stepping-stone to friendship and love.

These conversational methods are straightforward and usually very effective. I *know*, because I use them myself over and over every day and they work like a charm. I talk to strangers anywhere and I nearly always find that people interest me. I talk to people on the train, in the lines at grocery stores, or even when I'm standing at the corner waiting for the light to turn green. I've had wonderfully open, candid conversations with people I've just met. The world is filled with lonely people who would welcome the chance to exchange some ideas and feelings with someone who would reach out to them.

You may be skeptical and wonder why more people

didn't just apply these methods and become instantly popular. I've discovered that shy people often give themselves self-defeating messages which make them resist doing the very things that would be so helpful to them. A shy, lonely veterinary student complained that he had no friends and hadn't had a date in years. I suggested he make a plan to give out ten compliments to classmates in the following week. He told me angrily that he'd *never* do anything as stupid as that! He said this would be terribly peculiar and insisted that everybody would think he was a weirdo. Then I asked if he'd be willing to tell one of his friends he was feeling a little lonely and would like to get together or maybe meet some girls to date. He said he'd *never* consider doing something like that and explained that he'd rather die than have anyone find out how lonely he felt.

You may have similar inhibitions. You may feel that you could *never* reveal your inner feelings or tell a friend how nervous and shy you feel. You may believe that if you smiled at strangers and gave people compliments or asked them questions about themselves, they'd look down on you or react negatively. You may think that if you tried to make small talk at a social gathering, people wouldn't be interested in what you have to say. If you think these methods wouldn't work, do an experiment and see what kinds of results you actually get. Try complimenting ten people in the next week. When people talk to you, paraphrase what they say and ask them questions so they'll tell you more. Find little grains of truth in what they say. Take a chance and tell someone how you really feel inside. Tell them about your opinions and aspirations. The results might surprise you, and this could be a giant step toward greater intimacy and self-confidence.

How to Respond to Other People's Advances

You may not only be afraid to initiate contact with others but might also get nervous every time someone of the opposite sex approaches you. A divorced man named Dean was standing in the lobby of a movie theater putting salt on his popcorn when an attractive woman came up to him and said, "You shouldn't put that salt on your popcorn. It has too much salt on it already." Dean felt she was interested in him and wanted to start a conversation, but he got so nervous that he dropped his popcorn on the floor and muttered, "Gee, you're right." Then he practically ran back to his seat in the theater.

On another occasion he went to the neighborhood lounge for a beer. The owner, a woman, suggested that Dean and his friends might want to come on a particular night because they were having a male stripper and she thought there might be a number of ladies in the audience who wanted to meet some eligible bachelors. Dean decided to go. After he sat down at the bar the woman seated next to him made several flirtatious comments while the stripper did his act. First she said, "He looks like Lou Ferrigno. I may be a little bit older than he is, but I bet I could teach him a thing or two!" Dean just mumbled, "Gee. I guess you could." A few minutes later she said, "Boy, he certainly knows how to get somebody aroused. I think I'm going to run home and attack my neighbor." Dean got so excited by her comments that he was visibly shaking but he couldn't think of what to say, so he just said, "Do you think that would be okay with him?" At the end of the act he went home feeling lonely, frustrated, and humiliated and wondered what he could have done differently so he could get to know her.

While this situation might seem farfetched to some people, these days more and more women are making advances toward men and even inviting them out. For shy men this can be a very real problem.

Dean needed to learn how to respond to the woman in a friendly, lighthearted, flirtatious way that would help get the conversation rolling. To help him learn how to do this, I suggested he work with a form called "Revise Your Communication Style," which is illustrated in Figure 7-3. (A blank form for your use is included on page 308.) You will notice there are three columns, entitled "S/he Says," "I Ordinarily Say," and "Revised Version." In the left-hand column, write a brief description of the situation and put down what the other person said to you. In the middle column, write down what you said to them. As you think about what you said, it will usually become apparent to you why it wasn't effective. Then in the right-hand column substitute a revised version of what you could have said to them.

If you have trouble thinking of more effective statements to put in the right-hand column, ask a friend for suggestions. Don't be afraid of putting your foot in your mouth, because almost *anything* you say will work. The other person is probably feeling just as nervous as you are, and will be relieved to have something to talk about. Notice that Dean's "Revised Versions" often involve questions or compliments. Remember that people who initiate a conversation with you usually feel extremely vulnerable because they're afraid you might reject them and they're hoping that you'll express an interest in them. A few sincere questions and compliments can go a lot further toward developing a friendship than any attempt at being clever or cute. Everybody has the craving to be liked and admired, and if you're willing to express a little interest in others, they'll usually feel an immediate attraction to you. Dale Carnegie promoted this idea to earlier generations, but it's just as true today as it was several decades ago.

How to "Lighten Up"

Some readers may resist some of the techniques described in the last few chapters. You might think, "Oh, I couldn't wear an outrageous, sexy outfit because I'm basically a nice, sincere person. It wouldn't fit my personality to come on strong. I'm not the flashy type." Or you might say, "I'm not about to go around complimenting and flattering people or flirting because that would be phony. I don't want to lower myself by 'playing the game.' "

This is exactly how I felt for the first twenty-six years of my life. I saw myself as a "nice and sincere" person. And this was just exactly what was turning people off about me! Sometimes being overly serious can be a cover-up for a lack of self-confidence. It can be a way of being cold and keeping your distance. If you decide to lighten up and stop taking yourself so seriously, you can sometimes get closer to people.

The following excerpt from a therapy session with a shy

FIGURE 7-3
Revise Your Communication Style

S/HE SAYS	I ORDINARILY SAY	REVISED VERSION
In this column briefly describe the situation and write down what the other person said.	In this column write down what you said. Point out why your statement wasn't particularly effective.	Substitute a more effective statement here.
An attractive lady tapped me on the shoulder in the lobby of the theater and said, "I wouldn't put any more salt on there if I were you. It's got too much salt already."	I dropped the popcorn all over the floor and said, "Gee, you're right." Then I practically ran back to my seat in the theater! This didn't work out well because I didn't get to talk to her.	I could have said, "I'll take your advice. Are you playing hooky from work?"
While I was in the neighborhood lounge watching a male stripper, the woman sitting next to me turned to me and said, "He certainly knows how to get somebody aroused. I think I'll go home and attack my neighbor."	I was quaking in my boots and I said, "Do you think it would be okay with him?" This might have sounded insecure or even sarcastic.	I could have said, "You don't have to go all the way home to do that!"
Later on she said, "I may be a little older than him, but I bet I could teach him a thing or two!"	I said, "You don't look all that old to me." This was a compliment, but I didn't keep the conversation going.	I could have said, "You could show *me* a thing or two."

young man named Bill illustrates how people can resist applying the very techniques that would give them what they claim they want—namely, better relationships with others. Perhaps as you listen to Bill you will recognize some of your own fears and inhibitions. When you see a self-defeating attitude in someone else it sometimes makes it easier to recognize and change it in yourself.

Bill is a twenty-eight-year-old bachelor. He's good-looking, intelligent, and personable. He has a nice physique and dresses well. He has a solid career with his uncle's construction and real-estate investment business and drives a fancy sports car. His only real problem is that he's intensely shy, lonely, and overly serious. He lives with his parents and he's had very few dates for the past three years. He came to therapy so he could conquer some of his inhibitions and loosen up and enjoy life more.

The excerpted session took place after Bill and I had been working for several weeks on how to approach women by smiling, complimenting them, flirting, and making small talk, but it seemed as if between sessions he would resist practicing these skills. Bill always had elaborate rationalizations and excuses why he wouldn't try anything new or different. This will become quite evident as the session evolves:

Bill: Saturday I ah . . . I was sorta fighting myself. I can't stand to go to parties. I hate parties. Okay? And so a friend of mine who goes to Cornell said, "Hey, there's a party down there this weekend. Do you want to go?" Almost all the time he asks me and I say, "No, I don't want to go." And this week I said to myself, "Jeez, maybe I *better* go. You know, it's a good social thing to be able to meet some people. It's something that might benefit me." Come Saturday and he asked me again . . . but I didn't go. I wasn't only fighting him, I was fighting myself. Because half of me wanted to go and half of me didn't.

David: Well, that's kind of a tricky thing. You certainly are a free agent and you can do whatever you like, but I wonder why you decided not to go.

Bill: I was just telling myself that it wouldn't be a very good way to meet girls.

David: Yeah?

Bill: I don't like to date. Like a different girl every week the way some people do . . . so I said to myself, I doubt that I'm going to find someone. I don't know anybody who's ever gotten a good relationship as a result of going to a party. Because I figured the type of personality that is partygoer is not the type that I'd be interested in. Do you know what I mean?

David: I'm not sure that I do. What percentage of women enjoy going to parties at least on some occasions?

Bill: Most people like to go to parties on some occasions.

David: One hundred percent?

Bill: Close, yeah.

David: So when you say you don't want the kind of woman who enjoys parties, you're going to have a rather limited range of choices because the fact is that nearly *all* women enjoy going to parties some of the time!

Bill: (laughs) Maybe I was involved in some illogical thinking!

David: Right. You could call it all-or-nothing thinking, because you were thinking of women as being in one of two groups, the "partygoers" and the "nonpartygoers," and you were telling yourself that the "partygoers" weren't your type. That gave you a good excuse not to go.

Bill: I just felt the odds were against me, that's all. Even if I was involved in illogical thinking, that's what I *really* felt—that the odds were against meeting someone. . . .

David: At least it would give you the chance to practice some of the techniques for meeting people that we've been working on. If you do a little smiling and flirting and complimenting people, you might be surprised at how many interesting people you could meet.

Bill: Well, I hate parties.

David: Why do you hate parties?

Bill: I don't like . . . I don't like a lot of crowds and a lot of noise.

David: Why? Do you have a phobia about crowds? Do you get anxiety reactions, or what?

Bill: No. No. I just think there's too much B.S. floating around. . . . Everybody puts on a facade at parties.

David: Why is that a problem to you?

Bill: *To me it's just a lot of B.S. Nobody's telling the truth. Nobody's showing their real self.*

David: So?

Bill: So I don't like that.

David: Why?

Bill: I don't like to talk about nonsense kind of stuff. It's just a game.

David: Suppose you went to Africa to visit a tribe of cannibals. They might have a little gift ritual and if you bring them bottles of perfume or jewelry they decide you're their friend. If you don't bring them perfume or jewelry they decide you're an enemy and they eat you.

Bill: Make you a casserole!

David: Right! They enjoy you one way or the other! Now you could go there and insist they were being immature and refuse to give them any bottles of perfume because that isn't a reflection of your "true self" or because you think it's "phony B.S." But you'd just end up as a casserole. Or on the other hand, you could go and play that little game and accept their customs as a part of a ritual. Then you could get to know them better once they felt comfortable with you.

Bill: I can't do that. I hate it!

David: Well, it's not true that you *can't* do that. Maybe you mean you don't want to do it.

Bill: I don't want to do it at this point.

David: Why?

Bill: I don't want to *lower* myself like that.

David: I wonder if that sounds a little bit self-righteous.

Bill: (laughs) Well, maybe I do sound self-righteous. I don't want to be that way, but . . . I can't stand all the B.S. It's just that when you meet someone, male or female, it's like a . . . It immediately gets to be like one-upmanship situation.

David: Well who's setting it up that way? Who's thinking about "One-upmanship"?

Bill: Well that's how I see it . . . that's my experience.

David: Maybe if you went to one of these parties and focused on what's special about the people you meet you could begin to tune in on an entirely new way of experiencing people and you might even learn to have a good time. You might change your attitude and one day you might look back and say, "Yes, I was being defensive."

Bill: Well, that could be.

David: You might even say, "I actually enjoy parties now that I know how to fling a little B.S. as effectively as the rest of them."

Bill: (laugh) I only want to fling the B.S. with people I want to fling the B.S. with.

David: But how can you decide ahead of time whether or not you'd want to get to know someone?

Bill: I just don't wanna . . . I don't want to have to "win" them. I don't give a darn *what* they think of me at those parties!

David: If you really didn't care what other people thought about you, then I suspect you'd have no inhibitions about going to the party and talking to some women. I wonder if you're being honest with yourself when you insist that you aren't concerned with what people think of you. You claim to be sincere, but I wonder if what you're saying isn't a little phony. (Bill laughs)

Bill: You might have a line on me but I don't want to *constantly* use that B.S. attitude . . . flinging B.S. on *everybody*.

David: Did you think you'd *constantly* have to do it with *everybody?* What would you think about *occasionally* flinging a little B.S. with *some* people?

Bill: I was down in Florida once with a buddy and we went to this restaurant and they had like what we thought was a disco upstairs. Not that I'm a big disco freak but you know we went up to take a look—what the hell. So it ended up being a little disco and a big singles bar. So we went in and sat down and I'm like . . . We're at this little table near the bar. And it's like girl, boy, girl, boy, girl, boy, all the way down and it was pathetic. It was pathetic. I mean these guys were flinging out lines! Awkkkk!

David: Yeah?

Bill: Oh, yeah! Like "What's your sign?" You know, real B.S.! But these girls were eating it up!

David: Why don't you try it?

Bill: Ughhhhh. It'd turn my stomach. I wouldn't do it on a bet.

David: Why?

Bill: Because I don't want to *lower* myself.

David: Why would it be "lowering yourself"? Do you think that you're better than these people? And why would it be so terrible if you did "lower yourself"? Are they going to advertise it in the paper? "Smith lowers himself! Flings out line at party! Now impure, how like the rest of us!" (both laugh)

Bill: I just couldn't . . . That whole scene bummed me out. I wanted to get out of there. I said, "This is ridiculous. These guys are sick." I mean they were really losers. The whole thing is a game. Everything is a game.

David: Yeah, but you have to understand that the game is just the beginning of the relationship. Once you get to know someone, the relationship becomes genuine. Even birds do it. They play the game. Did you ever go to the zoo?

Bill: Yeah.

David: Did you ever see the male peacocks doing little mating rituals when they want a girl friend? They go out and they strut around and display their feathers. But do you say, "Ha Ha Ha, you're such an insincere bird. You shouldn't have to do that! It's transparent as all get out. It's not your 'true self.' No decent bird would do a silly dance like that."

Bill: It's not the same thing.

David: It *is* the same thing. Why do you think it isn't?

Bill: He shouldn't *have* to strut his feathers.

David: The birds?

Bill: Not the birds, the guys at the disco. They're just a bunch of phonies.

David: That may be more all-or-nothing thinking. You're telling yourself that some people are "phonies" and other people are "genuine." I believe that when you're trying to meet people, trying too hard to be genuine can sometimes be rather phony, and a little phoniness can sometimes be more genuine.

Bill: Wait, wait. What did you say?

David: Genuineness is phony . . .

Bill: No, I got that part. What was the other part?

David: And phoniness can be quite genuine.

Bill: I'm confused. What do you mean? How can you feel that way?

David: Because I believe it reflects the truth.

Bill: Why?

David: Because in social situations there are these little formulas that people use to make connnections. It's part of loving people. You take their social expectations into account and you realize that they need these little signals from you so they can feel relaxed during the first thirty seconds of an interaction.

Bill: I don't understand.

David: What I'm saying is that when you meet a girl she'll usually feel a lot more comfortable if you do ask her about her sign or make some small talk or give her a compliment. It lets her know that you're a single fellow who's interested in her. Once you start talking, you can get to know her in a more genuine way. Maybe you'll even end up becoming her husband and raising a family one day. But it's a part of loving humanity to bend enough to be a little phony and play the game at first. It sets people at ease, and it can be a way of caring. Your philosophy of remaining aloof because of your need to be sincere and real strikes me as pretty cold and lonely. You're a purist in an impure society, and you're asking people to be more than they really are.

Bill: Yeah.

David: They're just frail, insecure people in a tense social situation and they appreciate a little patter, a little small talk, a little B.S. as you call it.

Bill: Oh, I don't mind . . . I don't mind a little B.S. I just think I'm not going to tell her she's got a nice blouse if I don't like it. I'm not that kind of an idiot. And I'm not going to say "What's your sign" or something. I couldn't do that.

David: Well, make up your mind about what you *are* going to do. And don't be afraid of being playful or light-hearted or taking some chances and trying something new as an experiment. I think that once you get started you'll have some successes, and once you've had some success I predict you'll be singing a different tune.

Bill: I'm sure you're right. It's tough, though . . . and it seems incredible.

Bill's crusade for total sincerity was really a cover-up for his feelings of inadequacy. Although he spent a lot of time trying to persuade himself that he wasn't going to "lower himself" because he was better than other people, he really felt unsure of himself and didn't want to have to compete or expose himself to the possibility of rejection. His insistence that he wasn't going to "play games" gave him a perfect excuse to avoid life and all its disappointments—but it was also robbing him of opportunities for sharing and for getting involved with people.

I told Bill how trying some of these flirting techniques as an experiment helped me turn my life around when I was his age. You might recall from the introduction that up to the time I was halfway through medical school I had always been very tense and awkward around women. Then I learned the ropes from a friend who was incredibly successful with women. He taught me how to dress and how to flirt and turn people on. One evening I decided to go to a pub near the Stanford University campus to try some of the things he'd been teaching me. This was a place where people gathered and I had often gone there but I usually felt out of place. I'd notice everyone else talking and having fun and I'd wonder why I always seemed to be on the outside looking in. But that evening I was tired of being so serious and lonely and I was determined to try something new. I walked in and was standing alone near the front entrance when two tough-looking guys with Harley motorcycles and leather jackets came in with two extremely attractive, well-built girls. I felt nervous and looked over at one of the girls and blurted out, "Gee, that's really a cute blouse you're wearing," or something like that—in a real stiff way. It was dumb comment because she wasn't even wearing a blouse; she was just wearing a T-shirt without a bra. Making that comment was like forcing myself to jump off a high dive into a swimming pool for the first time, and I had no idea what would happen. Well, the most amazing thing happened. She walked up to me, wrapped her arms around me and hugged me and said, "Oh you're so *nice! I really like you!*" That was one of the first times in my entire life that I'd ever gotten a positive response from a girl. Wow! I started giving out compliments all the time because I felt like a child with a new toy. And the funny thing I discovered was that the more outrageous my compliments were, the more effective they were.

These experiences helped me stop taking myself so seriously, and as I became more flirtatious and devilish and a little less "sincere" I found that I stopped getting so many rejections. The more playful and lighthearted I became, the more women seemed to like me. Perhaps people felt more comfortable with me because I was becoming a little more comfortable with myself.

After many sessions of dealing with his fears, Bill did decide to make some changes in his life. He moved out of his parents' home, got his own apartment and began to take some chances. He started going to parties, asked friends to fix him up, and actually began flirting a little here and there. It made him seem more human and before long he was dating and getting more involved with other people.

If you have some doubts about trying some of these techniques, I would suggest that you try them as an experiment. You may find that it's okay to flirt and fling out a few lines, or you may find that it's better for you to be sincere and genuine. Try a variety of approaches and find out what style works best for you. Remember that you don't have to be "clever" or "charming." Sometimes just a natural, innocuous comment like saying hello or commenting on the weather can be enough to break the ice. Regardless of the results, you'll learn from your experiences and you'll be moving forward. And sometimes what you learn can be quite a revelation.

Remember that if you feel nervous and unsure of yourself, your sincerity and seriousness may be an important part of your identity and you may be reluctant to give it up. But remember that even after a little metamorphosis, you're still you. And once you get to know a person, you'll have plenty of opportunities to open up and become more genuine.

Also remember that you can do yourself a disservice by labeling small talk as B.S. the way Bill did. Small talk makes the world go round in just the same way that oil helps an engine run more smoothly. Small talk is a skill you have to work at, just like jogging or playing the piano. And even with effort and practice, you may not get as good at it as people who are naturally bubbly and outgoing. That's okay, because all you really need is to give people the chance to get to know you.

If you feel nervous, practice talking to people who aren't particularly threatening to you until you feel more confident. You can start out with someone totally "safe," like an old friend or a family member. Then you could practice talking to a nonthreatening stranger, like an elderly man or woman sitting on a park bench or a vendor selling hot dogs. Eventually you can try flirting with attractive strangers of the opposite sex. This step-by-step approach will allow you to develop the self-confidence to be able to talk to anyone anytime you want.

If you feel inhibited or nervous about trying any of these techniques, remember to write down your negative thoughts on a piece of paper. Here are some of the commonest thoughts that can keep you feeling lonely, along with some suggestions for more positive ones.

1. Negative Thought: "I shouldn't have to fling out lines or make small talk." Positive Response: "I don't *have* to fling out lines or make small talk, but it might help me meet people."

2. Negative Thought: "Friendship should come naturally." Positive Response: "Most things in life that are important come as a result of effort. If I work at it a little, eventually making friends will become more natural."

3. Negative Thought: "She [or he] probably won't like me. If I try to talk to her [or him] I might make a fool of myself." Positive Response: "Everybody makes a fool out of themselves sooner or later. If I do, so what? The world won't come to an end."

4. Negative Thought: "She [or he] will know how

nervous I am and think less of me." Positive Response: "It's natural to be nervous when you're trying to get to know someone. I can respect myself for trying."

5. Negative Thought: "She [or he] wouldn't be interested in someone like me." Positive Response: "I really can't know that ahead of time. It might be easier if I try to learn as much about her [or him] as I can and find out if I'm interested in her [or him]. Then I'll have to let the chips fall where they may."

6. Negative Thought: "I'm not really interested in her [or him]. She [or he] probably isn't my type." Positive Response: "That's just an excuse. I don't even know her [or him] and if we don't have good chemistry, it will still be good practice."

7. Negative Thought: "I don't feel like talking to her [or him]. I'm too nervous and I'm just not in the mood." Positive Response: "If I wait until I'm in the mood I'll probably be waiting forever. It's better to say hello whether or not I feel like it. Once the conversation gets going I'll probably feel more relaxed."

8. Negative Thought: "It wouldn't be appropriate to talk to a stranger in a place like this." ("This" could be a class, on the street, in a train or cafeteria, etc.) Positive Response: "People are entitled to meet each other anywhere they want."

9. Negative Thought: "She [or he] might think I'm cheap or easy if I try to flirt." Positive Response: "Saying hello to someone in a friendly way doesn't make me cheap or easy."

10. Negative Thought: "But what if I flub up and someone sees me and thinks I'm a jerk?" Positive Response: "It happens to everyone, and it only means I'm human, not a jerk."

8

How to Deal with Someone Who Gives You the Runaround

As you overcome your shyness and begin to flirt and express an interest in people, I suspect that people will begin to show interest in you. It can be a mistake to develop an exclusive relationship with the first person who expresses an interest in you. *Resist this temptation!* Getting too serious too fast is often just a way of avoiding anxiety. Your attraction may result more from your insecurities about dating and from your fears of being alone than from the qualities of the person you're dating. Over and over I see patients who don't follow this advice. They're so needy that they get too involved with the first person who gives them some little morsel of attention. Then when that person rejects them, they get desperate and hopeless again.

You can avoid this if you play the field and date a wide variety of people. This often makes others chase you because you'll be viewed as elusive and unavailable. Let's face it. Playing hard to get can be the key to success because most people want what they can't have. It's just human nature. Very few people think for themselves. They want what other people want. It's far easier to get a second friend when you have one. Once two people are pursuing you, a third will notice you're in demand, and that person will chase you, too. Soon you'll have three or four people to date and you'll be in hot demand. I call this the "Harem principle" or the "Queen bee phenomenon."

You may object to this and insist that you don't want several people to date, just that one special person. I hear this over and over from lonely people I treat. This is a nice romantic fantasy, but it isn't very realistic, and it frequently leads to heartbreak. You may have to date many people before you find that one special person you're looking for. If you have a lot of dating experience, you'll find out more about yourself and discover what you really like and dislike in others.

You may think, "I shouldn't have to play the game. I'm better than that. I'm a sincere and genuine type of person." But on one level, dating *is* a game, even though the purpose of the game is to find someone to form a rewarding, loving relationship with. One rule of the game is that some people are the pursuers and other people are the ones who get pursued.* The secret of winning is to be the one who gets pursued, not the pursuer. Once one person is chasing you, many people will chase you, and you can pick and choose. But the moment you chase someone, he or she will become elusive and reject you. Then you'll get discouraged and lonely and find that you lose your sex appeal. It will begin to seem as if no one wants you. You'll feel frustrated and try even harder. You can break out of this cycle and learn how to turn the tables on people who try to give you a hard time. Then *you'll* have the power and you can call the shots.

How to Deal with Women Who Play Hard to Get

Suppose you meet an attractive lady at a disco who gives you her phone number. She seems somewhat interested, but you're a little insecure and don't feel all that confident when you call her several days later. You invite her out to a fancy restaurant and a show on Saturday night. She politely tells you to call back and check with her on Saturday because she may be going out of town and she's not sure of her plans yet. What do you do?

---

*I do not mean to imply that you should sit back passively and wait for people to chase you. Certainly assertiveness and a willingness to initiate contact with a warm hello and an animated conversation are crucial first steps, as described in Chapter Six. What I'm really talking about is the self-confidence that allows you not to act desperate and needy.

Well, I'll tell you what many of my patients have done when they're confronted by this situation. They act extremely polite, humble, and appreciative and tell her they'll be glad to call on Saturday. They usually offer to go ahead and get the show tickets and a dinner reservation "just in case." They act as sincere and concerned as if they were visiting a sick friend in the hospital. Then they go out and lay out seventy-five hard-earned dollars for a Broadway show and hope she'll be suitably impressed.

So what happens? He calls her back on Saturday, and *inevitably* she's not available. He ends up feeling shafted and stuck with two expensive tickets to a show he never even wanted to see in the first place. He feels bitter about women and can't understand why all his genuineness and super-niceness weren't rewarded. All along she was giving him the runaround, and he just didn't handle it properly.

The hard truth is that in the early phase of dating "niceness" just doesn't work. Now, I know many readers will object to that statement. You may insist that being nice and sincere is the right way to be. But being too nice is usually just a way of encouraging people to take advantage of you—and they will. It's important to keep in mind that potential dates may test you to see how confident and self-assured you are. If a woman can wrap you around her finger, she'll lose respect for you and drop you like a hot brick. You can protest and say, "People shouldn't be like that! It's unfair!" But many people *are* like that, and if you act overly submissive and eager to please, you may just bring out their manipulative and aggressive tendencies. It's almost as if you're inviting them to dump on you—so they oblige!

A more effective response when the woman tells you to call back on Saturday to see if she's available would be to tell her in a friendly way that you can't do that because you'll be making other plans for the weekend. Explain that you like to make plans well ahead of time, not at the last minute, and ask if there is a day in the next few weeks when she would like to get together. If she acts vague, forget it. Don't pursue her. If she does want to go out, she'll name a day. Then make specific, definite plans. Tell her when you'll pick her up, where you'll go, and so on.

Your stature will increase in her eyes because you took the lead and you didn't let her manipulate you.

Women might also give you the runaround when you start to get intimate. Just as you're beginning to kiss and caress a woman, she may turn her head and say, "I'm not interested in a brief affair," or, "I'm not the type of person who likes to go to bed on the first [or second or third] date." You may make one of two universal mistakes: You may argue and pressure her or you may give up and feel rejected. Either way you'll lose. Arguing will make you appear hostile and demanding, and giving up will make you seem insecure. Neither reaction is very likely to arouse her to the heights of passion.

So how can you handle the situation? It's simple. Respond with empathy and use the disarming technique. Recognize that, more often than not, her statements will just be a way of saving face and expressing insecurities. If you simply *agree* with her and express an understanding for how she feels, she will often feel more relaxed because she won't perceive you as someone "on the make." Since trust is the basis of love, you may find that this will lead to the beginning of an intimate and sexually rewarding relationship.

Jeff met an attractive woman named Alice. At the end of their first date they were talking and enjoying a glass of wine on the couch at his apartment. Jeff leaned over to kiss her. Alice appeared shocked and pulled back, explaining that she was uncomfortable about having sex with someone she hardly knew. Jeff kept his cool and disarmed her by saying that he felt the same way. He emphasized how *terrible* it was that so many people who hardly knew or cared about each other just hopped into the sack the first time they met. Then he suggested that it might be fun just to cuddle and relax and get to know each other better, as long as they were both extremely careful not to let things get out of hand. Alice said this was a *wonderful* philosophy, and within minutes they were happily engaged in lovemaking. Alice later admitted that she'd really been quite attracted to Jeff all along, but she didn't want to appear overly "easy."

I don't mean to offend readers with strong moral convictions. It's your personal decision how much sexual intimacy you want to pursue when you're dating. I'm simply suggesting that you can often get much closer and avoid needless tension if you will simply listen to someone who begins to express negative feelings toward you. Show some concern for her point of view instead of giving up and pouting or getting annoyed and putting pressure on her. This can make life much sweeter for both of you!

Even when you've been dating someone regularly, it can be important not to pressure your partner when she's expressing mixed feelings about the relationship. I've recently been treating a lovable guy named Stan, who would remind you of a big teddy bear. Stan is a forty-eight-year-old divorced Toyota salesman who's been going with a woman named Sue for many years. It's been an on-again, off-again relationship. When they're separated for any length of time, Stan or Sue gets lonesome, and pretty soon they start dating and end up living together again. Eventually one or the other of them starts to get bored or unhappy with the relationship, and they break up for a few months. After a while the cycle starts up again. At the time of his referral to me, Stan and Sue had not been seeing each other for nearly half a year. The relationship was just starting to heat up again, largely as a result of Stan's phone calls to Sue.

Stan's complaint was that although Sue welcomed his calls and seemed interested in talking to him, whenever he expressed a desire to get together with her she'd resist and say things like, "Our relationship has no future." This would lead to an argument. Stan would pressure her for reasons why, and Sue would complain that he was doing his usual "sales job" and trying to win her back just because she was inaccessible again. He'd respond that that was nonsense, and they'd go round and round arguing. They'd both end up feeling exasperated with each other.

It's important to realize that Stan may in fact be chasing after Sue primarily because Sue's unavailable and because he's insecure and afraid of being alone. He's really using her as a tranquilizer instead of taking charge of his own life, so it's no surprise that she feels used and resists him. He needs to use the Pleasure Predicting Sheet (see Chapter

Three) and take responsibility for his own happiness instead of shifting the responsibility to Sue by telling himself that she's the key to his security and self-esteem.

I asked Stan to illustrate how their dialogue usually went, and he provided the following example of a typical telephone conversation:

STAN: Let's get together for dinner tonight. What do you say?

SUE: Stan, the real reason you're interested in me now is because I'm unavailable. This is just another sale for you.

STAN: You're crazy! I love ya! This is not a sale!

SUE: It'll never work. We've had so many differences in our likes and dislikes. We don't like the same people, we don't share the same interests.

STAN: That may be true, but don't people have differences? Why should that interfere? I want to see you!

Notice how Stan always contradicts what Sue says. Stan doesn't listen or explore what Sue's trying to say—he just cuts her off by arguing and insisting on his point of view—so she never has a chance to express her feelings. And the paradox is that by *contradicting* her, he proves that she's right. He *is* doing a "sales job," although an ineffective one, because he isn't expressing any genuine concern for her. His high-pressure tactics make Sue insecure, and she feels the need to avoid him. Stan is so obsessed with getting her back that he's simply driving her away.

What's his option? Instead of arguing with everything she says, Stan needs to be more open and receptive to Sue. He also needs to learn to *share* his feelings instead of expressing them in a demanding way, as illustrated in the following "revised version" of his conversation with Sue. After each of Stan's statements, I'll point out which of the basic communication skills are involved. You'll notice that the Disarming Technique is also used here. Disarming means finding some grain of truth in what the other person says instead of responding argumentatively.

SUE (PLAYED BY STAN): Stan, the real reason you're interested in me now is because I'm unavailable. This is just another sale for you.

STAN (PLAYED BY DAVID): I hear you saying that this is just another sale for me. *(Thought empathy)* I know you've been disappointed about how inconsistent our relationship has been in the past. *(Feeling empathy)* Are you afraid of getting involved and then being hurt again? *(Inquiry)*

SUE (PLAYED BY STAN): Exactly. Plus which, we've had so many differences in our likes and dislikes.

STAN (PLAYED BY DAVID): You're right. We do have our differences. *(Disarming technique)* Can you tell me how this has been a problem for you? *(Inquiry)*

SUE (PLAYED BY STAN): Well, you don't like my friends and you aren't interested in the theater. I always have to drag you along by your heels.

STAN (PLAYED BY DAVID): I have to admit that going to the theater isn't my cup of tea, and I guess I've been a drag when we went. *(Disarming technique)* That could take all the fun out of it for you. I can see how you might think, "Who needs this?" *(Feeling empathy)* Is that how you feel? *(Inquiry)*

SUE (PLAYED BY STAN): Yes! That's exactly why our relationship has no future.

STAN (PLAYED BY DAVID): Do you feel that our relationship has no future? *(Inquiry)* I want you to know that I still care about you a great deal *(Tactful self-expression)*, but I recognize we have a number of real problems that you have every right to be concerned about. *(Disarming technique)* Can you tell me more about how you feel? *(Inquiry)*

Stan and Sue need a lot of open exchange of feelings along these lines before there will be any significant chance of reconciliation. The only real way Stan can prove himself to Sue is to relate to her in a different way before they attempt any reconciliation. This means giving up his "need" for her so he can stop trying to manipulate her and start trying to listen to what she has to say. There's no guarantee that Sue will want to get romantically involved again, but it will give Sue the chance to get her feelings off her chest and feel understood. Then she'll feel free to become involved in the relationship again if she still has some feelings for Stan.

Giving your partner this freedom admittedly requires

tremendous courage. You must be genuinely willing to let him or her go if that's how it turns out. That means being convinced that your present and future happiness does *not* depend on your partner. If you feel you cannot live without someone, you'll be so anxious when you try to communicate that you'll inevitably come across in an insecure and manipulative way and your partner will feel trapped and resentful.

You can overcome these fears and insecurities with the Daily Mood Log, as illustrated in Figure 8-1. Write down all the negative thoughts you'd have if you broke up with the person you're now involved with. Ask yourself: "Would it really be so terrible if we broke up? What would it mean to me? How would I feel?" You can see from studying Stan's thoughts that he seems to be making two basic assumptions:

1. I cannot have a happy and fulfilled life without Sue's love.

2. I deserve Sue's love. If I'm a good fellow and I treat Sue well, then she should love me in return.

The first attitude is called "dependency" because it makes Stan think all his self-esteem and chances for happiness depend on Sue. It's actually quite unrealistic because Stan was quite happy before he met Sue and he's been happy on many occasions since they split up. Anytime you lose sight of this basic truth and start believing you're an empty shell without some particular person's love, you do yourself a grave injustice and you're headed for trouble.

The second attitude is called "demandingness" because it makes Stan feel that he's entitled to Sue's love. He'll become needy and coercive, and this will drive Sue away because she'll feel pressured and trapped. You can never demand someone's love. Love can only be given freely.

After he wrote down his "Automatic Thoughts" and answered them, Stan became aware that he was overinvested in his relationship with Sue. He decided to date a number of women and to stop putting so much pressure on Sue. He discovered that he enjoyed many of these relationships, and as so often happens, once he started to show less interest in Sue, she began to express more interest in him. Instead of complaining that their relationship had no fu-

FIGURE 8-1
The Daily Mood Log*

DESCRIBE THE UPSETTING EVENT—The one woman I love, Sue, will not see me on an intimate basis.

NEGATIVE FEELINGS—Record your emotions and rate each one on a scale from 0 (the least) to 100 (the most). Include feelings such as sad, anxious, angry, guilty, lonely, hopeless, frustrated, etc.

Emotion	Rating (0–100)	Emotion	Rating (0–100)	Emotion	Rating (0–100)
1. Sad	40%	3. Angry	90%	5.	
2. Anxious	90%	4.		6.	

AUTOMATIC THOUGHTS	DISTORTIONS	RATIONAL RESPONSES
Write down your negative thoughts and number them consecutively.	Identify the distortions in each "Automatic Thought."	Substitute more realistic and positive thoughts.
1. It's terrible that she won't see me. How can I be happy without Sue?	1. Magnification.	1. I've been quite happy without Sue on many occasions since we broke up. She's a fine woman, but she's not my only chance for happiness.
2. It's unfair that she won't see me!	2. Labeling.	2. It may be unfortunate that she doesn't want to see me, but it's not "unfair." There's no rule that says that people I care about are obligated to love me or want to see me.

AUTOMATIC THOUGHTS	DISTORTIONS	RATIONAL RESPONSES
3. I could never fall in love with anybody else.	3. Fortune-telling.	3. This is nonsense. I've been in love with many women in my life.
4. She's the *only* person in my life I can be myself with. I can talk about my insecurities and failures openly with Sue.	4. All-or-nothing thinking.	4. There are probably many people I could talk to more openly if I decided to. Maybe I'm making Sue a little too important to me right now. In fact, we can't really talk about our feelings very openly these days because we end up arguing all the time.

OUTCOME—Review your "Rational Responses" and put a check in the box that describes how you now feel:
☐ not at all better; ☐ somewhat better; ☑ quite a bit better; ☐ a lot better.

*Copyright © 1984, David D. Burns, M.D., from *Intimate Connections* (New York: William Morrow & Company).

ture, she started calling him more frequently, appeared to be getting jealous, and suggested they spend more time together. Coincidentally, when they were eating together in Philadelphia's Chinatown last week, Stan received the following message in his fortune cookie, which he brought in to his most recent session with a broad grin:

> A woman is like your shadow;
> Follow her, she flies;
> Fly from her, she follows.

How to Stop Idealizing Women

One habit that sets you up to be manipulated by women is the tendency to idealize them. When you're feeling lonely and insecure, you may fantasize about a woman in such a positive, romantic way that it begins to seem as if you couldn't possibly live without her or have a good relationship with anyone else. The picture you have of her is usually based on a mental distortion: You dwell on a few of her good qualities and filter out any negatives, so you turn her into a princess. This is why romance has been called a psychosis, because the person you're in love with may be primarily a figment of your imagination. It's sometimes difficult to give up this tendency, because these fantasies can feel very seductive and exciting. Learning to think more realistically about the woman you're dating can help you avoid a great deal of heartache.

Paul is a twenty-eight-year-old divorced architect who lives in a Philadelphia suburb. Following the breakup of his marriage, he had a stormy affair with a business asssociate named Susanne. He described her as a fascinating, creative individual. However, she had been in therapy since early adolescence because of serious emotional problems. Susanne found it difficult to form and maintain close, intimate relationships. Paul described his relationship with Susanne as a roller-coaster ride, with periods of intense closeness that were followed by equally intense periods of fighting and turbulence. She had warned him that she was threatened by serious commitment, and she'd back off and break up with Paul anytime she sensed they were getting close. They had broken up just prior to Paul's first therapy session. Although he was involved in partially satisfying relationships with other women, he would frequently lapse into spells of depression when he told himself, "Susanne is unique. I'll never find another woman like that again."

The therapy focused on the distorted way that Paul was thinking about his disintegrating relationship with Susanne:

DAVID: So you are convinced you can never find a relationship that will measure up to one you had with Susanne?

PAUL: That's the heart of it. It could never be quite the same with anyone else.

DAVID: Let's imagine a scale for rating your relationships with women going from 0 to 100 percent. A zero would be a relationship that was absolutely undesirable in every respect. A 98 percent would be living with an attractive heiress on the Riviera who is charming and deeply in love with you. The relationship with her is sexually, emotionally, and intellectually fulfilling.

PAUL: That sounds like perfection, 100 percent.

DAVID: And using this same scale, what rating would a relationship need for you to be satisfied and want to marry the woman?

PAUL: I think I'd want at least a 90 percent.

DAVID: I can see you have high standards. Now, what rating does Susanne get?

PAUL: She'd receive around a 95 percent.

DAVID: The answer to your problem is simple. Continue to pursue Susanne—in spite of all the unpleasantness of the relationship—and ask her to marry you. She's five points above 90 percent.

PAUL: But I couldn't endure all the misery and fighting. She would leave me and run away every two or three weeks.

DAVID: Then how can she get a 95 percent rating?

PAUL: I see what you mean. . . . Realistically, I could only give her a 60 to 70 percent rating.

DAVID: So, in point of fact, the relationship isn't so ideal. It's important to keep that in mind when you say you can never find anyone quite so desirable as Susanne.

PAUL: But I still feel that Susanne is unique and I can never find anyone exactly like her.

DAVID: Well, that is quite true. *Everyone* is different and unique. But suppose you could find one hundred women exactly like Susanne? Would that make you happy?

PAUL: Yes. That would be a dream come true.

DAVID: Then you have one hundred opportunities for repeating the same frustrating, painful relationship you had with Susanne. You could go through the same miserable affair over and over for the rest of your life. Do you really want that?

PAUL: That sounds like a nightmare . . . Actually, I'd like to find someone who has some of the qualities I loved in her, but who is basically different.

This dialogue helped Paul realize that he had been upsetting himself by idealizing his relationship with Susanne. As he learned to assess the relationship more realistically, by thinking about her liabilities as well as her assets, he began to feel less lonely and desperate about getting her back. In the week following the session, she called and told him she wanted to get back together again, but he decided not to. He explained that it wasn't out of spite, although he did feel quite angry about her inconsistency and explosiveness, but because he felt he could be happier without the constant turmoil of the relationship.

I first discovered the enormous power and truth in this when I was a medical student during my "wild oats" phase. I'd met a young woman, whom I'll call "Bobbie," and I started going with her steadily. Bobbie was not typical of most of the women I'd been dating, who tended to be somewhat idealistic and "safe." Bobbie, in contrast, was a "tough chick." She was independent and curvaceous and wore cut-off Levi's and hung around with Palo Alto's rough crowd.

One evening I noticed a car driving back and forth in front of her house, flashing its lights. I thought that was peculiar and asked Bobbie about it, but she just shrugged it off. The next night I noticed the same thing, and the car even pulled into the driveway and the lights flashed. I pointed this out and she acted vague. When I pressed her, she owned up to the fact that it was Mike, an old boyfriend who wanted to get together with her. My anxiety levels suddenly escalated, and the fact that she'd pretended not to know what was going on made me doubly anxious. About thirty minutes later a strange man who I assumed was Mike called and asked to talk to Bobbie. Like a jerk, I told him in an overly protective, annoyed voice that Bobbie wasn't available or interested in talking to him. I told him to stop bothering us and hung up. He seemed quite angry, and Bobbie was annoyed with me as well.

Later that night there was a knock at the door. I opened it and two men barged in. One of them was a menacing six-foot-four muscle man who looked like a thug from a TV detective series. The other one, who wasn't very big or impressive-looking, was Mike. The thug stared at me icily and announced that Mike had come to see Bobbie. I'd never been much of a fighter, and I sensed these guys were *way* out of my league. To make matters even worse, my jaw had been broken in an accident several weeks earlier. It was wired shut and quite fragile, and I'd lost a great deal of weight because I could only take in liquids. I felt especially vulnerable and frightened.

What I did next was quite cowardly. I ignored them and walked over to the phone, dialed the police emergency number, and said, "Please send the police immediately to 18937 Allen Boulevard. There are unwanted guests in the house." Then I turned to them, feeling for a moment that I'd "beaten" them and managed to "control" the situation. But they simply backed out the door and said, "We'll get you, buddy!"

Horrors! What had I done? I figured they probably already had multiple arrests for burglary, assault, and worse. I foresaw my life turning into a nightmare of fear. But to make matters worse, Bobbie—who'd been observing the whole scene from an adjacent room—was *furious* with me. She acted as if our relationship was over and I was the biggest wimp in the world. She berated me and wouldn't let me touch her.

That night it was impossible for me to sleep. I was drowning in waves of panic and humiliation. What could I do? It seemed I'd dug a bottomless pit for myself and fallen into it. I felt I had only one chance. I remembered an older friend whom I'll call Matt who I thought might be able to help me. Matt was a part-time professional gambler and psychodrama leader. I'd seen him in action leading encounter groups on numerous occasions, and I'd never seen anyone get the better of him. He had an incredible ability to intimidate people and turn the most difficult situations to his advantage. Of the many "gurus" circulating through California in the mid-1960s, he was considered one of the most powerful. Whether he would be able or willing to show me the way out of my predicament remained to be seen.

At 3:00 A.M. I called Matt in desperation and told him something terrible had happened. After I explained the situation, he told me the solution was extremely simple. He suggested that I call Mike at 6:00 A.M. and admit that I'd made a mistake. He said to explain that I'd thought things over and realized it was wrong for me to stand between him and Bobbie because they needed the chance to explore what they had in common. Matt said to emphasize that they might, in fact, be ideal for each other and that I would spend the day away so he could come over to visit Bobbie and spend all the time with her he wanted. Matt predicted that Mike would probably be waking up with a bad hangover from a wild night and that women would be the last thing on his mind. Inviting him to spend the day with Bobbie would probably make her seem even less interesting. Finally, Matt said to tell Bobbie about the arrangement to get her together with Mike and then to forget all about them and get on my motorcycle and drive up in the hills and have the best day of my life.

I followed Matt's advice to the T. I called Mike at six in the morning and apologized for waking him up but said I had something important to tell him. I explained how I'd made a mistake and that he had *every right* to see Bobbie because maybe she was the girl for him. I urged him to come and spend the entire day with her and explained that I'd be gone and that Bobbie would be there waiting for him. Mike was stunned. After a long silence, he explained in a groggy, meek, apologetic voice that they'd never gotten along very well and that he would "try" to come by to see her, but he couldn't "guarantee" it. He thanked me profusely and said I was a hell of a guy.

I then explained the arrangements to Bobbie. I told her that since she wanted to spend time with Mike, it was insensitive of me to try to prevent this. To make up for my mistake, I'd decided to spend the day away from home and told her she was free to call Mike and to invite him to spend the day with her. She acted as if a bolt of lightning had hit her. She immediately started protesting that she wasn't really the slightest bit interested in Mike anymore and had never even been particularly attracted to him in the first place.

I told her she shouldn't jump to any conclusions, and that she should at least call him and talk things over. Then I got on my motorcycle and headed for the hills above Palo Alto. I was still feeling a little hurt and jealous, but it was almost an aesthetic, pleasing experience because I felt so proud of the way I'd handled the situation. The cool early morning air felt good on my face and the motorcycle engine's roar was reassuring. What a relief to have been rescued from the jaws of a lion!

The day turned out to be one of the most incredible of my life. As I was driving the motorcycle along a trail through the woods I met two gorgeous young women riding horses through the hills. They lived in a cabin commune with a group of students, and we played music, talked, and frolicked all day long. I ended up cuddling with one of the women in the backyard hammock during the afternoon. It was a magical, emotionally opening adventure!

Around 7:00 P.M. I headed home with my mind reeling. I was dying to see what had happened at Bobbie's house. Bobbie met me at the door wearing a long dress—something she'd never worn before. She explained that Mike had called her and after a brief chat they'd both decided they didn't really have anything in common anymore. Bobbie had spent the entire day cleaning the house and cooking a beautiful meal—two things she'd *never* been willing to do before—and the dining room table looked as if it were prepared for a king!

This experience taught me that you cannot *"get"* someone until you're prepared to lose them. Chasing a woman who's giving you the runaround will never work. When a woman is giving you a hard time, don't plead or try to persuade her. These are fatal mistakes! Instead, click your heels and strut off in the opposite direction. Pretty soon she'll be chasing you!

How to Turn the Tables on That Elusive Man

In my office yesterday an attractive thirty-year-old divorced woman named Beth voiced a familiar complaint. "Why can't I ever trust men? For the past several months I've been seeing a fellow named George who lives in New York. The problem is that George keeps getting involved with old girl friends. Last month he said his former fiancée was coming to visit him. I pleaded with him not to see her, but he said, *'Trust me!* I'll be available if you need me the entire time she's here! We're *only friends* and I feel I owe it to her to see her. It's the only decent thing to do.'

"So I gave in and he ended up living with her for ten days. I couldn't get a hold of him the whole time. Then the s.o.b. had the nerve to tell me he got some kind of urinary tract infection, which was a way of broadcasting the fact that they were sleeping together! The frosting on the cake is that now another ex-girl friend is coming to town to visit him, and he's saying, *'Trust me,'* again. But I'm going to make him promise not to see her. Don't you think I have the right, Dr. Burns?" Beth added that she didn't really "blame" George because she thought he was immature and under the influence of these women. She explained she felt she could "help" him learn to resist them so he could be faithful to her.

The only problem with this strategy is that it won't work. Trying to get George to agree not to see these women is as likely to be successful as asking your cat not to chase mice. Either Beth will get in an argument with him about his "rights" and his "freedom" or he'll passively agree to be faithful but then sneak around behind her back. If he doesn't feel ready for an exclusive relationship, he may feel trapped and bitter and think she's trying to control him. Ultimately she may lose him.

So what's her option? First, Beth has to stop telling herself she *needs* him. Believing this makes her seem like a horse wearing blinders, because all she can think about is *getting* him. But most people don't want to be "gotten." Letting go of her "need" for George will open up a number of more creative options.

Sometimes the most enlightened and effective response to a frustrating situation involves doing just the *opposite* of what you're now doing. Maybe if Beth stops trying to snare George and tries to push him away, she'll have better luck! Instead of trying to demand a pledge of faithfulness, she could tell him, "George, I've been thinking about how you feel about these other women and I realize you *do* need some time to explore these relationships. One of them may very well be the right woman for you. I've decided that I need some time on my own for the next month or two as well. I don't want you to feel badly, because I do think you're a real sweet guy, but I've decided that I can't see you for a while. I need a break from our relationship. Why don't you take this time and pursue these other relationships? If at the end of a couple of months you still think we might have something in common, give me a call. If I'm still available, we can see if there would be a basis for continuing to see each other."

I'm sure you know the probable result. George is like the rest of us. He wants what he can't get. The moment he senses that he may be losing Beth, her value in his eyes will suddenly and dramatically escalate. George thought he had her in the palm of his hand, and in a flash he'll realize he doesn't. He'll probably pursue her, and she can call the shots. It's a simple strategy, and all it takes is a little courage. It usually works like a charm. When George starts to sing his new tune and he tells Beth how *dear* she is to him, then she can spell out the terms of the relationship more effectively. Their conversation might evolve like this:

GEORGE: What do you mean? Are you saying you don't want to see me for the next two months?

BETH: Yes, I feel I need a break from our relationship and you need some time, too. I'm not ruling out the possibility of seeing you again, though.

GEORGE: What do you mean, you need "a break"? I really want to see you. Don't *my* feelings count?

BETH: Oh, your feelings *do* count. But look at the bright side. You can date all the people you want. I realized that I was putting pressure you and you're the kind of guy who needs a lot of freedom. I want you to explore all your options.

GEORGE: But I don't *need* to do a lot of dating and explore these "options." Those women are only friends. I want to see *you*!

BETH: Well, that may be, but I realize how dear Sarah and Barbara are to you, and how you don't want to hurt them by not seeing them anymore. This way you can continue to see them and give them a chance. I know that's very important to you.

GEORGE: Well, *they're* not important to me! *You're* important to me!

BETH: It's really nice of you to say that. I think the world of you, too.

GEORGE: So let's get together this weekend!

BETH: Oh, I'm sorry. I have some other plans. As I mentioned, I need some time to think things through a little. I have to decide what's right for me.

GEORGE: That's unfair! So who are you going out with this weekend? What do you need all this "time" for?

BETH: Well, my plans for the weekend are personal. But to be completely honest, I'm not convinced that you're ready for a steady relationship yet, and I'm not sure you're the right guy for me. There are a lot of things about you that are terrific, but there are some things we don't see eye to eye on that are very important to me. You seem to need to go out with a number of women, and you have every right to do just that. It's just that I don't care to be one of them. In the future, if things change for you, let me know.

What if the conversation doesn't evolve like this? What if George doesn't pursue Beth? This is the crucial issue. If she tells herself that she *needs* George and cannot live without him, then *any* strategy, including the one I've just outlined, is doomed to failure. Simply mimicking so-called correct behavior rarely ever works. If you don't believe in yourself, the fear and the hurt in your voice will betray you, even if the lines you say are correct. But if you're really willing to tell yourself. "This man is an interesting option but he's not a necessity because I can still survive and accept my life without him," then you'll succeed whether or not he pursues you. Your *real* battle is with your self-doubt and insecurity, not with your boyfriend, and the ultimate triumph isn't "getting" him but learning to love and respect yourself.

How Not to Get Used by a Man

Not getting used by a man depends entirely on believing in yourself. The biggest mistake is to tell yourself you can't live without someone you're attracted to. The moment you start thinking along these lines, you're in trouble.

A common problem single women confront is the man who habitually calls at the last minute to see if they're available. While it can be extremely tempting to say yes—especially if you're desperately afraid of being alone—you must realize that any man who will ask you out only at the last minute is treating you in a disrespectful way. Why does he always ask you out at the last minute? Does he just want sex? Is he so disorganized he can't plan ahead? Is he married and running around behind his wife's back? Is he calling you because someone else stood him up? Or because everyone else turned him down and he couldn't get anyone better? Ask yourself if you want to get used this way. What does it say to him about your self-esteem?

If you want to turn the tables on the gentleman, you'll have to stick up for yourself and be more assertive, as in the following dialogue. Notice that when he puts pressure on you, you don't need to get hostile and sarcastic or to respond in an apologetic, self-effacing way. Instead, you firmly and politely refuse to let yourself get used.

RALPH: (ON THE PHONE) Hi, Janie! I'm in town. I just arrived this morning.

YOU: Hi, Ralph! It's nice to talk to you.

RALPH: Listen, I'll be off work in half an hour. What do you say we get together? I can meet you at your place for a drink.

YOU: Gee, I'm sorry but I already have plans. The next time you call, why don't you let me know a week or so ahead of time? I *would* like to see you.

RALPH: What do you mean, you have plans? What plans?

YOU: Oh, they're personal.

RALPH: You have "personal" plans? What kind of "personal" plans?

YOU: It sounds like you're interested in my plans.

RALPH: Well, I don't get to town very often and I *really* miss you. Can't you just change your plans a little bit? What do you have lined up that's so important?

YOU: That's sweet of you to miss me, Ralph. If you miss me enough, why not plan ahead next time? That way we'll be sure to get together.

RALPH: You know I *hate* to plan ahead. I like to do things on the spur of the moment. It's more fun to be spontaneous. Besides, my schedule's so unpredictable. It's just *impossible* for me to know if I'm going to be in town a week ahead of time because my boss always schedules these trips for me at the last minute. That's just the nature of my business. Come on, now. You can change your plans tonight for little old Ralph.

YOU: Gee, I'm really sorry it's impossible for you to plan ahead. I've been hoping to see you, but it sounds like it'll be really difficult for us to get together. If you find you can work things out with your boss or you decide to plan a trip this way on your own, let me know ahead of time.

Comment. Ralph will either drop you and find someone else to take advantage of, or he'll start singing a different tune and treat you with more respect. Either way you'll be ahead of the game because you'll be in control of the situation. In contrast, if you give in to Ralph, you'll probably end up getting used and you'll feel bitter about what scoundrels men are. Is it worth it?

Giving Up the "Need" for Love

Many men and women have a hard time giving up the notion that they "need" a partner to feel happy and worthwhile. But in point of fact, you may not be able to find love until you stop "needing" it. If you're lonely, the idea that you don't "need" love may be about as appealing as the sound of fingernails across a blackboard. It's especially difficult because our entire culture is based on the idea that love *is* a basic human need. We see this theme in our advertising and we hear it in our music. Barbra Streisand sings that "people who need people are the luckiest people in the world." Harry Stack Sullivan, one of the most influential twentieth-century psychiatrists, agreed. He viewed intimate relationships as a need that stays with every being for life. He wrote: "There is no way that I know of by which one can, all by oneself, satisfy the need for intimacy."* Even the book of Genesis emphasizes the pain of solitude and notes that God created Eve because "it is not good that the man should be alone. I will make him a helpmate."

My research and my work with lonely single people and disturbed couples has convinced me that a different point of view is much closer to the truth. The fact is that the "need" for love can often deprive you of the intimacy you most desire. This insight is drawn from Eastern philosophy, which suggests that you can't really gain what you want until you give up the idea that you "need" it. Once you give up the idea that you "need" love, you may suddenly discover far more love than you ever thought you needed.

Some people initially feel annoyed when I suggest that the "need" for love can be unhealthy. Shortly after my first book, *Feeling Good: The New Mood Therapy*, was released, I was interviewed by a journalist from a San Francisco newspaper who said she was shocked by a sentence in the chapter called "The Love Addiction" that read "love is not an adult human need." She protested: "Isn't it *healthy* to need love?" She then went on to reveal that a man she was in love with had broken up with her a year earlier and she had been severely depressed ever since. Why? Because she told herself that she *needed* his love to feel worthwhile and happy! She thought she felt empty and unfulfilled because she was alone, and it was difficult for her to see that her misery actually resulted from the unrealistic way she was thinking. And yet, amazingly enough, she was defending the very value system that was the source of her misery and loneliness. She wasn't aware that the "need" for love, like many other

---

*H. S. Sullivan, *The Interpersonal Theory of Psychiatry* (New York: W. W. Norton & Co., 1953), p. 57.

attitudes about love, is essentially two-sided with the potential either to enhance or to devastate you.

Please don't misinterpret what I'm saying. I'm *not* claiming that love is unimportant or that all loneliness is neurotic. Basically we are social creatures, and the tension and lack of fulfillment we feel when we're cut off from others can be an important motivating force, just as the joy of tenderness and intimacy, can be. If you respect yourself and find life fulfilling, then your love for others can only enhance your life—and theirs. But when you tell yourself you can't exist without another person's love, you sell yourself short and you lose sight of life's incredible potential for richness and joy.

This chapter has been about power—how to get what you want, how to turn the tables on people who are giving you a hard time. But it's also about surrender, because sometimes you have to decide that you're willing to lose before you can win. Ultimately, you can never control someone else; you can only control yourself. You can never force a person to love or respect you; you can only choose to love and respect yourself. If you chase people, they'll become elusive and run away. If you try to grab them, they'll resist you and feel the urge to pull away. Sometimes you have to open up your hand and let go of them—then they'll feel free to reach out to touch you.

But this involves taking a risk. What if you lose them and end up being alone? The courage to take this risk results from trust—trust in yourself. You must believe that you're worthwhile and lovable regardless of whether someone treats you in a loving way or rejects you. Being dominated by the fear of being alone will simply make you appear insecure, and people will want to avoid you. The self-confidence you project when you decide you can live without someone will give you self-respect and make you suddenly more elusive and desirable. Telling yourself you "need" someone is the fastest road to loneliness, and letting go of that "need" is the path to intimacy.

Does this mean that love is nothing more than a cheap game of power in which you learn to outmanipulate someone? Nothing could be further from the truth. The basis of any relationship is mutual respect. Love is the opportunity for two people to share their lives openly and honestly and without pretense. But in the early phases of dating certain games *are* played, and if you don't take this into account, all your pride and idealism may turn into bitterness and loneliness. You play the game, not to "win" or to put someone down, but to have the chance to share your life with someone in a deeper, more genuine manner. That's the real victory!

PART FOUR

GETTING CLOSE

9

Liking and Loving Others: How to Overcome Romantic Perfectionism

As you overcome your fears of rejection and begin dating more regularly, you may find that a new problem develops: How do you learn to love and appreciate the people who care about you? The most popular people seem to have an infectious capacity to enjoy others. William, the friend of mine from medical school days, never had a bad thing to say about anybody. He was a genuine lover in the sense that he seemed to be attracted by everybody. That was one of the secrets of his success. People felt so good around him they had trouble resisting him. I sometimes heard women talking behind his back about what a scoundrel he was. They'd complain bitterly about how much he was sleeping around. But when William was with them, he'd smile and whisper something charming and their resistance would instantly melt.

You can get close to people if you project positive vibrations as he did. Your warmth and friendliness can show people that you really do like and desire them. This isn't always as easy as it might at first appear. Many shy and lonely people often give the impression they don't really like anybody very much. Inside, they may have a reservoir of disillusionment and hurt feelings that come spilling out whenever they get close to someone. They get irritable and defensive, and they're always looking for little signs of rejection and noticing things about their dates or partners that annoy them. They're so picky that nobody ever seems quite good enough for them. This is often just an expression of their insecurity. After all, if you're sufficiently critical and choosey you won't ever find anyone who's good enough and you'll never have to run the risk of rejection—or intimacy.

One of the causes of this is "romantic perfectionism." You may be a romantic perfectionist if you constantly find fault with people because they don't quite measure up to your ideas of what your partner *should* be like. They may not be as good-looking or intelligent or sensitive or successful as the person you've been dreaming about. Of course, you have every right to look for someone who's exciting and appealing to you, but dwelling on everyone's shortcomings will only prevent you from getting close to anyone. When you expect the most from others, you often end up with the least satisfying personal relationships because nobody's ever good enough for you. Instead of experiencing dating as a challenging adventure, you'll feel constantly frustrated and deprived. You'll forever be reaching for the stars and clutching at empty air.

Loneliness researchers have documented this tendency. Dr. Warren Jones, an associate professor of psychology at the University of Tulsa, has observed that lonely people frequently have cynical and rejecting attitudes toward other people and toward life in general.* In his research he observed that lonely people appear to be less caring and responsive to the needs, concerns, and feelings of others. He discovered that loneliness was less related to the actual number of friendships, dates, and family contacts that people had, and more to the inability of lonely people to enjoy others and to find satisfaction in the relationships they do have. In other words, loneliness may result less from a lack of quantity and more from a lack of quality in personal relationships.

In one study, Dr. Jones and his collaborators examined the way college students responded to strangers of the opposite sex who they were asked to talk to and "get

*W. H. Jones, "Loneliness and Social Behavior," in *Loneliness: A Sourcebook of Current Theory, Research and Therapy*, L. A. Peplau and D. Perlman, eds. (New York: John Wiley & Sons, 1982).

acquainted" with.* He observed that the more lonely students were quite judgmental and felt less attracted to the people they were paired with. They were also less likely to want to spend more time with their partners. Dr. Jones speculates that these negative attitudes toward others stem from unrealistic and rigid expectations about relationships. The cynicism and hostility of lonely people may represent disappointment over the failure of others to live up to their standards for the ideal friend, lover, or spouse. These expectations may be so high and exacting that no one could ever possibly satisfy them.

I've observed this perfectionism over and over in my clinical work with shy and lonely people. A lonely twenty-five-year-old man named Larry told me that his mother suggested that he go and meet an attractive young woman she knew who was working at Bloomingdale's department store. Larry described his experience when he went to "check her out": "I looked at her from twenty feet away, and even though she was attractive and pretty I felt real disappointed. I left instead of talking to her, and then I got mad at myself. I meet so few people that I *really count* on the few I do meet. I was like a hungry man lost on a desert island. After two weeks of starvation he finally manages to catch a fish, and then he cuts his line in disgust because the fish isn't good enough."

Larry was quite distressed with the way he behaved, so I suggested he write down his automatic thoughts using the Daily Mood Log, as illustrated in Figure 9-1. As you review his negative thoughts, it will be clear to you just how judgmental Larry was. Not only did he make a snap judgment about this particular woman, he was equally hard on himself for backing off because he wasn't immediately attracted to her. Talking back to these negative thoughts helped him ease up on himself.

It was clear from the way Larry reacted that he was making a number of assumptions that were causing real problems in his social life. We made a list of these "silent

---

*W. H. Jones, J. A. Freeman, and R. A. Gonich. "The Persistence of Loneliness: Self and Other Determinants," *Journal of Personality* (1981, 49), pp. 27–48.

FIGURE 9-1
The Daily Mood Log*

DESCRIBE THE UPSETTING EVENT—I looked at a prospective date from twenty feet away and I felt very disappointed because she didn't meet my expectations. Then I left and got annoyed with myself because I didn't talk to her.

NEGATIVE FEELINGS—Record your emotions and rate each one on a scale from 0 (the least) to 100 (the most). Include feelings such as sad, anxious, angry, guilty, lonely, hopeless, frustrated, etc.

Emotion	Rating (0–100)	Emotion	Rating (0–100)	Emotion	Rating (0–100)
1. Angry & upset	90%	3. Guilty	30%	5.	
2. Anxious	90%	4. Frustrated	90%	6.	

AUTOMATIC THOUGHTS Write down your negative thoughts and number them consecutively.	DISTORTIONS Identify the distortions in each "Automatic Thought."	RATIONAL RESPONSES Substitute more realistic and positive thoughts.
1. Jeez, I may never get another chance.	1. All-or-nothing thinking.	1. This is extremely unlikely, since I've had a number of opportunities to meet women in the past. I'm sure I'll have many more chances in the future. I could even come back and talk to her tomorrow if I wanted.

AUTOMATIC THOUGHTS	DISTORTIONS	RATIONAL RESPONSES
2. If she doesn't ring my chimes visually, why bother to talk to her?	2. All-or-nothing thinking; fortune-telling.	2. If I get to know her and give the relationship a chance, it may turn out to be more enjoyable than I thought. It would be nice to have someone "ring my chimes" visually, but that isn't all there is to a relationship.
3. I get so few chances and I throw them away!	3. "Should" statement.	3. I didn't necessarily do the wrong thing and I wasn't obligated to talk to her. On the other hand, if I did make a mistake, there's no reason to beat myself up about it.
4. I may never get out of the trap of looking for somebody perfect.	4. Fortune-telling; all-or-nothing thinking.	4. I'm working on getting out of that trap right now, so there's every reason to predict some success in this area.

AUTOMATIC THOUGHTS	DISTORTIONS	RATIONAL RESPONSES
5. Time is running out on me. I'm already twenty-five-years old.	5. All-or-nothing thinking.	5. Everyone is on their own timetable. Some people don't get married until they're in their fifties or sixties. What happened today can be a growth experience that I can learn from.

OUTCOME—Review your "Rational Responses" and put a check in the box that describes how you now feel:
☐ not at all better; ☐ somewhat better; ☑ quite a bit better; ☐ a lot better.

*Copyright © 1984, David D. Burns, M.D., from *Intimate Connections* (New York: William Morrow & Company).

Figure 9-2
My "Silent Assumptions"

1. There's no point in forming a relationship with someone who doesn't meet all of my qualifications. She has to be perfect. Since I have no confidence in myself, I need a perfect mate, a perfect car, and a perfect environment so I can feel good about myself.

2. A relationship with someone who isn't perfect won't go anywhere. (I won't allow it to.) Since it won't become a long-term relationship, there's no point in pursuing it. I don't want to start anything I can't finish.

3. If I'm not immediately attracted to someone, I won't be able to have an exciting sexual relationship with them.

4. If someone doesn't meet all of my qualifications, I can't have a satisfying relationship with them.

assumptions'' (see Figure 9-2). You can see from this list that Larry is a romantic perfectionist. Romantic perfectionism is defined as the need to have a perfect partner or a perfect relationship before you can feel happy and fulfilled.

One way of overcoming this attitude is to make a list of the advantages and disadvantages of looking for a perfect mate. How will this mind-set help you and how will it hurt you? Larry's Cost-Benefit Analysis is illustrated in Figure 9-3. This helped him realize how self-defeating it was to

Figure 9-3
Cost-Benefit Analysis

Attitude: There's no point in forming a relationship with someone who doesn't meet all of my qualifications. She has to be perfect.

Advantages of Believing This	Disadvantages of Believing This
1. I'll be very choosy and not get stuck with somebody who's beneath my expectations.	1. I'll have very few dates.
2. I can avoid the anxiety of dating, since there are so few women around who meet all my expectations and qualifications.	2. I may miss out on a lot of good times.
	3. I may never meet someone who meets all of my qualifications and end up a bachelor for life.
	4. I'll be trying to find the self-esteem that I'm lacking in myself in someone else. That doesn't seem like a good idea.
(25)	(75)

Revised Attitude: It would be to my advantage to date many women, even if they don't meet all of my qualifications. This will improve my social life, and once I'm dating more frequently, I can afford to be a little more choosy.

be so picky and critical. Once he saw that his perfectionism wasn't working in a positive way for him, he decided to revise it and develop a more realistic and self-enhancing attitude, as indicated at the bottom of Figure 9-3.

Consistent with his new philosophy, Larry decided to go back to Bloomingdale's to introduce himself to the woman he'd seen there. To his surprise, he discovered that the woman he had seen was not the woman his mother had picked out but someone entirely different. When he made the connection with the "correct" woman, he found her quite appealing and they began to date regularly.

Another way of overcoming romantic perfectionism is to make a list of what you're really looking for in a mate. You might include qualities such as faithfulness, honesty, emotional openness, sensitivity, maturity, and attractiveness. I recommend that you make a list of twenty desired qualities like the ones illustrated in Figure 9-4 (a blank copy of this form is available on page 312). Once you complete your list, rate people you have met or dated between 0 (the lowest rating) and 5 (the highest rating) in each of the twenty categories. If someone has an outstanding sense of humor, you might give him or her a 4 or a 5 in this category. If persons are in the appropriate age range, you can give them a 5 in that category. If they rejected you and they're not basically interested in dating, you you could give them a 0 in the category of "Available." (It's important to make "Available" one of your twenty desired characteristics, since a partner who is available to you would presumably be more desirable than someone who isn't.) If you don't know people well enough to rate them in one or two of your categories, simply make a guess based on your intuition. Later on, when you get to know them better, you can rate them again.

After you have rated several people in each of the twenty categories, add up their total scores. This will give you their overall ratings between 0 percent (if they scored 0 in each of the twenty categories) and 100 percent (if they scored 5 in each category). Ask yourself what overall rating someone would have to have in order for you to date that person once. That might be 60 percent. Now ask yourself what overall rating someone would need in order

Figure 9-4
Qualities I'm Looking for in a Mate

Qualities	Ben	Herb
1. Someone I can trust.	4	3
2. Good communication.	5	3
3. Similar interests.	4	4
4. Available.	5	1
5. Self-confident.	3	5
6. Intelligent	4	5
7. Sense of humor.	3	3
8. Easygoing.	3	4
9. Good-looking and attractive (to me, but not necessarily to everyone).	4	5
10. Hardworking and ambitious.	5	4
11. Individualistic.	4	4
12. Not ego-centered or macho.	4	2
13. Likes himself and his life.	3	4
14. Likes me (but not in an overly dependent way).	4	2
15. Flexible.	4	3
16. Not jealous and possessive.	3	3
17. Similar religious background.	5	5
18. Between 25 and 35.	5	5
19. Caring and affectionate (but not overly eager to please).	4	2
20. Natural—not trying too hard to impress people.	4	3
TOTAL	80	70

for you to have several dates. Your requirement might be a little higher, say 65 percent. Then ask yourself what rating someone would have to have for you to go out with that person on a regular, exclusive basis. Here you might require a minimum rating of 70 percent. Finally, ask yourself what someone's rating would have to be for you to desire marriage. Your requirement for marriage might be 75 percent. (One of my associates suggested that if you can find someone who scores 65 percent or better, marry that person instantly!) The secret of a good relationship has less to do with finding that "perfect partner" and more to do with your willingness to solve problems together and make a commitment to your relationship.

Some people might think it's crass to rate people, but this can actually lead to greater intimacy because it will help you learn to accept people as they are. The ratings will force you to come to terms with any unrealistic expectations you might have. You'll quickly see that nobody will average out to 100 percent. If you insist on perfection, then you'll be insisting on loneliness.

You may find that some people you might ordinarily reject will actually have rather favorable ratings. This doesn't mean that you're *obligated* to date them, but if you're avoiding someone with good ratings you might want to ask yourself why. You might be telling yourself, "Well, Sam [or Mary] doesn't seem all that attractive and exciting," or, "They aren't quite as ambitious as I had in mind." These expectations can cut off your options for fulfilling relationships. As an experiment, date someone with good ratings who doesn't initially excite you. Before you go out with him or her, predict how satisfying the evening will be between 0 percent (for the least enjoyable evening a human being could possibly have) and 99 percent (for the most satisfying evening imaginable). Don't use 100 percent, since you can always imagine how an experience could be even better.

After the date, decide how satisfying it actually was on the same 0-to-99 percent scale and compare this with your prediction. You might be surprised to discover that some dates you think will be absolutely thrilling turn out to be real duds, and vice versa.

Another reason to date people with less than perfect ratings is because of the old saying "The rich get richer and the poor get poorer." The more dates you have, the more you'll get. People who date a lot seem to be more in demand. Everyone figures that if you go out a lot you must be a pretty hot number, so they decide they want you, too. Dating people who are less than ideal on your rating scale will give you the experience you need to develop more polished social skills and overcome your inhibitions and insecurities. The more people you date, the more relaxed you'll become. Eventually you'll find that you will begin to attract people with higher and higher ratings, and you'll have the self-confidence you need to form a lasting relationship.

Dating many people can help you overcome the belief that you have to find that one special person who will make you feel happy and worthwhile. Telling yourself that you need someone fantastic in order to feel good is a myth. There is only one person who could ever make you happy, and that person is you. A loving partner might enhance your happiness, but ultimately you will have to take responsibility for your life and your moods.

Many single people tell me they're not overly choosy or looking for an ideal relationship. They insist the real problem is that they don't want to get stuck with a dull or boring date. Single people aren't the only ones who have this problem. You might at times think that your friends or associates are basically boring. A psychiatrist I was training recently asked me what he was supposed to do when he had a patient who wasn't very interesting. A thirty-six-year-old lonely divorced man who was independently wealthy told me that most of his old friends just didn't interest him anymore because they'd settled into predictable routines with typical wives and ordinary careers. After you've been married for several years, you may begin to think that you're stuck in a lackluster marriage with a—let's admit it—rather dull and predictable partner. So what do you do? Take up golf? Have a secret affair with a lover who's more exciting and adventuresome? Put up with the boredom and decide that's just the way life *really* is? Or what?

The first thing you have to realize is that there are no boring or uninteresting people in the world. That's right! There's not one person who's even *slightly* uninteresting. There are only dull, boring interactions between people. But even these are quite fascinating, and furthermore they can nearly always be instantly transformed into dynamic, exciting ones.

How? It's very simple. If you feel bored with someone, say so. That's guaranteed to liven things up quickly! Just acknowledge how bored you're feeling and ask if the other person feels the same way. See if you can find out why the two of you are interacting in such a stuffy, dull way. The aim of this maneuver is not to reject or put the other person down, but to encourage more openness and directness in both of you. If you feel "bored" with someone, it's almost a sure bet that you're both being pretty inhibited about expressing what you're really feeling. Maybe you're trying too hard to be polite or impress each other, or perhaps you're annoyed because you want something you're not getting. Instead of expressing yourself openly and directly, you may be censoring your feelings because you're telling yourself, "I shouldn't be feeling like that." Being more assertive and honest is generally an instant cure!

Another form of romantic perfectionism stems from the fear that family members or friends won't like the person you're dating. Jack, a divorced economics professor who will be described in greater detail in the chapter on the sexual problems of single people (see page 227), overcame his shyness and sexual insecurities and developed an excellent relationship with a woman named Jean. Jean had high overall ratings on Jack's list of "Qualities I'm Looking for in a Mate," and her only area of weakness was that she wasn't quite as intelligent as Jack hoped his wife would be. Jack was afraid that his academic friends might think less of him if he married a woman who wasn't an intellectual superstar.

Jack and I worked on this, using the Feared-Fantasy Technique. I asked him to pretend to be a critical friend who was trying to put him down because Jean wasn't smart enough. I played his role so he could see how to talk back to these criticisms. I urged him to verbalize what he thought other people might be thinking but would never have the courage to actually say to his face:

JACK (IN THE ROLE OF THE CRITIC): Gee, how did you get linked up with that girl, Jean? Couldn't you do any better than that?

DAVID (IN THE ROLE OF JACK): Well, I happen to love Jean and I feel very committed to her. I get the idea you aren't too impressed with her. Why is that?

JACK (AS CRITIC): Well, she seems very nice and very good-looking, but she's not really all that bright, is she?

DAVID (AS JACK): Jean's above-average, but she's certainly not a genius. I understand that your wife is particularly gifted. Do you think any less of Jean because she's not as smart? Do you think any less of me because I love her? Would you feel too uncomfortable to get together with us for dinner or to play cards or have fun?

It didn't take Jack long to see how ludicrous his concerns were. If a friend thought less of him because Jean wasn't smart enough, so what? I then reversed roles so Jack could practice talking back to the imaginary critic. He was able to handle the put-downs as effectively as I had without feeling perturbed, and this helped him feel more comfortable with his commitment to Jean.

We often evaluate ourselves and the people we love in a materialistic, narcissistic way. We measure people on the basis of their intelligence, beauty, or success. We believe that if we fall short of some ideal concept, then we're inferior or defectve. We may search for the perfection that's lacking in ourselves by trying to find a perfect mate. But this isn't real love, it's just a way of using someone else to cope with our own insecurities and lack of self-esteem.

Some people believe there's no point in dating someone unless they find the other person terribly exciting. They feel they have to be swept off their feet and have intense, romantic feelings before they allow themselves to get involved. This can be a real problem unless you're fortunate enough to fall in love regularly. A starry-eyed, lovely young lady named Debbie who was having trouble finding people to date asked me, "What's the point of a relationship if there's no romance?"

You can certainly form a good relationship in spite of your romantic feelings—but rarely because of them. The most that romance can do is to draw two people together initially, but these feelings tend not to last and they don't guarantee a satisfying long-term relationship. In fact, it may be more difficult to have a successful relationship with someone who seems terribly intoxicating, because your expectations may become unrealistically high. When the romantic feelings fade and your partner's very human foibles become apparent to you, as they inevitably will, you may begin to feel bitterly disillusioned.

One way out of this trap is to list the practical advantages of having a partner. Debbie's list is illustrated in

Figure 9-5. You can see that she included companionship, communication, and sex. This pragmatic approach to a relationship does not mean that romantic feelings are unhealthy or undesirable, it just means they are unnecessary. Some of the very best marriages are those in which there is no romantic love at all. In certain cultures your mate would be selected for you at the time of birth. You would enter into the relationship without any preconceived notion that your marriage would be filled with exotic, romantic feelings. Viewing your marriage as a challenging opportunity for growth can often lead to a richer and more rewarding relationship than insisting your partner make all your dreams come true. The satisfaction you feel when you and your partner have made a commitment to each other and struggled to resolve your differences can lead to feelings of tenderness and intimacy that are deeper and more gratifying than any feelings of romantic excitement. Quite often the secret of happiness doesn't involve getting what you want but letting go of the cruel illusion that you really needed it in the first place.

Figure 9-5
Advantages of Having a Relationship

1. Communication—someone to share feelings and ideas with.
2. Companionship—doing things and going places together.
3. Caring—giving and receiving emotional support.
4. Sex.
5. Convenience—many things are easier for couples.
6. Raising a family.
7. Learning from each other and getting help with difficult decisions.
8. Financial advantages, such as in buying a house.
9. Someone to fight with when you feel annoyed.

The last type of romantic perfectionism that can get in the way of developing an intimate relationship is the belief that you and your partner should always have positive feelings and never fight or feel indifferent toward each other. Some people have the misguided notion that love means always being warm and excited and free of conflict. A single forty-five-year-old chemical engineer named Murray who lived with his elderly mother decided it was time to develop more of a life of his own. He got a separate apartment and started to date more frequently. Murray is an affectionate and sensitive individual, and he quickly developed a serious relationship with a divorced professional woman named Diane. Diane seemed to have a pragmatic bent, while Murray was more of a dreamer and a procrastinator, so their personalities complemented each other nicely. Diane was attracted to Murray's idealism and gentleness, while Murray admired Diane's gumption and persistence.

One Sunday morning, after they'd spent the previous evening and night together, Murray realized that he didn't feel particularly close to Diane and wanted to spend the day alone getting caught up on things. This made him anxious and despondent because he told himself he should have stronger feelings and be more involved with Diane. He began to think there was something terribly wrong with him and that his relationship with Diane was over.

Writing down his negative thoughts on a Daily Mood Log (see Figure 9-6) made Murray more aware just how unreasonable he was being. After he substituted more realistic responses, his self-critical feelings faded and he began to feel more positively toward Diane again. As you study his responses, I think you'll be impressed by the wisdom they contain. They illustrate a principle I call the "acceptance paradox": By accepting yourself the way you are, instead of putting yourself down and insisting that you measure up to some imaginary and impossible ideal of how you think you *should* be, you'll often feel much better about yourself and others. You'll get into the flow of life and grow instead of staying stuck the way you are. Self-acceptance becomes the doorway to intimacy and growth.

FIGURE 9-6
The Daily Mood Log*

DESCRIBE THE UPSETTING EVENT—Arriving home after a date with Diane and thinking about my feelings.

NEGATIVE FEELINGS—Record your emotions and rate each one on a scale from 0 (the least) to 100 (the most). Include feelings such as sad, anxious, angry, guilty, lonely, hopeless, frustrated, etc.

Emotion	Rating (0–100)	Emotion	Rating (0–100)	Emotion	Rating (0–100)
1. Sad & depressed	80%	3. Hopeless	85%	5.	
2. Guilty	90%	4.		6.	

AUTOMATIC THOUGHTS	DISTORTIONS	RATIONAL RESPONSES
Write down your negative thoughts and number them consecutively.	Identify the distortions in each "Automatic Thought."	Substitute more realistic and positive thoughts.
1. I should feel more empathy and emotion for her and for our relationship.	1. "Should" statement.	1. Where is the legislation, the rule book, that says how I *should* feel? A characteristic of humans is that they are very individualistic about how they feel. Do I *always* have to feel more empathy and emotion for her? Didn't I have strong feelings when we were talking and cuddling yesterday? Is it reasonable to expect our relationship to stay on the same emotional level at all times?

AUTOMATIC THOUGHTS	DISTORTIONS	RATIONAL RESPONSES
2. There must be something wrong with me for not being able to feel more involved in the relationship.	2. All-or-nothing thinking.	2. Maybe I *want* to feel more strongly but I'm holding back at times—perhaps I'm afraid of the commitment and the loss of my freedom. Since I've been a bachelor and avoided involvements for a long time, it seems reasonable to expect that there will be times when I will prefer to spend time by myself. Does this mean there's something "wrong" with me? Basically I'm saying that other people must be much more in touch with their feelings than I am and that they never have to struggle with uncertainty, but that seems

AUTOMATIC THOUGHTS	DISTORTIONS	RATIONAL RESPONSES
		unrealistic. I may *want* to have more feelings for Diane, but if I had strong feelings for her *all* the time I'd be so preoccupied with her that I couldn't do or think of anything else.

OUTCOME—Review your "Rational Responses" and put a check in the box that describes how you now feel:
☐ not at all better; ☐ somewhat better; ☑ quite a bit better; ☐ a lot better.

---

*Copyright © 1984, by David D. Burns, M.D. from *Intimate Connections* (New York: William Morrow & Company).

10

The Trapped Factor:
Are You a Prisoner of Love?

Once you've found someone to date regularly, a new problem may crop up: You or your partner may begin to feel trapped by the relationship. Just when you're beginning to feel intimate and you're finally sharing a satisfying sex life, you may start to notice that you also feel claustrophobic and confined, and you may be terrified by the thought that you're losing your freedom. When you realize you feel trapped, you'll be determined to escape. Escape generally means breaking up, having affairs on the side, or trying to prevent the relationship from getting "too serious."

The following symptoms suggest that this may be a problem for you:

• You feel your romantic relationships don't give you an adequate amount of personal freedom.

• The idea of making a commitment to your partner seems less like an adventure and more like a burden. Love seems to involve more duty and self-sacrifice than reward.

• The more involved you get in a relationship, the less spontaneous, sexually excited, and affectionate you feel. A relationship quickly loses its magic and begins to feel like drudgery.

• You're more interested in quick affairs or one-night stands—which seem enormously stimulating and enticing—than in an enduring commitment to one person—which seems about as thrilling as going to a long church service.

• It sometimes seems as if the person you're dating

needs an excessive amount of your time and attention. When she or he makes demands on you, it's hard for you to say no, even when saying yes isn't in your best self-interest. You may get into disagreements about how often you should date and how much time you should spend together.

• It may be difficult for you to tell your partner how you feel or what you really want. When you get upset or angry, you may deny your feelings and hold them in rather than expressing them openly. You want to avoid getting into a fight or hurting your partner's feelings, but you often end up tense and secretly annoyed with your partner.

• If the person you're dating seems unhappy or depressed, you have a tendency to feel guilty and blame yourself. If he or she has a personal problem, you feel as if it's up to you to solve it. At first this "helper" or "teacher" role is gratifying and makes you feel important, but after a while it begins to wear thin because your partner leans on you more and more. As the feelings of romance fade, the relationship becomes more work than pleasure.

Recent research with couples and with lonely single people has indicated that these problems often result from your attitudes and from certain illogical ways you think about romantic relationships. By developing healthier and more realistic attitudes, you can learn to experience love, not as a trap that limits you, but as an adventure that can enhance your freedom and your potential for joy.

One self-defeating belief that often leads to trapped feelings is the idea that you must cater to all of your partner's needs and demands. You may feel obligated to please your partner because you believe he or she is weak and needs your love in the same way that a diabetic needs insulin to survive. Or you may be afraid of your partner's disapproval or rejection if you don't meet all of his or her expectations and demands. This preoccupation with pleasing your partner makes each relationship an oppressive burden instead of an opportunity for growth and sharing.

A divorced woman recently told me, "I feel like a grotesque evil witch. Whenever someone falls in love with me I end up leaving him and hurting him. What's wrong with me? Why am I so hard and cruel? Do I hate men?" Her problem does not stem from hate but from her inability to say, "I don't care to be with you now because I need to be alone for a while." She thinks the men she dates are inadequate weaklings who can't exist without her love and attention. This belief destroys her capacity to give or receive love freely and spontaneously. Her fear of hurting them is a disguised insult that carries the message: "I am convinced that you can't exist without me. You're weak. You need me. I am the oxygen that allows you to breathe."

Once you begin to feel trapped, it will appear that you actually are trapped—even though you really aren't. Suppose the woman you're dating suggests that the two of you get together Saturday afternoon and do some shopping. You had previously decided that you might like to spend the afternoon with a buddy going to the track. You have two choices: You can say no to her or you can say yes to her. You are reluctant to say no because you feel guilty about disappointing her. But what happens when you say yes? If you agree to spend the afternoon with her, she'll notice that you seem tense. She may feel hurt and wonder what's wrong. You have given her a mixed message because your words say yes but your heart says no. She may ask, "Are you *sure* you want to go?" You insist that you *really do* and that it's "fine," but the tension in your face and the lack of genuine warmth and enthusiasm in your voice will project the message "I really don't want to be with you." So off you go shopping—you feel trapped and unhappy and she feels insecure. Neither of you has a very good time.

Suppose you try it the other way. You tell her you have other plans for Saturday afternoon, but you feel guilty about leaving her alone. She notices how uncomfortable you are, and this makes her upset. She wonders what's wrong. When you're at the track you don't have that great a time because you know she was upset and you feel guilty. You feel that you're in a can't-win situation, because whatever you do seems to make both of you feel bad. You're damned if you do, and you're damned if you don't. This is the essence of the "trap."

So what's the solution? You need to transform these can't-win situations into can't-lose situations. This means changing the way you think about your relationship as well as the way you communicate with your partner. Too much of anything—even the person you care about—can become a curse. This means there will be times when you'll have to tell your partner you can't join him or her in an activity because you have other plans. The way you do this will depend on the stage of the relationship you're in, as well as your needs and expectations. It's not always easy to ask for what you want even if what you want is simply a few hours of being alone, and there's a natural tendency to believe that if two people care about each other they'll want to spend every moment together. In reality, this idealism just doesn't work out well, and sooner or later you're going to have to learn to set limits on your relationship and negotiate for what you want.

Ben, the man whose Daily Mood Log is illustrated in Figure 10-1, felt guilty because Kathy, a woman he'd been dating on and off for several months, called him at five on a Saturday evening "just to say hello." Ben had plans to go out for a beer with a friend, and he started to feel self-critical and trapped because he thought her phone call was a hint she wanted him to ask her out. You can see from examining Ben's "Automatic Thoughts" that he was involved in a number of familiar distortions, including:

• Mind reading—Ben assumed that Kathy couldn't tolerate being alone, that she had no other plans for the evening, and that she'd be hurt if he didn't ask her out.

• Personalization—Ben told himself that if she did have a lousy evening it would be his fault.

• "Should" statements—Ben told himself he *should* want to be with Kathy and he didn't have the right to want to spend an evening with a friend.

• Labeling—Ben labels himself as "selfish" and "rotten" because he can't meet all her needs.

While it's important to be concerned about the feelings and needs of someone you've been dating, Ben's thoughts were rather inappropriate, since he and Kathy had no understanding that they would date each other steadily or that their relationship was an exclusive one. However, his self-critical thoughts *seemed* entirely valid because he felt so guilty and upset. Feelings can be quite deceptive in this regard. If you accept them at face value—as most of us nearly always do—there's a good chance of being misled. In contrast, when you write down your negative thoughts, it becomes far easier to examine the messages you're giving yourself and to see how illogical they are.

Ben's "Rational Responses" reminded him that although Kathy might have been hoping he'd ask her out, he really had no obligation to change his plans, just as she wouldn't have been obligated to go out with him if he had asked her out at the last minute. He realized that sticking to his plans that night didn't make him a "rotten person" and that it was unnecessary to feel pressured by her phone call. As Ben thought about the situation, it dawned on him that he'd been making a certain assumption about loving relationships that was getting him into trouble: He assumed that it was his duty to meet all of Kathy's needs and expectations, and that anytime he didn't, it meant he wasn't doing a good job in the relationship.

I suggested that Ben list the advantages and disadvantages of believing this (see Figure 10-2). This Cost-Benefit Analysis convinced him that his attitude wasn't going to be helpful to him *or to Kathy*. He decided to substitute a new attitude that would be more realistic and fair to both of them (see his "Revised Version" in Figure 10-2).

Does this mean Ben should *ignore* Kathy's feelings and think only of himself? Nothing could be further from the truth. A loving relationship should involve a balanced concern for your own feelings and those of the other person. But just as it would be unethical to take advantage of someone else to get what you want, it's equally unethical to make yourself miserable just to please another person. And it's really an illusion that you could do this, anyway. Anytime you don't take your needs and feelings into account, you're likely to become unhappy and resentful. Your resentment makes it very unlikely that you could really make someone else very happy in the long run.

I've mentioned that negotiating with your partner can be the key to eliminating those trapped feelings and reestablishing a mutually rewarding relationship. But what exactly do I mean by negotiation? Ben needs to learn how to communicate his feelings to Kathy without hurting her

FIGURE 10-1
The Daily Mood Log*

DESCRIBE THE UPSETTING EVENT—Kathy called me at 5:00 Saturday night. I had plans to go out for a beer with a buddy, and I felt torn about whether I should ask her out and cancel my plans or ignore her needs and do what I planned. I didn't ask her out but felt upset.

NEGATIVE FEELINGS—Record your emotions and rate each one on a scale from 0 (the least) to 100 (the most). Include feelings such as sad, anxious, angry, guilty, lonely, hopeless, frustrated, etc.

Emotion	Rating (0–100)	Emotion	Rating (0–100)	Emotion	Rating (0–100)
1. Guilty	80%	3.		5.	
2. Trapped	80%	4.		6.	

AUTOMATIC THOUGHTS Write down your negative thoughts and number them consecutively.	DISTORTIONS Identify the distortions in each "Automatic Thought."	RATIONAL RESPONSES Substitute more realistic and positive thoughts.
1. She might have nothing to do tonight and I could have asked her to join me.	1. Mind reading.	1. She had plenty of time to plan her weekend without me. I have every right to spend time with my friends.
2. I should have asked her to join me because she might be alone tonight.	2. "Should" statement.	2. If she was alone tonight, it was by her own decision. It's not so terrible to spend an evening alone unless you mope and feel sorry for yourself.

AUTOMATIC THOUGHTS	DISTORTIONS	RATIONAL RESPONSES
3. If she's unhappy because she has nothing to do, that's my fault.	3. Personalization.	3. I am not responsible for her happiness—she is. If she's afraid of spending time by herself, this is something she needs to deal with.
4. Since I didn't ask her to join me, I'm a rotten person.	4. Personalization.	4. I'm not a rotten person for spending an evening with a friend.
5. Since I'm a rotten, insensitive person, I don't deserve to have a good time tonight.	5. Labeling.	5. Even if I was insensitive (and I'm not sure that I was) that doesn't make me a rotten person. There's no reason to punish myself. If I didn't handle the situation particularly well, I can try to learn from it so I can deal with situations like this more effectively in the future. I really didn't

AUTOMATIC THOUGHTS	DISTORTIONS	RATIONAL RESPONSES
		know what the right thing to do was, and this makes me human, not rotten.

OUTCOME—Review your "Rational Responses" and put a check in the box that describes how you now feel:

☐ not at all better; ☐ somewhat better; ☑ quite a bit better; ☐ a lot better.

*Copyright © 1984, David D. Burns, M.D., from *Intimate Connections* (New York: William Morrow & Company).

feelings or putting her down. The following basic communication skills helped him, and they can help you negotiate personal differences in a way that takes both people's needs into account.

Inquiry. You ask questions to learn more about how the other person is thinking and feeling. Since many people are unassertive and afraid to say what's on their mind, you cannot assume that someone will tell you what they're thinking unless you ask. This is especially true when someone is upset with you or when they want something from you. Often a simple, direct question is enough to open things up.

When Kathy called, the first thing she said was "Hi, Ben, this is Kathy!" He replied, "Oh, hi, Kathy." This led to an awkward silence. He might have handled it by adding, "It's nice to hear from you. What's on your mind?" She might say why she called, which would break the ice, or she might act vague and say, "Oh, nothing, really. I was just calling to say hello." In the latter case, further inquiry might sound patronizing and make Kathy feel put down. Instead, Ben could simply say, "Oh, I'm glad you did, but I was just heading out. I'd love to get together with you next Friday. Would you be available?" or alternatively, "Could I call you back tomorrow?" This illustrates the second communication skill:

Figure 10-2
Cost-Benefit Analysis

Silent Assumption: I must make Kathy happy and meet all of her needs. If she's feeling upset, it means I haven't done my part in the relationship.

Advantages of Believing This	Disadvantages of Believing This
1. When Kathy's happy I'll feel good because I'll think I'm doing a good job.	1. When Kathy's unhappy I may feel guilty and blame myself.
2. I'll try very hard to make her happy, and that seems like the morally correct thing to do.	2. I may become resentful of her because she'll have too much power to manipulate me. If I don't give her what she wants and she gets upset, I'll feel like a failure.
3. When she's upset, I won't ignore her but I'll do my best to help her.	3. I'll have a hard time saying no or telling her what I want.
	4. I may actually end up making her unhappy because she'll notice how unhappy I feel and this will be upsetting to her.
(40)	(60)

Revised Version: It's important that both Kathy and I feel good about our relationship. That means we'll have to talk about what we want and negotiate. If she's upset we can talk it over and share our feelings. Sometimes we'll have to compromise. I can't be expected to meet *all* her needs, and I can't expect her to meet all of mine. We can work these problems through in a spirit of fairness and mutual respect.

Tactful Self-expression. You express your own feelings openly and directly. Kathy will probably get the message and agree to go out Friday, or to speak with him tomorrow. Ben will avoid feeling trapped, but he hasn't rejected her either. Asserting his needs will allow the relationship to evolve in a natural way that he feels comfortable with. By not asking her out that night, he's communicated his expectations about the degree of involvement and commitment he feels ready for at this time. He can go out and have fun without feeling guilty.

Let's assume the worst. Suppose Kathy doesn't get the message and she begins to pressure Ben in a demanding, manipulative way. She might sound hurt and say, "Oh, you're going out tonight?" Ben can respond by asserting his position directly again, but he can also ask questions that will invite Kathy to state what's on her mind: "Yes, I was just on my way out. I'm a little concerned, though. Did we have an arrangement to go out tonight? Perhaps there's been some misunderstanding." This will make his position clear without being insulting and will allow her to express her feelings.

Suppose that Kathy decides to make things difficult and blatantly tries to make Ben feel guilty. She might sigh and say, "Oh, gee. I was kind of counting on us getting together tonight. Who are you going out with?" Instead of getting uptight or defensive, Ben can use a third listening skill:

Empathy. You show an appreciation for how other people are thinking (thought empathy) and feeling (feeling empathy). You can do this by paraphrasing what they say. Repeat their words. Reflect what they're saying, and try to convey an awareness for how they might be feeling. Ben could say, "I'm sorry to disappoint you. It sounds like you were counting on going out tonight, but I've had other plans for some time. I'd love to see you next Friday if you're available, but I didn't think we'd talked about tonight. Did we?" Notice that this statement contains a balance of assertiveness—Ben again expresses his position and feelings—along with empathy—he demonstrates a concern for Kathy's feelings and gives her the opportunity to say what's on her mind.

Too much emphasis on your own thoughts and needs leads to self-centeredness and insensitivity. Too much preoccupation with what the other person wants and feels leads to submissiveness and a lack of self-respect. A balance between your needs and the desires of others can be difficult to achieve. Some people go to one extreme and come across in an overly selfish, manipulative way, while others go to the opposite extreme and come across as overly helpful and "nice." Being concerned about yourself *and* others is the essence of caring as well as personal freedom. If you learn to express your feelings openly and without hostility, you can listen to your partner without having to feel guilty, defensive, or trapped.

Although popular stereotypes suggest that men like Ben are the ones who are most likely to be afraid of intimacy and commitment, my clinical experience and research suggest that this is a myth. Women are just as likely to feel trapped by intimate relationships and to have trouble sharing their feelings and getting close. I saw in my office today an attractive nineteen-year-old woman named Inga who has this problem. Inga is trying to develop a career as an artist. She has been dating Roger, a man she described as "a free-lance writer with a harem of women who are pursuing him." Inga said she felt insecure because Roger was older and seemed considerably wiser and more worldly, and she was concerned that he'd eventually lose interest in her and drop her.

During the course of treatment, Inga worked on boosting her own self-esteem so she could overcome her feelings of inferiority and her fears of losing Roger. Once she began to feel more self-confident, the delicate balance of her relationship with Roger suddenly and dramatically shifted. The very week that she decided she wanted but didn't really "need" a relationship with Roger, he suddenly decided he didn't want to date anybody else, dropped all his other lady friends, and announced that he wanted an exclusive relationship with Inga. (That, incidentally, is why it's *so* important for you to master the concepts in Chapters Three and Four. Self-esteem is the key to success in any relationship. The moment you stop "needing" people, they'll need you. If you respect yourself, you'll be in hot demand. It works like magic!)

Roger's sudden attentiveness was a pleasant change, but it created a new problem for Inga. She told me, "Dr. Burns, I'm afraid the same thing is happening to me that's happened in several previous relationships. When a man decides he wants to get really close, I suddenly start to feel cold and distant. Am I afraid of intimacy? Is something wrong with me?"

Inga described how Roger had invited her over Sunday evening to spend the night together. After she arrived they began teasing and tickling each other, the way they usually did before they made love. Inga felt she really wasn't in the mood for sex but felt *obligated* to make love. To make matters even more awkward, two days earlier they'd played a "bondage" game, and she'd let Roger tie her up. This led to some exciting lovemaking. She sensed that Roger was in the same mood and wanted a repeat performance because of the "lusty look" in his eyes. But because she was already feeling like a prisoner, she was in no mood to play the game again that night. She began to feel trapped and uncomfortable.

I asked Inga what negative thoughts had been going through her mind. Her first thought was "I shouldn't be feeling so cold. If I'm not more responsive, he's going to get turned off and I'll lose him." This involves all-or-nothing thinking, since she's predicting their relationship will fall apart if she doesn't feel warm, loving, and responsive at every moment. She's also making a "should" statement, since she's telling herself she doesn't have the right to feel the way she does and that she should measure up to some imaginary ideal of how people should feel. In fact, my recent studies have indicated that perfectionism and the fear of expressing inner feelings can predispose women to feeling trapped by intimate relationships. This suggests that it may be Inga's unrealistic expectations for herself, not Roger's demands, that are at the heart of the problem. She's the real warden, and the prison is a creation of her mind.

After we discussed these distortions, Inga decided to think about it like this instead: "It's hardly likely that

Roger is going to leave me if I'm not feeling affectionate tonight, since he's been getting closer and closer lately. Nobody can feel loving or sexually excited all the time. Our relationship isn't so weak that I have to live in the fear that any little thing will end it. And even if he did leave me, it wouldn't be the end of the world. He's not the only man out there." Thinking about it this way took some of the pressure off and Inga felt less trapped.

A second thought that was making Inga upset was "If Roger feels excited, I'm obligated to perform and to respond sexually." This also involves all-or-nothing thinking, since she's telling herself she *always* has to want sex whenever Roger does. It's certainly important for Inga to take Roger's sexual desires into account along with her own, but telling herself she has to meet all of his needs is sexual perfectionism. In fact, Inga and Roger have been having excellent sexual experiences several times a week, so one could hardly argue that she was unjustly depriving him if she wasn't in the mood for sex on a given Sunday night.

After thinking about these issues, Inga decided to tell herself that she wasn't *obligated* to respond sexually. You can't *demand* that anybody be sexually aroused. If Inga wasn't comfortable about having sex, she had every right to share this with Roger and find out how he felt. Sexual expectations have to be negotiated, just like any other aspect of a relationship.

Inga saw that she was making a basic assumption about relationships that was causing her to feel trapped. It was "I must be totally open to Roger's needs and mold myself to him and please him at all times. If I don't, the relationship will be over." Her excessive preoccupation with his feelings may *seem* loving, but she makes herself unhappy and it becomes much harder to love him and respond sexually. Inga needs to change her value system and to emphasize a balanced concern for her needs as well as Roger's.

Although Inga agreed to this on principle, when I suggested she would have to work on being more assertive she acted as if she were in a lightning storm. She said, "You mean I should just *tell* Roger openly that I'm not feeling interested in sex? Why, he'd get angry and say, "Then what are you here for?' Then he might give me an ultimatum. I think it's better not to talk about these things, because then I won't have to hear something that might be upsetting." I see this fear of self-expression over and over every day. Many people seem to feel that they don't have the right to express their own feelings and needs, and they think that if they do, something terrible will happen.

I suggested that we practice how she might respond if Roger became upset. In the following dialogue, I played Inga's role and suggested that she could be Roger and criticize me for not wanting to have sex that night.

ROGER (PLAYED BY INGA): You're not in the mood for sex! Then what are you here for?

INGA (PLAYED BY DAVID): I'm here for your company.

ROGER (PLAYED BY INGA): That's all very well and good . . . that's great . . . but relationships are sexual, also.

INGA (PLAYED BY DAVID): I think we have a great sexual relationship, but I'm not really in the mood for sex tonight. I'm feeling a little bit tense and pressured.

ROGER (PLAYED BY INGA): But I've been thinking about you all afternoon!

INGA (PLAYED BY DAVID): I'm flattered. You turn me on, too. But I'm not feeling very sexy just now.

ROGER (PLAYED BY INGA): But I want to have sex tonight!

INGA (PLAYED BY DAVID): It sounds like having sex tonight is pretty important to you. Why is this?

ROGER (PLAYED BY INGA): If you don't want to have sex, it means you're just *using* me for my company.

INGA (PLAYED BY DAVID): Do you think I'd use you for your company? I hate it when I feel used by someone. Are there other things I've done or said that gave you the impression I was using you?

ROGER (PLAYED BY INGA): No, but I'm afraid this might get to be a regular thing where you don't want sex and you just turn out to be a cock-tease!

INGA (PLAYED BY DAVID): Have I been doing things that made you feel like I was just a "cock-tease"?

ROGER (PLAYED BY INGA): Well, no, I just don't want things to go in that direction.

INGA (PLAYED BY DAVID): I wouldn't like that, either. Tell me—how often would you like sex?

ROGER (PLAYED BY INGA): Three times a week.

INGA (PLAYED BY DAVID): That sounds good to me, too. I think that's actually about how often we've been having sex. Would it be a problem if we don't have sex tonight?

Notice that in playing Inga's role I didn't give in or get argumentative or defensive. My responses illustrate the same three basic communication skills described earlier:

1. *Inquiry.* You ask questions to find out how your partner is thinking and feeling. Encourage him or her to express the hidden feelings and needs that are just under the surface. Try to discover what the real fears are. The real problem isn't sex but Roger's fears that if he doesn't get what he wants, it means he's being used.

2. *Empathy.* You paraphrase what your partner says. You put yourself in his or her shoes and try to understand how she or he thinks and feels *without getting judgmental*. Roger really wants to know that Inga respects him and cares about him. If the sharing of fears and insecurities is an important part of love, then simply listening and understanding can be a very loving act. This type of deep emotional exchange is the very essence of intimacy, trust, and freedom.

3. *Tactful self-expression.* You express your feelings openly and directly and without putting your partner down. You stick to your guns and state your point of view, but you encourage your partner to express his or her feelings as well as using the inquiry technique and empathy.

I don't mean to imply that increased assertiveness, better negotiations about sex, or even the ability to say no will entirely resolve Inga's tendency to feel trapped. Inga needs to become more aware of her deeper feelings and to have the courage and self-confidence to share them with Roger. Instead of taking all her cues from him and wondering whether she's meeting all his needs and expectations, she needs to look inside and ask herself how she's feeling. Why isn't she in the mood for sex? Is she annoyed with Roger? Perhaps she feels disturbed about her work. This kind of openness represents a profound emotional freedom that's the ultimate antidote to feeling trapped.

Once the trust and openness and sharing of feelings are there, the so-called real problems—such as when to have sex or how much time to spend together—are usually far easier to deal with, and they often simply dissolve entirely.

Summary

Trapped feelings are a common barrier to intimacy. Recent research and clinical work with people who feel trapped suggest that the real prison exists not in reality but in your own mind. Certain self-defeating attitudes tend to trigger trapped feelings. These include:

• I must meet all my partner's needs and expectations.

• I'm responsible for my partner's happiness. If she (or he) is unhappy, this is necessarily my fault.

• My partner is very weak and needy and can't exist without my constant attention and reassurance.

• It would be too risky to assert my own needs and feelings and to negotiate for what I really want in my relationship.

Most people try to deal with trapped feelings by escaping from a relationship. They break up, they have affairs, or they become emotionally detached and less involved. The real solution is actually the opposite—to become more assertive, more involved, more emotionally open. This means believing in yourself—in the importance of your own needs and feelings—and believing in your partner—as someone who isn't really so weak and fragile but as a human being who can endure the discomfort of resolving conflicts, negotiating, and communicating more openly and honestly.

The following methods can help you achieve these goals:

• Daily Mood Log—You write down the distorted, self-critical thoughts that make you feel guilty, frustrated, and trapped every time you want to express your feelings.

• Cost-Benefit Analysis—You make a list of the advantages and disadvantages of believing you have to meet all of your partner's needs and expectations. You develop a new value system in which both partners' needs and feelings are important.

• Listening Skills—Instead of avoiding a conflict, you

ask how your partner feels (inquiry), you paraphrase what your partner says (empathy), and you find some truth in it (the disarming technique).

• Self-expression Skills—At the same time, you express your own needs and feelings instead of withdrawing or pouting, but you do it in a way that doesn't put your partner down or threaten his or her self-esteem.

• Negotiation—Instead of trying to meet all your partner's needs, you learn to negotiate and to compromise. This may take some of the magic and romance out of a relationship, but in exchange it gives you a greater measure of intimacy and satisfaction. You can express a loving relationship not as a trap, but as an opportunity for growth.

11

How to Repair a Broken Heart: Conquering Fears of Rejection and Success

As you apply the principles in the previous chapters, you'll begin to feel better about yourself and you'll project greater self-confidence in your personal relationships. As you start to date more frequently, two things will happen. You'll experience a number of rejections—since *nobody* on earth can attract everyone they're interested in—and you'll also begin to experience a certain measure of success because you'll be looking and feeling more attractive and flirting and communicating more effectively. As this happens, two deep fears, the fear of rejection and the fear of success, may start to cause problems for you. Some readers will be terrified by the prospect of intimacy and success. After all, there's a *comfort* in being lonely and rejected—you may have been that way for ten or twenty years or even longer, and although it's not much fun, at least it's familiar. The prospect of sudden change can be frightening and overwhelming.

In this chapter we'll take a look at these two fears. You'll discover that many of your apprehensions are not due to the realities of being rejected or to being close, but to certain illogical thoughts and self-defeating attitudes. As you begin to think about your relationships more positively and realistically, you can conquer these needless barriers to intimacy.

The Fear of Rejection

If you feel shy and lonely, you may be so afraid of

rejection that you're reluctant to look your best and smile and flirt with people you're attracted to. You may think, "What if someone rejects me? I couldn't stand it! It would be terrible!" But why is rejection so terrible? In point of fact, rejection, per se, can *never* be overly upsetting unless you think about it in an illogical way. Once you learn to think about the experience more objectively, it will lose most of its power to upset you.

This doesn't mean that you're supposed to *enjoy* rejection! It's natural to feel good when you're accepted and disappointed when someone gives you the cold shoulder. However, you can learn to put these experiences in a more realistic perspective so that they won't involve a blow to your self-esteem. Then your fears will no longer prevent you from taking a few chances so you can get close to other people again.

It's important to take a close look at your negative thoughts when you feel rejected. You'll notice many of the distortions that are listed in Table 4-1 on page 51. One of the commonest distortions to look for is overgeneralization— you will probably be assuming that since this person rejected you, everyone will. You may tell yourself, "I'll probably *never* have anyone to love. I'll *always* be alone." This thought may seem realistic, but it's actually absurd because everyone's taste is so very different. Beauty is in the eye of the beholder, and no two people can ever have identical tastes. If you're willing to persist, sooner or later you'll discover someone who does find you interesting and appealing.

Another way you may overgeneralize is when you tell yourself that you were rejected because of some inherent inadequacy in your "self" rather than because of some specific problem in this particular relationship. You may think, "I'm such a loser. There must be something wrong with me. I just don't have what it takes to get close to anybody." Then you feel as if your "essence" or "identity" has been judged by a panel of authorities and you've been found to be defective and stamped as unlovable for time eternal.

You will see just how unrealistic this attitude is if you carefully examine the specific reasons why people might reject you:

• They may feel angry and frustrated with you.

• They may not be attracted to you because of certain physical characteristics, such as your appearance, your age, or your race.

• They may reject you because the relationship is going well and they're afraid of intimacy or commitment.

• They may have found someone else they're more attracted to.

You will notice that these reasons sometimes reflect the other person's taste. The most obvious example would be someone who rejects you because you're black or blond and they're looking for a lover who is quite different. In this case, the rejection really has little or nothing to do with how desirable you are.

One of my patients, Dan, is a handsome thirty-two-year-old man in the publishing business. He likes women who are at least twenty-seven to thirty years of age, and he generally considers any woman in her early or mid-twenties too young. Another patient of mine, John, is an attractive thirty-three-year-old accountant. He happens to be attracted to women who are no older than twenty-five. If a twenty-four-year-old woman happens to go out with Dan, she'll probably get the brush-off. If she happens to go out with John, he'll probably pursue her eagerly. She's the same person, and the outcome will almost entirely depend on the other person's subjective preferences.

A second distortion that leads to the pain of rejection is a personalization, or self-blame. You tell yourself, "It's all my fault. If only I had been more loving" (or sexually responsive, or whatever). Blaming yourself is generally unrealistic because both people contribute to the success or failure of any relationship. Telling yourself it's all your fault is really quite self-centered and grandiose. It's as if the entire relationship depended only on you and was entirely under your control. Other people aren't just extensions of your ego, they are separate and unique and have minds of their own. It may be a pleasant fantasy to believe that if you behave in just the right way you can make everyone love and desire you, but the world doesn't work that way.

Instead of blaming yourself, try to pinpoint what the

specific problems in the relationship were. Did the two of you argue a lot? Why? Was there a sexual problem? Did you both have trouble sharing your feelings? How come? Try to understand what you both might have done that contributed to the breakup. If there's a problem you can do something about, such as being overweight or self-centered or defensive, don't waste your energy putting yourself down and getting depressed. Instead, get some counseling or make a plan for correcting it so that you can grow and learn to get closer to people in the future.

Even when there's something genuinely negative about you that makes it hard for people to feel close to you, it's still unnecessary to blame yourself. A twenty-eight-year-old woman named Sally came to me after years of loneliness and depression. She'd lost her job and felt as if most of her friends were abandoning her as well. Several months earlier, one of her best friends unexpectedly told her during a telephone conversation that she thought it would be best for them not to continue their friendship. Her friend was unwilling to talk about it or give Sally any explanation of what the problem was. Sally felt frustrated and convinced she was unlovable. She thought that all these rejections really were her fault. Even a counselor she'd seen told her she seemed quite irritable and had a tendency to put people on the defensive. Sally felt that even the counselor didn't like her, and wept as she told me how hopeless and inadequate she felt.

I asked Sally why she thought her best friend might have rejected her. She suggested, crying profusely the entire time she spoke, that she was so depressed all the time she was probably a "big downer" to be around. Sally's probably right. Research by Dr. James Coyne at the Palo Alto Mental Research Institute has indicated that people often do find it frustrating to relate to someone who's feeling depressed. The depressed person's lack of self-esteem, fragility, and defensiveness can easily put others on edge. Does it follow that Sally is "to blame" or "at fault" for being rejected?

No. The problem is not that Sally is to blame. The real problem is that she blames herself. Self-blame is not the same as personal responsibility, as indicated in Table 11-1.

Table 11-1
Three Key Differences Between Self-Blame and Personal Responsibility

Self-Blame	Personal Responsibility
1. *Causes of rejections always seem internal:* You automatically assume that you are entirely responsible for any problems in your personal relationships.	1. *Causes of rejections are usually seen as mutual:* You try to understand how both you and the other person might have contributed to a conflict.
2. *Rejections seem global and overwhelming:* You feel that any shortcoming or rejection proves what a basically inadequate, undesirable person you are. Then you feel defeated, depressed, and defective.	2. *Problems seem specific:* You think of a personal shortcoming as a problem in how you felt or acted and not as a reflection on your self-esteem. This gives you the motivation to do something constructive to change.
3. *Rejections seem permanent and irreversible:* You feel hopeless that things could ever be better or that your problems could ever be resolved.	3. *Problems seem temporary and reversible:* You see the problem as an opportunity to grow so you can make your next relationship even better.

Personal responsibility involves accepting your shortcomings without any loss of self-esteem so you can change and grow. But Sally's so hard on herself and spends so much of her time blaming and despising herself that even the gentlest criticism from a friend becomes more than she can bear. She lashes out defensively because it's just too dangerous to listen to what other people have to say. Her poor listening skills make her seem self-centered and difficult to be around. Her self-blaming tendencies alienate others and create the rejection she most fears. Sally will have to work hard on modifying this tendency during her therapy. As her self-esteem goes up, she will learn how to tolerate the ups and downs of close personal relationships without becoming so self-blaming and defensive. As she becomes more open and self-confident, people will begin to respond to her in a more positive way.

A third type of distortion that's common in rejection is all-or-nothing thinking. When you break up with someone, you may tell yourself that you "failed" or that the relationship was a "failure." These thoughts are unrealistic because there's really no such thing as an unsuccessful relationship. At the very least, you successfully discovered that the two of you weren't suitable for each other. Think of all the different ways the adequacy of a relationship can be measured. You might include sexual satisfaction, openness, having common interests, faithfulness, trust, mutual respect, honesty, loyalty, the capacity to laugh and have fun, the ability to communicate, the willingness to solve problems, and so on. Now rate the relationship on a 0-to-10 scale in each of these areas. I think you'll see that some of the ratings will be higher and others will be lower, and that you were at least somewhat successful in most areas. This should make it clear to you that no relationship is a "total failure" or a "total success."

A fourth type of distortion that leads to the pain of rejection is the fortune-telling error: You tell yourself that you'll never develop an enduring steady, loving relationship with anyone. People who have been rejected often tell me, "As I look back on my life, all I can see is a long string of rejections. My marriage broke up. All the relationships I had before I got married eventually fell apart. I've never had a truly permanent relationship with anyone. Doesn't this mean I'm hopeless? Let's face the facts, Dr. Burns. I'll *never* have the kind of lasting relationship I really want."

This argument may *sound* persuasive, but it's quite misleading. Consider all the people in the United States who are now involved in a successful marriage or love affair. Let's assume that there are at least 100 million people like this. Prior to their current relationship, what percentage of their *previous* relationships ended in rejection?

After you think about it, I suspect it will dawn on you that the answer is 100 percent. Up until the time you meet the person you finally settle down with, *all* your romantic relationships will eventually break up. Either you will decide the other person isn't right for you, or vice versa. Sometimes it will be a mutual decision. But this doesn't mean you're "hopeless." It just means you're dating and actively searching for a partner. Frequent rejections are an absolutely necessary part of the process of getting close to others. You can think of each rejection or broken relationship as climbing one step up a ladder. You grow and learn from each of these experiences, and this knowledge can help you make your next relationship more intimate and satisfying.

It is crucial to remember that rejection can *never* mean that you are an uninteresting or undesirable person. There really *is* no such thing as an uninteresting or unlovable person. Someone can reject you only on the basis of some *speeific* problem, not because of some vague, global notion, such as your being "a loser." If someone has a *valid* criticism—let's say you dress sloppily or you have a tendency to be insensitive, selfish, or defensive—then you can *agree* with them and try to correct the problem. This has nothing to do with how worthwhile or lovable you are. Remember that your imperfections make you more human, not less worthwhile, and accepting them without a sense of shame can be the basis for *increased* self-respect. If someone refuses to continue a relationship without trying to work things out in spite of your willingness to change, this person may be more interested in getting revenge than in solving the problem. He or she may be overwhelmed by feelings of anger and frustration and not be very good at working out the problems in a relationship. That's a reflection on them, not on you. It shows that he or she is human and has limits, but it has nothing to do with how lovable or worthwhile you are. Why not make the decision to love and accept yourself in spite of your imperfections? This doesn't mean *ignoring* your faults. Admit every one of them, and try to correct the ones you can do something about. But do it in the spirit of self-love.

Suppose you have poor social skills. Maybe you turn people off because you dress poorly. Maybe you go around with a chip on your shoulder. If so, work on these problems. But realize that you will never help yourself by labeling yourself as a second-rate human being. Thinking of yourself as inferior will only make your problems worse, but loving yourself unconditionally can give you the motivation and courage to grow and share yourself with others.

Rejection Practice. How can you turn these rational insights into an emotional reality? Even though you *logically* understand that all human beings are lovable, you may still *feel* bad about yourself when you get rejected. And you know that other people don't operate in such an enlightened way and they will make value judgments about you and you *will* get rejected at times.

The repeated exposure to something you're afraid of is one of the most effective ways of overcoming your fears at a gut level. If you're afraid of rejection, you need as much rejection experience as possible. I would recommend that you try to collect at least five rejections a week for at *least* two months. One way you can do this is to flirt with attractive strangers and get to know as many people as possible using the techniques described in Chapter Five and Six. You can smile and talk to people you meet on the street, in stores, in restaurants, at clubs, or wherever you want. When people respond in a friendly way, you can ask them out for coffee or for a date. Each time someone turns you down or rejects you, you get a point. Once you accumulate 20 points, you can give yourself a special reward, such as buying that exotic new outfit you've had your eye on or giving yourself a weekend holiday at the shore.

This "rejection practice" has many payoffs. Once you've been rejected a certain number of times, your fear of rejection will tend to go away because you'll discover that you do survive and the world really doesn't come to an end. As you become less and less afraid of rejection, you'll become more and more assertive and adventuresome in your flirting and dating. You may have to date lots of people before you find a suitable mate. If you let your shyness hold you back because you can't stand the thought of being rejected, you may be ninety years old before you find that special person you're looking for.

Another advantage of rejection practice is that you'll

find you have a certain batting average. No one is 100 percent successful, and no one is 0 percent successful. Even if you "score" with only 10 or 20 percent of the people who interest you, this means that for every twenty rejections you collect, you will find between two and four people who are attracted to you. Having that many people to date is not a bad start, and you can build on those successes to improve your social life.

When you're involved in your rejection practice and you see someone attractive, you may get nervous because you may tell yourself, "She [or he] probably wouldn't be interested in someone like me. I'm not attractive or intelligent or charming enough." When you get rejected or turned down for a date, you may tell yourself, "I'm really no good. This shows what a loser I am." These negative thoughts can sabotage your efforts to connect with people. One way to overcome these thoughts is with the Daily Mood Log. If you write them down and talk back to them, you can keep a more realistic perspective and develop the warmth and self-confidence that will make people feel more attracted to you.

A lonely young woman named Sandy described how bitchy she acted when a good-looking male classmate stopped to say hello to her while she was walking across campus. While they spoke Sandy began to feel lonely and inferior and found herself getting angry, frustrated, and nervous. The kinds of messages Sandy was giving herself are illustrated in Figure 11-1. You can see how her lack of self-esteem undermines her. She tells herself that he couldn't *possibly* be interested in her and that he's just talking to her to be polite or because he has some ulterior motive. Then she feels rejected and tries to compensate for her hurt feelings by trying to convince herself that he's a loser who she couldn't possibly be interested in! It's little wonder she feels lonely and has trouble getting close to men.

Once Sandy wrote down these negative, self-defeating thoughts, it was easier for her to see how arbitrary and illogical they were (see Figure 11-1). Practicing this exercise with the Daily Mood Log over a period of time helped her feel more relaxed around men, and as she began to feel better about herself, her fear of rejection diminished and

FIGURE 11-1
The Daily Mood Log*

DESCRIBE THE UPSETTING EVENT—While I was walking across campus, Frank stopped me and began to chat. I've always thought he was attractive, but I felt annoyed while we were talking and I didn't act very friendly.

NEGATIVE FEELINGS—Record your emotions and rate each one on a scale from 0 (the least) to 100 (the most). Include feelings such as sad, anxious, angry, guilty, lonely, hopeless, frustrated, etc.

Emotion	Rating (0–100)	Emotion	Rating (0–100)	Emotion	Rating (0–100)
1. Defensive	90%	3. Frustrated	90%	5. Inferior	90%
2. Angry	90%	4. Lonely	90%	6.	

AUTOMATIC THOUGHTS Write down your negative thoughts and number them consecutively.	DISTORTIONS Identify the distortions in each "Automatic Thought."	RATIONAL RESPONSES Substitute more realistic and positive thoughts.
1. He probably just wants to walk away.	1. Mind reading.	1. I have no idea that he just wants to walk away. He's probably talking to me because he wants to.
2. He's prejudged me without giving me a chance.	2. Mind reading.	2. I have no evidence that he's prejudged me. The fact is that he's talking to me, and this can be my chance to get to know him.

AUTOMATIC THOUGHTS	DISTORTIONS	RATIONAL RESPONSES
3. I feel so uncomfortable when I'm around him that I wouldn't consider him a potential friend.	3. Emotional reasoning.	3. I feel uncomfortable because I'm inexperienced around men and I'm afraid of rejection. If I think of him as a potential friend and treat him in a positive way, I'll probably feel more relaxed.
4. He probably doesn't want to talk to me. He's just saying hello to be polite.	4. Disqualifying the positive.	4. He could be saying hello because he wants to. After all, he wasn't obligated to stop and talk to me.
5. He's a member of the Student Council so he probably feels superior.	5. Mind-reading; all-or-nothing thinking.	5. I'm probably the one who feels inferior and so I assume he thinks he's superior.
6. The only reason he's talking to me is because I'm a friend of Helen and he probably wants a date with Helen.	6. Disqualifying the positive.	6. If he wants a date with Helen he can ask her himself. He doesn't have to go through me.

AUTOMATIC THOUGHTS	DISTORTIONS	RATIONAL RESPONSES
7. I'm not interested in him.	7. Disqualifying the positive.	7. How do I know I'm not interested in him until I get to know him? He's attractive and intelligent and he might be a very interesting date.

OUTCOME—Review your "Rational Responses" and put a check in the box that describes how you now feel:
☐ not at all better; ☐ somewhat better; ☑ quite a bit better; ☐ a lot better.

---

*Copyright © 1984, David D. Burns, M.D., from *Intimate Connections* (New York: William Morrow & Company).

she discovered that men responded to her in a more positive, affectionate manner.

Men often feel just as shy and insecure. Nick is a lonely, thirty-four-year-old man who has a business selling appliances to builders. Although he's done very well in his work, it has been at the expense of his social life, because he's put in long, long hours in order to make a success of himself. Recently Nick began to feel lonely and unfulfilled, and he sought therapy to try to build his self-confidence so he could date, find a partner, and raise a family.

Like Sandy, Nick has many negative thoughts about rejection that make him tense and insecure whenever he tries to approach a woman who interests him. Figure 11-2 illustrates what he told himself when he noticed an attractive woman at a disco who was glancing at him. As you

FIGURE 11-2
The Daily Mood Log*

DESCRIBE THE UPSETTING EVENT—I see an attractive blond woman at a club. I'm afraid to go up and speak to her.

NEGATIVE FEELINGS—Record your emotions and rate each one on a scale from 0 (the least) to 100 (the most). Include feelings such as sad, anxious, angry, guilty, lonely, hopeless, frustrated, etc.

Emotion	Rating (0–100)	Emotion	Rating (0–100)	Emotion	Rating (0–100)
1. Anxious	80%	3.		5.	
2.		4.		6.	

AUTOMATIC THOUGHTS Write down your negative thoughts and number them consecutively.	DISTORTIONS Identify the distortions in each "Automatic Thought."	RATIONAL RESPONSES Substitute more realistic and positive thoughts.
1. I'm not attractive enough.	1. Fortune-telling; mind reading; all-or-nothing thinking.	1. I may not be unusually attractive but I look okay and there might be a certain chemistry between us.
2. I'm not the kind of stud she's looking for.	2. Labeling; mind reading.	2. I don't know her, so I don't know what turns her on. It's possible sbe may find me interesting and be attracted to me. She

AUTOMATIC THOUGHTS	DISTORTIONS	RATIONAL RESPONSES
		might be lonely and happy to have the chance to go out with me.
3. She's probably not what I'm looking for in a woman.	3. All-or-nothing thinking; emotional reasoning; fortune-telling.	3. I'm just making excuses for not going up to her because it's scary. Since I don't know her, I couldn't know what she's like.
4. She seems very sexy and desirable. She could get a better guy than me.	4. Jumping to conclusions; disqualifying the positive.	4. She does seem sexy and desirable, but I don't have to write myself off. What does the term "better guy" mean? Some things about me are "better," and some things about other people are "better." I may be better-looking than some men, and some men may be better-looking than I am. I won't know if she's interested in me until I go up and speak to her.

AUTOMATIC THOUGHTS	DISTORTIONS	RATIONAL RESPONSES
5. I will look like a fool trying to talk to her.	5. Fortune-telling; labeling.	5. I don't know what other people will think about me if I talk to her. They may not care one way or the other, or they may admire me for trying. If they think I'm "a fool," it will have to be their problem because this is something I want to do.

OUTCOME—Review your "Rational Responses" and put a check in the box that describes how you now feel:
☐ not at all better; ☑ somewhat better; ☐ quite a bit better; ☐ a lot better.

---

*Copyright © 1984, David D. Burns, M.D., from *Intimate Connections* (New York: William Morrow & Company).

can see, he began telling himself that he wasn't good enough for her and that she couldn't possibly be interested in him. Then, as a defense, he decided that he couldn't possibly be interested in her either. He defeats himself with a one-two punch within the first several seconds after their eyes meet! It's easy to understand why he feels insecure and inhibited about dating!

After he jotted down his negative thoughts on a napkin and talked back to them, he got enough courage to go up and say hello to her. After a brief conversation he invited her to a quiet nearby restaurant for a drink. She agreed, but the chemistry wasn't right and after a couple of drinks she left without giving him her phone number. Nick felt angry and discouraged, but he wrote down his negative thoughts and talked back to them again, as illustrated in Figure 11-3. This helped him give himself a little moral support instead of catastrophizing and telling himself he was a loser whose fate was sealed forever.

The idea that every human being is eminently lovable and interesting seems to me to be quite obvious but also quite revolutionary. Your capacity to be close to people has more to do with your willingness to be open and to solve the problems in your relationships than with some mystical quality of "worthwhileness" or "lovability." If it turns out that you're not someone's cup of tea, that's unfortunate. You may, in fact, be less intelligent or attractive than many other people. Who isn't? There are millions of people in the world who are smarter or sexier than both you and me. So what? How intelligent and attractive do we have to be to be worthwhile? To give and receive love? To feel joy and to be excited by our lives and by the people we meet?

The Fear of Success

Some readers who apply the principles I've outlined in these chapters will have the opposite problem. You may become *so* successful in your dating that you get frightened and overwhelmed. The sudden discovery that many people are very attracted to you can be just as nerve-racking as the prospect of constant rejection and loneliness. Maybe our Calvinist work ethic makes us suspicious of great levels of joy. You may feel that if things are going *too* well it means you've made a pact with the devil or that something has to be dreadfully wrong and your whole life is about to collapse.

A college student named Rex suffered from severe depression for many years. He was rigid and excessively serious. Although he was dating a young woman regularly, he was prone to jealousy attacks and was constantly ob-

FIGURE 11-3
The Daily Mood Log*

DESCRIBE THE UPSETTING EVENT—I met her and we went to a restaurant for a couple of drinks. I asked her if she wanted me to call her and she said no.

NEGATIVE FEELINGS—Record your emotions and rate each one on a scale from 0 (the least) to 100 (the most). Include feelings such as sad, anxious, angry, guilty, lonely, hopeless, frustrated, etc.

Emotion	Rating (0–100)	Emotion	Rating (0–100)	Emotion	Rating (0–100)
1. Sad	90%	3. Depressed	90%	5.	
2. Angry	90%	4.		6.	

AUTOMATIC THOUGHTS Write down your negative thoughts and number them consecutively.	DISTORTIONS Identify the distortions in each "Automatic Thought."	RATIONAL RESPONSES Substitute more realistic and positive thoughts.
1. I'm a loser.	1. All-or-nothing thinking; labeling.	1. She didn't want to go out with me. How does that make me "a loser"? Not evrybody is going to be turned on by me, and vice versa.
2. I'll never get a date or meet somebody.	2. Overgeneralization; fortune-telling.	2. I didn't get a date with her, but I am getting better at meeting women. If I

AUTOMATIC THOUGHTS	DISTORTIONS	RATIONAL RESPONSES
		hang in there, eventually I will meet somebody who's interested in me.

OUTCOME—Review your "Rational Responses" and put a check in the box that describes how you now feel:
☐ not at all better; ☐ somewhat better; ☑ quite a bit better; ☐ a lot better.

*Copyright © 1984, David D. Burns, M.D., from *Intimate Connections* (New York: William Morrow & Company).

sessed with the fear that she would reject him. He felt so insecure that he used to go and spy on her when she was at work to make sure she wasn't flirting with any customers.

Rex was a delightful patient because he worked incredibly hard to overcome his depression. Prior to our first meeting he had read my book *Feeling Good: The New Mood Therapy* from cover to cover and had completed over 600 pages of self-help assignments!

His depression was severe and intractable. We struggled together for over nine months. Little by little he conquered it and began to experience greater happiness and self-confidence. Once the depression was gone, he continued to work on his personal relationships. He wanted to learn to be more lighthearted and to date more. He followed all my suggestions to the T. He started lifting weights to improve his physique, and pretty soon he looked like Superman. He bought some spiffy clothing and worked on flirting and smiling and coming across in a more sensual, relaxed way. He became enormously charming and women seemed to find him irresistible. He seemed like a child with a new toy. Everywhere he went he would talk to people, and he seemed to make friends instantly because he felt turned on by almost everyone he met. Women were giving him their phone numbers left and right, and he started going out more and more. More often than not these women developed crushes on him, and vice versa. The only problem was that this began happening almost every day because he was radiating so much warmth and self-confidence. For someone who had spent years and years drowning in self-doubt and obsessive worry, the sudden transformation was remarkable.

Once it dawned on Rex just how popular he was getting, he began to get terrified. Things were just *too* good, and so it seemed there just had to be a catch somewhere. Would he get a reputation as a Romeo? What would his parents think of him if they found out what an incredible social life he was having? What if all his friends started to hate him because they felt jealous of all his success?

Writing down his negative thoughts and talking back to them (see Figure 11-4) helped Rex understand and overcome these fears so he could enjoy all these marvelous experiences. He discovered that underneath his fear of success was the fear of rejection. As he thought this through more realistically, he realized that while some people would be envious and a few might reject him, most of his friends were attracted to him because of his warmth and his genuine liking for people. He began to fall in love on a weekly basis. Life became a joyous adventure.

I think that most of us have that same potential within ourselves to unleash great feelings of intimacy and excitement. This is not magic or fantasy—it's simply the power of love and self-esteem. The sad thing is how much joy we miss out on when we give in to our self-doubts and fears.

I recently received a letter from Rex. I thought you might enjoy reading it, and with his kind permission I am reproducing it here.

June 10, 1984

Dear David,

Please accept my apologies for such a long period of silence. While the silence itself is not a good thing, I know that there is a truly positive aspect to it. I've been maintaining a "zero" BDI* since our last meeting—in fact I want to say that it's been better than "zero." I've been feeling great! I often wish I could videotape a couple of days from the past few months and send it to you. Then you could really see how I've come out of the "insecure shell" and into the real world as a talented individual with a lot of popularity, nonstop smiles, good humor, and plenty of radiating self-esteem. My personality is bubbling out at its best. I think you understand how I'm feeling since you have tried so hard (and quite successfully, I might add) to get me to realize my full potential.

FIGURE 11-4
The Daily Mood Log*

DESCRIBE THE UPSETTING EVENT—I'm beginning to meet and date more and more women, but at times I get frightened and feel like climbing back into my old shell.

NEGATIVE FEELINGS—Record your emotions and rate each one on a scale from 0 (the least) to 100 (the most). Include feelings such as sad, anxious, angry, guilty, lonely, hopeless, frustrated, etc.

Emotion	Rating (0–100)	Emotion	Rating (0–100)	Emotion	Rating (0–100)
1. Anxious	90%	3.		5.	
2. Guilty	90%	4.		6.	

AUTOMATIC THOUGHTS	DISTORTIONS	RATIONAL RESPONSES
Write down your negative thoughts and number them consecutively.	Identify the distortions in each "Automatic Thought."	Substitute more realistic and positive thoughts.

*The "BDI" is a test to measure depression. A zero is an extremely low score that indicates virtually no symptoms of depression. For further information, see D. D. Burns, M.D., "Diagnosing Your Moods," Chapter 2 of *Feeling Good: The New Mood Therapy,* op. cit.

AUTOMATIC THOUGHTS	DISTORTIONS	RATIONAL RESPONSES
1. If I keep this up, I'll be under constant pressure to mantain the image. Then if I don't live up to the image, I'll be rejected. I'll end up all by myself—I'll be a nobody.	1. Fortune-telling; mind reading.	1. I don't have to maintain any "image." I can date as much or as little as I want. It's unlikely that everyone will reject me. In fact, I have more friends than ever before.
2. Other people will get jealous of me and dislike me. They could even confront me and try to make a fool of me.	2. Fortune-telling; mind reading; labeling.	2. Some people may get jealous, and others will become better friends. I may act foolish at times, but that's not the end of the world.
3. Girls will want to get as close to me as they can, and if I tell them I don't want to get attached yet, they'll become depressed and reject me. They'll think I'm a shameless womanizer.	3. Personalization.	3. It's true that when you break up with someone who's still attracted to you, they might have hurt feelings. This is all a part of dating. It can work the other way, too.

AUTOMATIC THOUGHTS	DISTORTIONS	RATIONAL RESPONSES
4. People are probably getting jealous of me because I'm in such a good mood most of the time.	4. Mind reading; disqualifying the positive.	4. Most people enjoy someone who's in a good mood, as long as you don't get arrogant or insensitive.
5. Even girls who have boyfriends look at me, make eyes at me, and flirt. It makes it seem like I'm a home wrecker.	5. Labeling; disqualifying the positive; personalization.	5. I'm not responsible if a woman flirts with me. It means I'm attractive and I can enjoy it. If she's not married, I have every right to date her.
6. If my parents knew about my reputation, they'd be upset with me. They would tell me that I shouldn't be fooling around or having fun but concentrating on my studies instead.	6. Personalization; mind reading.	6. My parents are probably glad I'm having fun and am no longer depressed. As long as I keep up with my studies, they have no reason to feel concerned about my social success.

AUTOMATIC THOUGHTS	DISTORTIONS	RATIONAL RESPONSES
7. I feel strange going to the disco because when I dance, people look at me. They probably think I'm strange or just trying to show off. They are probably making jokes about me behind my back.	7. Disqualifying the positive; mind reading.	7. I have a good physique and I'm an excellent dancer. People probably enjoy seeing me dance. If someone wants to joke about me, that's okay.
8. Other guys will dislike me and think that I'm just showing off because I know all those girls.	8. Mind reading; disqualifying the positive.	8. If I don't act like a know-it-all, other guys will probably admire all my success and want me to show them how to do it!

OUTCOME—Review your "Rational Responses" and put a check in the box that describes how you now feel:
☐ not at all better; ☐ somewhat better; ☐ quite a bit better; ☑ a lot better.

*Copyright © 1984, David D. Burns, M.D., from *Intimate Connections* (New York: William Morrow & Company).

I'll attempt to give you some examples of my success—a difficult task in such a short text. On May 24 I celebrated my twenty-second birthday and a group of my friends gave me a surprise birthday party. The gifts I received amazed me—nice shirts, cologne, dinner at a nice restaurant, cakes—the list goes on. My birthday was last week and I'm still getting things.

Another example. Breaking myself from the "compulsion" of falling in love and getting serious with every girl I meet and go out with has been one of the most exciting events of my life. I've been taking different girls out and having girls ask me out.

In July my ex-fiancée came back from Germany and I decided to break up with her entirely—one of the best decisions that I've made! We still see each other on occasion just to exchange greetings.

One thing I did want to mention was about the fear of success. I remember our discussion concerning that fear and how that could be a cause for my not using my full potential. With my success I've confronted that fear. I guess I get scared of the idea that people could be jealous or dislike me because of my popularity. They could think that I'm just an insecure show-off (why would that bother me if they did?). Anyway, I welcome the challenge to overcome the fear.

I hope that all has been well with you. As we had discussed before, if you would like me to review the manuscript for your new book, please let me know and I'd be glad to help out. I will be a better letter writer from now on to keep you posted as how things are going. In the meantime, I wish you the best of success on everything that you are currently working on.

Most sincerely,
Rex

PART FIVE

MAKING LOVE: YOUR PERSONAL SEXUAL GROWTH PROGRAM

12

For Men Only: New Ways to Overcome Impotence and Sexual Insecurity

As intimate relationships with the people you're dating begin to evolve, you'll be confronted with the challenges of sexuality. This means the potential for enhancing your relationship and adding greater trust and joy, but it also raises the possibility of a number of new sources of insecurity. What if you're starting to make love with a woman and your penis won't respond by getting hard? What if you come too quickly? Or can't come at all?

These problems are often caused by feelings of anxiety and insecurity. While writers and sexual counselors emphasize the enormous importance that our feelings can have on our capacity for sexual satisfaction, few, if any, systematic methods have been developed to help people identify and modify the thought patterns that lead to sexual anxiety and inhibitions. Men who have trouble with erections because of "performance anxiety" are advised to relax and to stop being so preoccupied with sexual success or failure. They are told to avoid "spectatoring"—constantly watching to see whether their penises are erect as if they were under the spotlight in a crucial stage performance. Instead they are advised to try to get into the here and now and to enjoy themselves. But how, precisely, are they to do this? How can you relax when your wife or girl friend is frantically trying to "help" stimulate your flaccid penis with her hand or mouth because it just won't respond? How can you "flow with the here and now" when your every muscle is rigid and you're telling yourself, "I'm blowing it again! This is terrible! What's wrong with me? What will she think of me?''

I've developed specific techniques to help men modify the negative thinking patterns that can lead to sexual problems. As you learn to change your attitudes about sex, you can gain greater self-confidence and overcome your sexual fears and inhibitions. This can enhance your capacity to enjoy sex and make you feel more creative and erotic. It can also help you learn to communicate more frankly and openly with your partner.

Suppose that a slim, attractive blonde walked into a cocktail party. How would the men in the room feel? One man might feel sexually turned on, because he thinks: "Gee, she looks exciting. I wonder if she's available.'' A second man might feel anxious and shy, because he tells himself: "She's really gorgeous, but she probably wouldn't be interested in someone like me.'' A third man might feel guilty, because he has a sexual fantasy about her and tells himself: "I really shouldn't have fantasies about someone other than my wife.'' A fourth man might feel angry, because he has the thought: "She's probably the stuck-up type.'' And if there are ten different men in the room, they may *all* have different reactions to her.

Now—who creates all these feelings in the men? Does she? Is she simultaneously "turning on" the men who feel attracted to her and "turning off" the men who aren't? This is obviously absurd. They actually create their own reactions because of the different ways they think about her. This insight is the basis for the cognitive approach to sexuality, which depends on several simple ideas. The first idea is that your thoughts and "cognitions"—what you are telling yourself and thinking—turn you on and off sexually. This means that your sexual excitement originates *above* your neck. The second premise is that when you are having sexual problems, such as impotence or guilt or a loss of interest in sex, negative thoughts and irrational attitudes about sex will often contribute to the problem. The final premise is that if you are willing to get rid of these self-defeating beliefs and learn to think about yourself and your sexual partner in a more realistic and positive way, you can become a better lover and improve your sex life.

One disclaimer is necessary. While thoughts and attitudes can play a major role in your sexual functioning, there are numerous factors that may cause sexual difficulties. Anyone with a persistent sexual problem should seek professional consultation with a qualified clinic or physician specializing in sexual disorders so that the problem can be properly diagnosed and treated. There are many effective interventions, including education, medical and surgical treatments, individual psychotherapy or couples therapy, as well as behavioral therapies like the "Sensate Focus" techniques pioneered by Dr. William H. Masters and Virginia E. Johnson.

Overcoming Impotence and Erection Anxiety: Jack is an intense, good-looking thirty-four-year-old divorced professor with dark hair and eyes who teaches economics at a prominent New York university. After he separated from his wife several years ago, Jack began to feel lonely and down on himself and had a hard time getting close to women. Part of the problem was that he was just too eager. He came on a little too strong because he was trying so hard, and then women would get turned off and dump him. Jack believed these continual rejections meant he was basically inferior or that something was wrong with him. This made him feel even more insecure, so he'd try harder, creating a vicious cycle of rejection.

Toward the beginning of therapy, Jack worked on building up his low self-esteem and overcoming his shyness and loneliness using methods similar to the ones described in the previous chapters. The solution involved overcoming the fear of rejection and learning how to feel happy and contented when he was alone. Using the Pleasure Predicting Sheet described in Chapter Three put the lie to his belief that he *needed* a woman to feel fulfilled, because he discovered he was often as happy as a lark when he was by himself, involved in his work. Although that might seem trivial or obvious to some people, to Jack it was an incredible revelation and freed him from the desperate neediness that was driving women away. As Jack discovered how to feel relaxed and comfortable with himself, dating became less important to him. And women immediately began to show much more interest in him. That's the way it almost always works—once you stop needing women so much, they become much more interested in you.

Soon he began dating a young woman named Jean on a regular basis. He was thrilled but apprehensive, because a new problem surfaced—he was terrified that he might not be able to get an erection when the time came to perform in bed. Although he'd functioned adequately with his wife, they'd had some sexual difficulties that were resolved in therapy. But Jack felt that making love to Jean for the first time would put tremendous pressure on him. He was afraid that if he failed sexually he'd be rejected and might never have the chance to develop the kind of intimate, relaxed relationship that would allow him to have erections during lovemaking.

I asked Jack to fantasize that he and Jean were in bed for the first time and to tell me about his thoughts and feelings so I could learn more about his fears.

JACK: I'm imagining that we're lying in bed caressing each other. She's playing with my penis but it takes a longer time to get erect than it used to with my wife. That's because I was more relaxed with my wife.

DR. BURNS: And how would you be feeling if your penis didn't become erect?

JACK: I'd feel worried! What if I can't get it up? What will she think of me? I'd get frustrated and angry and feel humiliated.

DR. BURNS: And why would you be feeling that way? What are you thinking?

JACK: I'm thinking that she won't like me if I can't perform adequately. She might despise me. This might mean there was something permanently wrong with me. And what if she told the fellow who introduced us? Then he'd look down on me because I was so unmanly. She'd jilt me and tell her friends that I had "a problem." Then the word would get around and people would think I was weird.

This brief dialogue revealed several irrational beliefs that were making Jack feel anxious:

Belief Number 1. Impotence is unusual and shameful. If you don't get an erection it means you're less of a man.

Belief Number 2. Not getting an erection necessarily

means there's something seriously wrong with you. The problem will probably get worse and worse and become a constant pattern of failure.

Belief Number 3. You must impress a woman with your penis and your sexual experience so she'll respect you and know how special and worthwhile you are. She'll necessarily look down on you if you don't get an erection. Any sexual failure makes you less lovable and desirable.

Belief Number 4. If one woman rejects you, every woman will reject you because they're all clones who think exactly alike. The news that you're a loser will spread like wildfire and soon you'll be totally alone and miserable.

Nearly all the single men I've treated who feel insecure about getting erections buy into these beliefs. Let's examine each one of them. Jack's first belief is that the failure to get an erection is very unusual and would mean that he wasn't very manly. This attitude is almost universal among men with impotence problems, but it's hardly realistic. Since only a man can fail to get an erection, it is, by definition, a uniquely "manly" experience. So it can hardly make you *less* of a man! Few men, if any, are perfect erection machines throughout their lives. In fact, the majority of men have experienced at least one episode of impotence at some time in their lives. Jack's real problem is *not* lack of an erection, but the *fear and shame* he feels because of the harsh judgments he levels against himself whenever he falls short of his expectations for himself. This lack of compassion and self-acceptance is a far greater barrier to love and intimacy than any technical problems he might have with sex. Jack's inability to love and accept himself was one of the problems that initially led to his loneliness and shyness as well as his sexual insecurities.

The lack of an erection need not diminish any man's ability to give and receive love or to participate as a fully competent sexual partner. Many men with spinal cord injuries that prevent erections can satisfy their wives with oral or manual sex. Many couples find their sexual pleasure enhanced with the use of sexual devices such as vibrators. As long as you have self-esteem and are willing to love your partner without putting yourself down, the lack of an erection need not be an insurmountable problem.

Jack's second belief is the idea that failure to get an erection would mean there was something seriously wrong with him. Certainly there are a number of medical conditions and interpersonal problems that can lead to impotence (see Table 12-1), but by far the commonest cause is performance anxiety—the constant self-monitoring and the negative messages you give yourself that failure to get an erection would be catastrophic. Most frequently, the problem is not that there really is something wrong with you, but that you are telling yourself there is.

Table 12-1
Causes of Impotence*

1. *Alcohol*. Although some people believe alcohol is an aphrodisiac because it can lower your inhibitions, significant alcohol intoxication as well as chronic alcohol abuse frequently lead to impotence and a loss of libido.

2. *Street drugs*. Many drugs can cause sexual problems, including impotence, delayed ejaculation, and decreased sexual drive. Common offenders include:
   - Sedatives such as Quaaludes or barbiturates.
   - Narcotics such as heroin.
   - Cocaine.
   - Amphetamines.
   - Amyl nitrite.
   - Hallucinogens such as LSD.
   - Marijuana, in chronic use.

3. *Prescription drugs*. Many drugs your physician might prescribe can lead to impotence, decreased sexual drive, or delayed ejaculation. If you are taking any prescription drug and have concerns about sexual difficulties, check with your druggist or physician. Some of the commonest offenders include:
   - Certain drugs used in the treatment of hypertension or heart disorders, such as guanethidine (Esimil or Ismelin), alpha-methyldopa (Aldomet), propranalol (Inderal), or clonidine (Catapres).
   - The anabolic steroids used by weight lifters are frequently taken far in excess of the prescribed dose. This turns off the hypothalamus in the brain and causes the testicles to shrink. The

*This table was adapted from lecture materials presented by Robert Kolodny, M.D., the associate director of the Masters and Johnson Institute.

weight lifters may erroneously attribute their loss of sexual drive to the rigors of training.

• Some major tranquilizers: Mellaril can delay or retard ejaculation, and Haldol is associated with impotence in 20 percent or more of users.

• Certain antidepressants, such as the mono-amine oxidase inhibitor Nardil, can lead to delayed ejaculation.

• Lithium—as many as 20 percent of men may develop erection difficulties.

• Anticholinergic agents, such as atropine.

• Sleeping pills and sedatives.

• Antabuse.

• Antihistamines—women may develop insufficient vaginal lubrication for intercourse.

4. *Medical Disorders*. The following list is not comprehensive. Any man or woman with significant, recurrent sexual difficulties should have a consultation with a urologist or other physician so that any illness or condition that may contribute to the problem can be properly diagnosed and treated.

• Hormonal diseases, including diabetes, thyroid abnormalities, and pituitary or adrenal tumors.

• Urologic problems such as urinary tract infections, suprapubic prostatectomy, and Peyronie's disease.

• Heart, lung, and vascular diseases such as emphysema or uncontrolled congestive heart failure.

• Neurologic disorders, including multiple sclerosis, spinal cord tumors, Parkinsonism, and cerebral palsy.

• Liver or kidney failure.

• Obesity.

• Lead or herbicide poisoning.

• Vaginismus (involuntary vaginal spasms in the woman which make penile penetration difficult).

5. *Emotional Problems*. A psychological, emotional cause of impotence is suspected when:

• The problem occurs with some sexual partners but not with others.

• The man can attain a satisfactory erection during masturbation but not during intercourse.

• The man sometimes wakes up in the middle of the night or in the morning with an adequate erection.

• The problem is sporadic and occurs on some occasions but not on others.

Psychological causes of sexual problems can include:

• Depression—a loss of libido is one of the commonest symptoms of depression. Other symptoms of depression include sadness, guilt, a loss of interest in life, irritability, indecisiveness, low self-esteem, insomnia, loss of motivation, fatigue, and feelings of discouragement.

• Fears and Phobias—concerns about pregnancy or venereal diseases such as herpes can lead to impotence.

• Performance anxiety—sexual insecurity and fear of failure are among the commonest causes of impotence.

• Relationship conflicts—sexual problems can often result from unexpressed anger, unresolved power struggles, or jealousy.

• Guilt and shame due to strong religious and moral prohibitions against sex can lead to impotence.

Jack's third belief involves the idea that Jean will necessarily love him less if he experiences a sexual failure. Although there may be some women who would be so demanding, most of them don't function like this. And if Jean *did* reject him because he had difficulties getting an erection the first time they made love, would that really be the end of the world? Would Jack want to spend his life with someone so insecure and uncompassionate? In point of fact, Jean is probably far more concerned with being loved and cared about than with being impressed by the stiffness or size of Jack's erect penis. I do not mean to imply that sexual technique is irrelevant, but if Jack gets fixated on his anatomy he may selfishly lose sight of how Jean feels and forget about the importance of touching and sharing intimate feelings with her.

The preoccupation with getting an erection sometimes results from sexual perfectionism. Our society is so obsessed with success that we may feel immense anxiety when we fail to achieve all our goals. Little boys are told they must always try to win the race because there's something extra special about being Number One. You buy into this destructive value system when you tell yourself that you're a failure if you don't perform perfectly in every sexual situation. How sad to think you must *earn* a woman's love by impressing her with how smart or macho you are. How lonely it must be to feel convinced that you can't be loved and accepted as a fallible, vulnerable human being. You may become so involved with making judgments about your sexual "success" or "failure" that you become blind to your partner's needs and feelings. In reality, there is no such thing as success or failure. These are just imaginary concepts we make up. When you apply these concepts to problems involving sexuality and intimacy, they can be very destructive. Real intimacy has more to do with sharing yourself—including your positive and negative experiences—openly and without shame.

Some men will say, "But success *is* important, because if I don't get an erection I *really might* be rejected." Okay, let's assume you don't get an erection and your partner gets tense or annoyed. Ask yourself why she might be reacting this way. Why is she so uptight about the situation? Perhaps she's thinking it's *her* fault—maybe she feels she's not sexy or attractive enough. Maybe she feels hurt and she's putting pressure on you so she won't have to feel inadequate. Either way, it's a mistake to assume that her tension means that you don't measure up. What's really going on is a *folie à deux:* Your insecurities and lack of self-esteem trigger hers, and vice versa, and you both end up feeling awkward and miserable.

Jack's fourth belief is that if Jean rejects him, then every woman will. I call this the "brushfire fallacy." It's the idea that one rejection will spread like wildfire and soon you'll end up isolated and ostracized by the whole human race. This is quite unrealistic, because people react so differently. What turns one person on may turn another person off. The idea that all human beings will react to you the same way is sheer nonsense.

Daily Mood Log. You can often modify these self-defeating attitudes with the Daily Mood Log, as illustrated in Figure 12-1. Try to pinpoint what you would be telling yourself if you were having difficulties getting an erection and write them down in the "Automatic Thoughts" column. You might be thinking "What's wrong with me? Why isn't it getting hard yet? What's she going to think of me? She probably thinks I'm gay. She'll think I'm no good in bed. She'll think my penis is small. The last guy she slept with probably had a nine-inch rod!" Now try to

FIGURE 12-1
The Daily Mood Log*

DESCRIBE THE UPSETTING EVENT—I imagine trying to make love and being unable to get an erection.

NEGATIVE FEELINGS—Record your emotions and rate each one on a scale from 0 (the least) to 100 (the most). Include feelings such as sad, anxious, angry, guilty, lonely, hopeless, frustrated, etc.

Emotion	Rating (0–100)	Emotion	Rating (0–100)	Emotion	Rating (0–100)
1. Anxious	99%	3. Inadequate	99%	5.	
2. Frustrated	99%	4.		6.	

AUTOMATIC THOUGHTS Write down your negative thoughts and number them consecutively.	DISTORTIONS Identify the distortions in each "Automatic Thought."	RATIONAL RESPONSES Substitute more realistic and positive thoughts.
1. She'll think I have an awfully small penis.	1. Mind reading.	1. I can't file for an extension! She'll have to learn to appreciate the penis I've got.
2. She'll think I'm gay.	2. Mind reading.	2. There's no reason to believe she'll think I'm gay. Many men have difficulties getting erections at some time in their lives.

AUTOMATIC THOUGHTS	DISTORTIONS	RATIONAL RESPONSES
3. She'll think I'm no good in bed.	3. Mind reading.	3. I can ask her about this. She's may think that *she* isn't sexy enough. Talking it out might make both of us feel better. Anyway, there's nothing shameful about being sexually inexperienced.
4. What's wrong with me? I should be able to get it up.	4. "Should" statement.	4. There's nothing "wrong" with me. I'm feeling nervous and that's perfectly natural.
5. But what if I *never* get an erection again?	5. Overgeneralization; fortune-telling.	5. I've gotten erections in the past, so I'll undoubtedly get them again in the future.
6. It would be awful not to get an erection. She'd probably reject me.	6. Magnification.	6. There's nothing "awful" about not getting an erection. I can give and receive pleasure through massage and touching whether or not I have an

AUTOMATIC THOUGHTS	DISTORTIONS	RATIONAL RESPONSES
		erection. If she rejected me it would be uncomfortable but it wouldn't be the end of the world, because it would mean she was awfully narrow-minded. I've been happy without her in the past, so I can be happy without her in the future if I have to.

OUTCOME—Review your "Rational Responses" and put a check in the box that describes how you now feel:
☐ not at all better; ☐ somewhat better; ☑ quite a bit better; ☐ a lot better.

---

*Copyright © 1984, David D. Burns, M.D., from *Intimate Connections* (New York: William Morrow & Company).

---

identify the distortions in these thoughts. Here are some of the commonest ones:

• Mind reading. You automatically assume that a woman will think less of you if you don't get an erection.

• Fortune-telling. You work yourself into a state of panic before and during sex by predicting that you're not going to get an erection.

• "Should" statements. You try to force your penis to get stiff by telling yourself you "should" or "must" or "have to" get an erection.

• Overgeneralization. You assume that one bad sexual

experience will become a never-ending pattern of humiliation and sexual failure.

• Personalization. You assume it's entirely your responsibility to make your partner feel happy and sexually excited. If she isn't excited or she gets angry, you tell yourself it's all your fault.

• Magnification. You feel that if you don't get an erection it will be a catastrophe.

Once you've identified these distortions in your negative thoughts, substitute others that are more objective and compassionate in the right-hand column. If you have trouble thinking of rational responses, ask yourself what you'd say to a friend who had trouble getting an erection. Would you put him down and tell him he's an unmanly wimp? Or would you be supportive and encouraging? Then why not talk to yourself in the same reassuring way you would talk to a friend? That's the meaning of self-esteem and self-esteem is the basis of a good sexual relationship.

The Feared-Fantasy Technique. Men with difficulties getting erections nearly always assume that anyone who found out about their difficulties would look down on them. One of Jack's fear was that if he failed to get an erection Jean would tell the fellow who introduced them and then the word would spread that he was a "weirdo." During therapy I helped him confront these fears with the Feared-Fantasy Technique that was described in Chapter Four. I asked Jack to play the role of a hostile critic who was trying to put him down because he was unable to get an erection with Jean. I played his role to show him how to respond to this criticism. The Feared-Fantasy Technique can be enormously useful because you discover that you could handle the worst things that a person could say to you about a sexual failure without being perturbed. Although such a sadistic dialogue would rarely, if ever, happen in reality, it helped Jack see how unnecessary it was to be afraid of putdowns and insults.

JACK (AS HOSTILE CRITIC): I heard you couldn't get it up with Jean the other night. Is that true?

DR. B (PLAYING JACK'S ROLE): That's true. I was feeling nervous and I had trouble getting an erection.

JACK (AS CRITIC): Well, what's wrong with you? You some kind of a fag or something?

DR. B (AS JACK): Far from it. But I am a little inexperienced and shy when I go to bed with someone the first time. Do you think that means I'm a "fag"?

JACK (AS CRITIC): Well, Jean was telling all her friends what a little dork you have and they were laughing at you.

DR. B (AS JACK): I'm glad you told me that. It sounds like Jean and her friends are very interested in the size of my penis. It sounds like you're quite concerned about my penis, too. Are you?

JACK (AS CRITIC): Well, what's wrong with you? A real man can get it up! Is Jean too much woman for you?

DR. B (AS JACK): It's interesting that you think a "real man" should always be able to get it up. I know I feel a little nervous sometimes, especially at first. How does that make me less of a man? Don't you ever feel nervous? Do you think a "real man" has to feel confident all the time?

JACK (AS CRITIC): Well I do! I *never* feel nervous and I always have magnificent erections that thrill the ladies.

DR. B (AS JACK): Well it sounds like you're much more sexually experienced than I am. Do you think less of me for that?

JACK (AS CRITIC): Of course I think less of you!

DR. B. (AS JACK): And why is that? Do you only associate with men who always feel supremely self-confident and always get stiff erections? Why are you so obsessed with men's erections?

JACK (AS CRITIC): Touché!

This dialogue helped Jack see that even in the event that people found out he had trouble getting an erection, any negativity they felt toward him was likely to be the result of their own immaturity rather than any lack of manliness on his part. We also reversed roles so he could learn to talk back to the imaginary critic. Jack and I also used the Feared-Fantasy Technique to show how he could respond to a hostile woman who was trying to put him down because he didn't get an erection when he went to bed with her.

If you have this type of fear, try writing out an imaginary dialogue of this type. If you have a creative, uninhibited friend, try role-playing the way Jack and I did. Acting out your fears or seeing on paper just how ridiculous the critic's worst insults really are can be surprisingly liberating!

Fantasy Enhancement: In addition to thinking about sex in a self-defeating way and arousing yourself to panic states by predicting failure and humiliation, you may fill your mind with frightening fantasies instead of sexually exciting ones. Before sex you may picture yourself lying in bed feeling tense and miserable as you desperately try to get your limp penis up. During sex you may have all kinds of unpleasant fantasies. You may think of mowing the lawn or being fired as you ask your boss for a raise. The negative effects of these pictures are just as destructive as your self-critical thoughts because they turn off the pleasure centers in your brain and activate negative emotions like fear and guilt.

One antidote to this was suggested by a patient of mine named Mark, who sought treatment because of his lifelong homosexual fixation on young boys. Although Mark was married, he had never found women sexually interesting and his fantasies had always involved boys. On two occasions he had tried to act on these homosexual impulses and had gotten into trouble with the police and with the parents of the boys with devastating emotional effects. In spite of the fact that he was overwhelmed with shame and sexual frustration, he was hesitant to give up these fantasies because they were the only thing in life that gave him any pleasure at all. The prognosis did not seem especially bright, since he had not responded to more than a decade of psychotherapy with several talented therapists using a variety of approaches.

After Mark and I tried a number of techniques that weren't particularly productive, he came up with an unusual suggestion I was initially quite skeptical about. He reasoned that if he would simply practice putting sexual fantasies about women in his mind over and over again, eventually they might start to activate the sexual centers in his brain so he could become more attracted to women. It seemed like a harmless idea, so I instructed him to get a wrist counter*

---

*A wrist counter resembles a watch, and you can use it to count things; golfers often use them to keep track of their scores. You can purchase them for under $10 in golf shops or sporting-good stores.

and whenever he saw a woman—regardless of her age or appearance—he was to create a sexual fantasy about her and to count it on his wrist clicker *whether or not he found the fantasy stimulating or exciting*. For example, when he saw an elderly man and woman sitting on a park bench, he imagined them making love on the spot after she did a strip tease for him. The fantasy was not particularly arousing or sexually exciting to him, but Mark counted it on his wrist clicker because he remembered to create it.

Initially he found the exercise quite unappealing, so he would do it only once a week before his sessions. He would walk around the university campus for an hour, making up sexual fantasies about the coeds, and click his wrist counter over and over. None of the fantasies were stimulating to him, but he dutifully continued the exercise. He gradually accumulated more and more counts. After a period of six to eight weeks, his total fantasy count had risen to over one thousand, and a funny thing happened. Some of the images began to seem mildly interesting to him, so he became motivated to create the fantasies more and more frequently. As his sexual fantasy total approached two thousand he began to experience some pronounced sexual reactions from them. As the total rose toward three thousand these effects became stronger and stronger, and once he surpassed three thousand they became extremely profound. He said that he would often remain in a state of sustained sexual excitement with more or less continual erections that lasted for several days at a time! He began to think about women constantly, and his brain became so programmed by this exercise that he found he would get spontaneous erections simply by reaching over and touching the counter on his wrist!

Next he started developing fantasies about his wife. After a period of time these, too, became arousing. The proof of the effectiveness of the method was the forty-fifth birthday card he got from his wife which read: "HAPPY BIRTHDAY, HOT STUFF!" This was a dramatic change for someone who'd had such an impoverished sex life.

I was sufficiently impressed with this method that I began to try it with other men who had less severe sexual inhibitions and problems. I would instruct them to put sexual fantasies in their minds every time they saw a woman and to keep track of the total number of these fantasies with wrist counters or by putting marks on three-by-five cards. After several days or weeks they would usually report a powerful increase in their sexual desires.

You might want to try this method and see how well it works for you. Over the next several days, whenever you see people of the opposite sex, create sexual fantasies about them. Count each one, *whether or not you find it exciting*. The sexual excitement will usually begin after you have generated enough of these fantasies.

You can also modify your spontaneous sexual fantasies. You may find that you inadvertently turn yourself off during sex with unhappy memories or thoughts of filling out your federal income tax forms. You're not obligated to do this to yourself! Instead, substitute creative positive fantasies for the negative ones that are causing the problems for you. There's no law against it!

You may be afraid of your fantasies—you may think they are dangerously "kinky" or odd, or you may think that it isn't "nice" or morally acceptable to have thoughts of sex with someone other than your partner. Trying to turn these strange fantasies off during lovemaking will simply create anxiety and inhibit your spontaneity and pleasure. The fantasies themselves are generally harmless and can even enhance and enrich your lovemaking. The real problem is probably your fear of these fantasies and your attempt to control them. Accepting them as a normal, healthy part of sexuality without resisting or fighting them is usually far more effective.

A high school teacher named Harold was disturbed because during intercourse he'd sometimes get stimulated by fantasies of being tied up and teased by some domineering woman. He believed these impulses were terribly abnormal and felt he needed some deep prolonged psychotherapy to try to understand their origin so he could get rid of them. I suggested to Harold that most of us are "stuck" with a number of these unusual fantasies. Even if it seemed inappropriate to act on them, he could nonetheless consider the option of simply accepting and enjoying them instead of berating himself for having them. That way he wouldn't have to spend years fighting off the images that most aroused him. He found it a relief to learn that it was okay to enjoy these fantasies, and he saved himself a prolonged, costly, and possibly unproductive course of treatment.

Paradoxical Techniques. One of the secrets of enjoying sex is to eliminate the pressure to perform, so that intercourse becomes an option but not a requirement. Many sex counselors handle this by instructing couples in therapy not to have intercourse during the early part of treatment. They are taught mutual pleasuring techniques, called "sensate focus" exercises, originally developed by Dr. William Masters and Virginia Johnson. These exercises involve touching and massage in the absence of any need to have intercourse. When you know you're not permitted to have intercourse, these exercises become so relaxing and exciting that many men experience spontaneous erections. Sensate focus training has helped many couples overcome problems like impotence and premature ejaculation and can help couples without any specific sexual problems enhance their sexual skills and satisfaction.*

Single men who are dating can also capitalize on the paradoxical idea that you can stimulate sexual excitement by "forbidding" intercourse. You have to be innovative in the way you do it, since you will probally feel you can't tell your date in so many words that you want to do sex therapy to overcome your impotence problem! However, with a little imagination you can make the paradoxical technique work for you, even if you're single.

A thirty-six-year-old medical technologist named Leonard was quite popular and had no problems getting dates, but he nearly always had difficulties getting an erection the first time he tried to make love. He felt so worried about whether or not he could perform that he simply couldn't get an erection. What made the problem even worse was

---

*Readers interested in learning more about sensate focus exercises may want to consult: P. E. Raley, *Making Love: How to Be Your Own Sex Therapist* (New York: Dial Press, 1976); B. W. McCarthy, M. Ryan, and F. A. Johnson, *Sexual Awareness* (San Francisco: Scrimshaw Press, 1975).

that on several occasions women had berated him for being a tease and enticing them to bed and then not "putting out."

Leonard and I talked about how he could feel more relaxed the first time he went to bed with a woman. We came up with a strategy that worked like a charm. I'm hesitant to share it with you because it might sound a little Machiavellian, but I suspect there are millions of anxious men out there who will benefit by reading about it. Here is the method: The first time Leonard found himself at a new girl friend's apartment, he would tell her he didn't like one-night stands or hopping into the sack with each woman he met, because he would like to get to know her better before they made love. He would then suggest it might be enjoyable to spend the night together so they could cuddle and relax, as long as she agreed not to have intercourse so early in their relationship.

The next session Leonard was quite animated. He'd tried this with a woman he'd been dating. She said she appreciated how sensitive he was and explained how she was tired of meeting men who would pressure her for sex the first chance they got. Following this conversation, they took off their clothes and got into bed and began to kiss and caress each other. Since it was clear that intercourse was strictly "prohibited," Leonard felt completely relaxed and aroused. Soon he had a marvelous erection, which led to some glorious lovemaking!

How a Woman Can Help You Overcome Erection Anxiety. Your date may inadvertently feed your insecurities about sex by trying too hard to help you get an erection through oral sex, the vigorous massage of your penis, and so on. These strategies usually backfire, because thy simply put extra pressure on you to get an erection, and this will intensify your preoccupation with your penis. If you're having trouble getting an erection, it can be far more effective to concentrate on exciting your partner. Ask her to guide your hands over her body and show you just how and where she likes to be touched, kissed, and pleasured. Instead of worrying about whether or not you're getting excited—which can be pretty selfish and uncomfortable—ignore your penis and see how excited you can make her feel. Make her the center of your attention. Tell her you want to be the pleasure giver and all she has to do is lie back and be the pleasure receiver. Tell her to let her fantasies run freely and to be selfish about it—this can be her moment.

If you follow these suggestions, you will discover that you don't need an erection to bring her to orgasm. You will also learn from her all the ways she loves to be touched and aroused, and this will make you a far better lover. Many men go through life and never learn this because they're so preoccupied with getting erections, having intercourse, and proving their masculinity.

While she's guiding your hands over her body, concentrate on *her* sexual responses instead of your own. Watch her as she's becoming more and more excited and look for each of the natural sexual reactions listed in Table 12-2. Watching her can be a powerful antidote to your self-preoccupation and the feelings of insecurity which lead to impotence. Remember that there's really nothing wrong with "spectatoring"—it just depends on whom you're watching! And because you will be giving her sexual pleasure, you'll feel more potent and sexy.

Table 12-2
Female Sexual Responses*

• Increased breathing: The rate and depth of her breathing will increase greatly as she becomes more and more sexually aroused.

• Hardening of her nipples: nipple erection is an early sign of female arousal.

• Breast enlargement: women who have not nursed babies may experience a 25 to 50 percent enlargement in the size of their breasts during sexual arousal. If you've always wanted a woman with larger breasts, just open your eyes. This is your opportunity!

• Lubrication of her vagina: within less than a minute of sexual excitement, vaginal "sweating" begins. Some women produce copious amounts of fluid, whereas others produce much less. The degree of wetness does not necessarily reflect how turned on she feels or the skillfulness of your sexual technique.

• Labial swelling: In women who have had children, the labia can swell to double or triple their normal size and may take on a deeper reddish or purplish tint.

---

*This table was adapted from lecture materials presented by the Masters and Johnson Institute.

• Sexual rash: About three quarters of women will develop a blush-like rash across their chest, breast, back, and neck during sexual excitement. This rash becomes most pronounced during orgasm.

• Muscle spasms: Orgasm brings a peak of muscle tension, especially in the arms and legs, sometimes with spasms or tremors of the entire body.

Summary

1. Anxiety is one of the commonest causes of sexual problems such as impotence or premature ejaculation. Since there are a wide variety of emotional and medical problems that can lead to sexual difficulties, anyone with a persistent problem should seek consultation with a qualified professional. If you or your partner is having trouble overcoming any sexual problem, it does not mean that you're abnormal but only that you're very human. Admitting this and seeking help are not proofs of weakness but signs of strength.

2. Sexual anxiety often results from distorted negative thoughts, such as mind reading (you assume your partner will necessarily think less of you if you're anxious or inexperienced or if you have trouble getting an erection); fortune-telling (you predict failure ahead of time); overgeneralization (you assume that one rejection or sexual failure will become a never-ending pattern); all-or-nothing thinking (you assume that one sexual failure makes you a complete failure as a human being); "should" statements (telling yourself you should get an erection or that there's something wrong with you if you don't); and personalization (you feel you're responsible for your partner's sexual satisfaction and you automatically blame yourself if she's unhappy.)

3. Sexual anxiety also results from irrational beliefs and self-defeating attitudes, such as the idea that sexual problems are very unusual, that sexual insecurities make you less worthwhile and lovable, and that if you're less than perfect you're not good enough.

4. You can often overcome these problems and enhance your capacity to enjoy sex with the following techniques.

• The Daily Mood Log—you write down and talk back to your negative thoughts.

• The Feared-Fantasy Technique—you write out a dialogue with a imaginary stranger who's trying to put you down because you couldn't get an erection.

• Fantasy Enhancement—you give yourself permission to enjoy your sexual fantasies and daydreams.

• Empathy—you try to understand your partner's needs, insecurities, and feelings without blaming yourself.

• Assertiveness—instead of hiding your needs and feelings, you frankly and openly discuss your sexual difficulties with your partner, and you develop a plan for working on the problem together in a spirit of love and caring. This sometimes requires a considerable degree of courage and determination because of the shame and embarrassment so many people feel when it comes to talking about sex or revealing feelings of inadequacy.

• Paradoxical Techniques—you learn to give and receive sexual pleasure without the demand for intercourse.

• Self-acceptance—you develop a personal value system based on unconditional self-esteem rather than on having to be a success in order to feel worthwhile and lovable.

5. It's important to keep sex in an appropriate perspective. While intercourse is an important part of any loving relationship, it is only one aspect of the entire spectrum of sexuality. You can express the love and nurturing you feel toward your partner through many forms of physical sharing, such as a casual touch, a tender hug, a massage, or even a flirtatious glance. You can even bring your partner to orgasm without an erection if you concentrate on giving her pleasure and ask her where and how she likes to be touched and aroused. Watch her become excited and make her the center of your attention. This will often make you feel sexier and more aroused, and it will make you a much better lover.

By the same token, difficulties with sex are often symptoms of other problems in your life or deeper feelings about your relationship that need to be expressed. These can include guilt, depression, fear, jealousy, job stress, resentment, and unexpressed anger. In the great majority of cases these problems can be corrected, with the result that you'll enjoy sex more and feel better about yourself as well as your partner.

13

For Women Only: How to Achieve Orgasm and Enhance Sexual Pleasure

Although we often think of men as being the ones who suffer from sexual performance anxiety, many women also experience insecurities about their bodies and about their sexuality. What if you're an inexperienced virgin and the man you're dating is far more experienced? Will he think less of you? What if the man you're dating is insensitive to the way you like to be touched and aroused? How do you know when your relationship is ready for sexual sharing and when someone is just trying to use you for a quick roll in the sack? These are just a few of the sexual dilemmas that single women face.

The great majority of these sexual problems result from fear and anxiety. Sexual insecurities can lead to:

• A loss of interest in sex—you get so nervous and worried that you lose your desire for sex.

• Difficulties with sexual arousal and orgasm—you may have difficulties feeling relaxed and excited and developing vaginal lubrication during love making. You may feel tense and unable to climax.

• Difficulties communicating about sex—you may be afraid to talk about sex or to tell your partner what you like and dislike.

• Inassertiveness—you may be afraid to initiate sex or to say no to your partner's sexual advances.

• Difficulties accepting your sexuality—you may feel disturbed about unusual sexual fantasies and urges that seem morally wrong, abnormal, or repulsive.

Feelings of Intensity: Lisa is an attractive college student (described in Chapter Six) who sought treatment because she felt anxious and lonely. At first it was hard for me to understand how such a charming young woman could be lonely, but I believe she had turned into a swan so suddenly that she still thought of herself as an ugly duckling. Although she was convinced men wouldn't be interested in her, she agreed with reluctance to do some flirting as an experiment, using some of the techniques described earlier. Needless to say, the men she flirted with responded to her with considerable enthusiasm. Lisa found this hard to believe. One of the first men she approached began to pursue her avidly and soon they were dating frequently.

This put Lisa under new pressure. The man she was dating was a little bit older than she was and seemed quite sexually experienced. Lisa was still a virgin, and although she hadn't made an absolute decision about this, she felt it might be best for her to keep her virginity until she got married. Curiously enough, Lisa's mother had been putting pressure on her to have intercourse because she felt Lisa's value system was old-fashioned!

Lisa's main concern was that she might be rejected when she revealed her sexual inexperience to her boyfriend. Her automatic thoughts are illustrated in Figure 13-1. You will notice that her concerns are remarkably similar to Jack's (see Figure 12-1) in spite of the fact that she and Jack differed in age, sex, and religious background. Her first two thoughts indicate her belief that her sexual inexperience made her less attractive and desirable. Although this attitude might seem strange, I have observed it over and over again in shy and inexperienced young women. It's quite unrealistic: Men often find a lovely and inexperienced woman even *more* attractive and desirable, because they enjoy playing the role of teacher.

The second theme you can see in her negative thoughts is her fear of exposing her inner feelings and becoming vulnerable. She believes that she always has to be in control or something unpleasant will happen. This attitude can lead to rigidity and a lack of openness and intimacy. Only when you surrender a certain amount of control in a

FIGURE 13-1
The Daily Mood Log*

DESCRIBE THE UPSETTING EVENT—I had a date with Fred tonight. He's very attractive and interesting, but I'm afraid he'll put pressure on me to have sex and once he finds out I'm a virgin he'll reject me.

NEGATIVE FEELINGS—Record your emotions and rate each one on a scale from 0 (the least) to 100 (the most). Include feelings such as sad, anxious, angry, guilty, lonely, hopeless, frustrated, etc.

Emotion	Rating (0–100)	Emotion	Rating (0–100)	Emotion	Rating 0–100
1. Anxiety	70%	3.		5.	
2.		4.		6.	

AUTOMATIC THOUGHTS Write down your negative thoughts and number them consecutively.	DISTORTIONS Identify the distortions in each "Automatic Thought."	RATIONAL RESPONSES Substitute more realistic and positive thoughts.
1. I can't stand the thought of confronting him with my inexperience.	1. Fortune-telling.	1. It will probably turn out okay, since he's obviously interested. If it doesn't turn out well, I can deal with it later.
2. He might reject me.	2. Fortune telling.	2. If he rejects me because of my sexual inexperience, it would be unpleasant but I could survive. There's no guarantee that everyone will like me.

AUTOMATIC THOUGHTS	DISTORTIONS	RATIONAL RESPONSES
3. Even if he doesn't reject me, I'll be in a situation where I don't have any control.	3. All-or-nothing thinking.	3. Loving someone involves surrendering a certain amount of control. That's where trust comes in and that's what makes love an exciting adventure. Letting go of my need to control every situation might make my life more intimate and magical.
4. I'll be at his mercy once he finds out how inexperienced I am. I will have lost the control I now have, since he probably thinks I'm a knowledgeable and experienced woman. This will make me vulnerable because he'll have the power to accept or reject me.	4. All-or-nothing thinking.	4. A relationship is a two-way street, and we both always have the right to accept or reject each other. I really lose nothing by being open and honest about myself because I'll find out about the kind of person he is.

AUTOMATIC THOUGHTS	DISTORTIONS	RATIONAL RESPONSES
5. But if he rejects me, I'll think less of myself, because he'll be rejecting my value system.	5. Personalization.	5. He can reject my value system if it isn't compatible with his, and vice versa. But I can't let him be the judge of my values and beliefs.
6. But if someone rejects me, it means I should be doing something differently.	6. "Should" statement.	6. Even if it turned out I *should* be doing something differently, is that so terrible? It would just give me the chance to learn something new!
7. If he rejects me I'll never be able to overcome my inexperience, because everyone else will also reject me once they find out.	7. Overgeneralization.	7. That's pure nonsense. Everyone is different. His tastes don't represent every man on earth!

OUTCOME—Review your "Rational Responses" and put a check in the box that describes how you now feel:
☐ not at all better; ☐ somewhat better; ☑ quite a bit better; ☐ a lot better.

*Copyright © 1984, David D. Burns, M.D., from *Intimate Connections* (New York: William Morrow & Company).

loving relationship can you take the risk of trusting your partner, and that's when love becomes an exciting adventure. Although we generally think of men as being the ones who are afraid of sharing their feelings and vulnerabilities, my recent research with couples of all ages has indicated that the fear of exposing feelings is actually as common in women as in men.

The third theme evident in Lisa's thoughts involves her fear of rejection. She tells herself that if he rejects her, it will mean she's less worthwhile and everyone will reject her. This puts her self-esteem into his hands. Why should she give this man whom she barely knows such power over the way she feels about herself?

Talking back to her negative thoughts helped her develop a greater degree of self-love and self-acceptance. When you come face to face with your imperfections, you can either turn against yourself and condemn yourself for not being as good as you ideally think you should be, or you can take the courageous step of trusting and believing in yourself even *more*. This can be a very difficult step to take when you believe you've fallen short of your goals and you feel insecure and self-critical, but it can also be your greatest opportunity to discover how to love yourself.

Difficulties Achieving Orgasm. Now that more and more couples are having sex before marriage, therapists are seeing a number of single women as well as married women who want treatment for difficulties experiencing sexual excitement or achieving orgasm during intercourse. Twenty years ago there wasn't much emphasis on a woman's sexuality, and neither women nor their partners thought it was abnormal if a woman didn't particularly enjoy sex. Recently this attitude has changed and there's a growing recognition of the importance of female sexuality. However, along with the acceptance of women's sexuality and the ability of women to enjoy orgasm came new expectations and definitions of what was normal. When it became clear from the studies of Masters and Johnson, and others, that women were capable not only of orgasm but of multiple orgasms, the capacity to respond in this way became a sign of womanliness, and many women who were not enjoying this degree of sexuality began to feel inferior. In fact, many women began to feel pressure to live up to these revised standards. What began as new opportunities for enhanced sexual enjoyment turned into a fresh source of anxiey and insecurity.

The sexual problem became more complicated. The pressure for women to achieve sexual satisfaction was felt by their husbands, who in turn put pressure on their wives so they could feel like good lovers. During a recent therapy session, a woman confessed to one of the therapists at our institute: "It was so much easier in the old days when the men didn't care so much whether or not we had orgasms." While it's not possible or even desirable to turn back the clock, these new problems need to be resolved. A combination of greater assertiveness and self-acceptance can often be an effective antidote to these sexual performance pressures.

In Chapter Two, I described a shy college student named Allison who almost broke up with her boyfriend because she didn't like the way he kissed her and she felt too embarrassed to talk to him about it. After our session she did become more assertive and began enjoying the relationship so much that they began going together steadily. Yesterday Allison came in for a "tune up" after a five-month hiatus. Things were going well in her relationship, and since I'd last seen her she had made the decision to give up her virginity. But she had one problem that had been upsetting her quite a bit. Although she experienced orgasm during oral sex, she had difficulty getting sexually excited during intercourse and was unable to achieve orgasm then. She said that during intercourse she would lie there thinking, "I wish I could feel something. There must be something wrong with me. Maybe I should have remained a virgin forever. I want to get this over with." Needless to say, these negative thoughts distracted and upset her and made it difficult to relax and respond sexually. She was also afraid to talk to her boyfriend about the problem because she didn't want to seem "bossy" or to hurt his feelings by letting him know she wasn't feeling excited during intercourse.

Many women carry this fear with them for years and sometimes resort to faking orgasm rather than dealing with the problem in a direct and honest way. This is unfortunate, because in the majority of cases these problems respond nicely to sexual education or couples therapy.

I suggested that Allison write down the negative thoughts she was having during intercourse, as illustrated in Figure 13-2. Substituting rational responses helped her feel a little less anxious and inhibited and more willing to discuss the problem with her boyfriend so that they could try some new approaches to making love.

One of the commonest reasons for a lack of excitement during intercourse is insufficient clitoral stimulation. Many couples solve this problem through direct manual stimulation of the woman's clitoris during intercourse. This can increase excitement and often leads to orgasm. In addition, some couples find that after a period of time the woman develops the capacity to achieve orgasm during intercourse without manual clitoral stimulation. Other couples adopt manual clitoral stimulation during intercourse as an ongoing part of their lovemaking style, and they feel this is a wonderful way of maximizing their sexual pleasure.

A second suggestion that Allison and I discussed would be for her boyfriend to stimulate her clitoris orally just up to the point of orgasm, and then they could begin intercourse before she climaxed. Her heightened state of excitement, along with the additional help of manual stimulation, would make it even more likely that she could experience sexual excitement and orgasm during intercourse.

Allison was relieved to be able to talk about a problem that had been so embarrassing to her, but she still felt inhibited about suggesting these techniques to her boyfriend. As you can see in Figure 13-3, she was thinking that if she stimulated herself during intercourse it would be like masturbating and being alone. She also thought this might be upsetting to her boyfriend, and that if he stimulated her clitoris he might not be able to concentrate on her. As we talked about ways of talking back to these thoughts, she was able to see that she was already quite "alone" during intercourse, since she was not responding to him but was simply being preoccupied with her own negative thoughts. In reality, these techniques might actually bring them close together because they would work

FIGURE 13-2
The Daily Mood Log*

DESCRIBE THE UPSETTING EVENT—Not feeling anything during intercourse.

NEGATIVE FEELINGS—Record your emotions and rate each one on a scale from 0 (the least) to 100 (the most). Include feelings such as sad, anxious, angry, guilty, lonely, hopeless, frustrated, etc.

Emotion	Rating (0–100)	Emotion	Rating (0–100)	Emotion	Rating (0–100)
1. Anxious	75%	3. Sad	75%	5.	
2. Frustrated	99%	4.		6.	

AUTOMATIC THOUGHTS	DISTORTIONS	RATIONAL RESPONSES
Write down your negative thoughts and number them consecutively.	Identify the distortions in each "Automatic Thought."	Substitute more realistic and positive thoughts.
1. I should be able to respond better. What's wrong with me?	1. "Should" statement; disqualifying the positive.	1. I do experience orgasm during oral sex, so its unlikely there's anything wrong with me. Learning to respond sexually takes time and I can be patient with myself. I'm just a beginner.
2. Forget it! I just want to get this over with!	2. Emotional reasoning.	2. If I "forget it," I'll just disconnect my mind and feel nothing. Maybe it would be better to talk about the problem and work on it together.

AUTOMATIC THOUGHTS	DISTORTIONS	RATIONAL RESPONSES
3. I don't want him to know I'm not turned on, because I might hurt his feelings.	3. Mind reading; fortune-telling; personalization.	3. If I don't tell him, we may never have the chance to improve our sex life. I don't know that it would hurt his feelings to talk about it, and if I approach him in a loving way perhaps we can learn to satisfy each other better. That would be worth a little discomfort now.

OUTCOME—Review your "Rational Responses" and put a check in the box that describes how you now feel:
☐ not at all better; ☐ somewhat better; ☑ quite a bit better; ☐ a lot better.

---

*Copyright © 1984, David D. Burns, M.D., from *Intimate Connections* (New York: William Morrow & Company).

as partners to share a more mutually gratifying sex life.

How to Overcome Inhibitions About Masturbation: Allison's negative attitudes about masturbation are typical of many lonely people. The idea that you need another person for a good sexual experience is just another extension of the belief that all happiness comes from other people. Physical and erotic fulfillment can be another dimension of self-love. Although there is a general superstition that masturbation is abnormal or shameful, surveys have indicated that the majority of human beings, even those who are married, do masturbate at times throughout their lives. Masturbation need not be viewed as an inferior sexual experience, but simply as an alternative one.

Many studies have shown that the degree of sexual arousal during masturbation can actually be equal or superior to the excitement during intercourse. Masturbation is much like any other experience in that the way you choose to view it will determine how you feel about it. If you put yourself down for masturbating and tell yourself how much more wonderful sex would be if you had a partner, you'll probably feel guilty and find masturbation a relatively empty experience. But if you approach this most intimate aspect of self-love with a positive, creative attitude, you may discover that it can be a rewarding sexual outlet when you have no other sexual partner. Dr. Laura Primakoff has pointed out that masturbation can offer several advantages over sex with a partner. These include the fact that it's always available, there is no pressure to perform, you don't have to feel judged, there's no danger of venereal disease, orgasm is usually guaranteed, and you can feel completely uninhibited and engage in unlimited erotic fantasies, which can sometimes be as arousing as an actual sexual encounter.

FIGURE 13-3
The Daily Mood Log*

DESCRIBE THE UPSETTING EVENT—Thinking about having John or me stimulate my clitoris by hand during intercourse.

NEGATIVE FEELINGS—Record your emotions and rate each one on a scale from 0 (the least) to 100 (the most). Include feelings such as sad, anxious, angry, guilty, lonely, hopeless, frustrated, etc.

Emotion	Rating (0–100)	Emotion	Rating (0–100)	Emotion	Rating (0–100)
1. Embarrassed	99%	3.		5.	
2.		4.		6.	

AUTOMATIC THOUGHTS Write down your negative thoughts and number them consecutively.	DISTORTIONS Identify the distortions in each "Automatic Thought."	RATIONAL RESPONSES Substitute more realistic and positive thoughts.
1. It would be strange to do that.	1. Fortune-telling.	1. It might feel strange at first, but it might improve our sex life.
2. If I stimulate myself, I would be masturbating myself in front of him.	2. "Should" statement.	2. It might be okay to masturbate in front of someone I love in an intimate situation.
3. Maybe he'd feel bad. He might feel left out if it's my hand. I might as well be alone!	3. Fortune-telling; mind reading.	3. We would actually be less alone, because we'd both be sharing a more satisfying and exciting sexual experience. I actually feel very alone now during intercourse.
4. If I ask him to stimulate me, he might not be able to concentrate on me.	4. Fortune-telling; mind reading.	4. We can try it and find out. He might enjoy me more if he knew that I was also excited during intercourse.

OUTCOME—Review your "Rational Responses" and put a check in the box that describes how you now feel:
☐ not at all better; ☐ somewhat better; ☑ quite a bit better; ☐ a lot better.

---

*Copyright © 1984, David D. Burns, M.D., from *Intimate Connections* (New York: William Morrow & Company).

If you still have the belief that masturbation is bound to be inferior, you can do an experiment to test this belief using the Pleasure Predicting Sheet. Predict how satisfying it will be to masturbate on a scale of 0 (for the least) to 99 (for the most satisfying). (If you have a sexual partner available, you can also make a second prediction of how satisfying it will be to make love to him or her, using the same 0 to 99 scale.) Then create a self-pleasuring experience for yourself. Put some caring and creativity into it, just as you might if you were having a date with someone special. You could light candles, put on your favorite music, and have a glass of wine. Indulge and pamper yourself and let your mind run free. You may be surprised that this experience, like any other when you're alone, can be extremely pleasurable if you approach it with a positive attitude. If you find it upsetting or you feel ashamed afterward, try to tune in to the negative thoughts that upset you. Write them down on a Daily Mood Log, as in Figure 13-4. The young woman whose automatic thoughts and rational responses are illustrated worked on an assembly line at night and was taking college classes part time during the day. One afternoon she masturbated while taking a shower at her apartment and then started to feel guilty and embarrassed about it. As you can see, she was telling herself that I would look down on her, that she was some kind of weirdo, that masturbation was bad for her and meant she was a selfish person. Talking back to these thoughts helped her feel better about herself and accept masturbation as a healthy and normal release of tension.

It may come as a shock to you that a professional would advocate masturbation when there's such a strong gut feeling in our society that masturbation, like being alone, is

FIGURE 13-4
The Daily Mood Log*

DESCRIBE THE UPSETTING EVENT—Thoughts about masturbating

NEGATIVE FEELINGS—Record your emotions and rate each one on a scale from 0 (the least) to 100 (the most). Include feelings such as sad, anxious, angry, guilty, lonely, hopeless, frustrated, etc.

Emotion	Rating (0–100)	Emotion	Rating (0–100)	Emotion	Rating (0–100)
1. Guilt	75%	3.		5.	
2. Embarrass-ment	75%	4.		6.	

AUTOMATIC THOUGHTS Write down your negative thoughts and number them consecutively.	DISTORTIONS Identify the distortions in each "Automatic Thought."	RATIONAL THOUGHTS Substitute more realistic and positive thoughts.
1. Dr. Burns will think I'm a no-good person because I told him I masturbate.	1. Mind reading.	1. I don't know what he thinks, but I'm really not a "no-good person" no matter what he thinks.
2. I think I'm a weirdo for masturbating in the afternoon.	2. Labeling.	2. I worked night work and felt like it in the afternoon because I knew I wouldn't have another chance that day.

AUTOMATIC THOUGHTS	DISTORTIONS	RATIONAL RESPONSES
3. I'll bet none of the other night workers did it.	3. Mind reading.	3. How can I tell what they did? Besides, a lot of them have husbands and wives to have fun with.
4. But it still doesn't mean its okay for me to masturbate.	4. "Should" statement.	4. Who says it isn't?
5. It must be bad for me somehow.	5. Jumping to conclusions.	5. It's a normal, healthy way of releasing tension and it's pleasurable besides.
6. But it's wrong because it's selfish and it's done alone.	6. Labeling; should statement.	6. Does it have to be done with others to make it right? Sex with someone else can be just as selfish.

OUTCOME—Review your "Rational Responses" and put a check in the box that describes how you now feel:
☐ not at all better; ☐ somewhat better; ☐ quite a bit better; ☑ a lot better.

*Copyright © 1984, David D. Burns, M.D., from *Intimate Connections* (New York: William Morrow & Company.)

somehow shameful or wrong. But masturbation can simply be a physical expression of self-love and the first step in accepting yourself as a sensual, sexual creature. And for many people, it can be an important step toward intimacy and love.

Sex and Intimacy. A common problem facing single women is when to have sex with someone they're dating. You may feel pressured to give in to a man's demands for intercourse, thinking you'll be rejected if you appear too cool and play hard to get. While this may sometimes happen, more often the opposite occurs. You may be pressured into having sex, thinking that a man will like you more and it will lead to greater intimacy. Once he's slept with you, you may not hear from him again and you end up feeling rejected.

This problem has been complicated by the tendency toward more liberal sexual standards during the last two decades. Whereas premarital sex was once considered wrong, these days a bride who's still a virgin is more the exception than the rule. As a result of these changing norms, women may rush into a sexual relationship prematurely because they don't want to appear old-fashioned or behind the times.

In my office yesterday an attractive college student named Carlene told me about a predicament along these lines. Carlene was shy and felt that most guys wouldn't be interested in her. I suggested that as an experiment, she pick out a young man from one of her classes and flirt with him using some of the techniques outlined in the previous chapters. She chose, with considerable reluctance, a fellow named Sam, and began smiling at him and talking to him between classes. As a result, he began to show more and more interest in her. This came as a surprise; she knew Sam already had a steady girl friend who'd graduated from their school the previous year. Nevertheless, the flirting methods worked like a charm and within several weeks Sam and Carlene were spending hours together, deeply engrossed in conversation, holding hands, looking longingly into each other's eyes. Carlene felt a strong sexual chemistry between them and suspected that before long Sam would be wanting more physical intimacy.

The only problem was that he was still dating his regular girl friend on weekends and she wasn't aware of Sam's interest in Carlene. Carlene talked the problem over with her roommate, who suggested that the "in" thing to do would be to go ahead and fool around sexually. She told Carlene she enjoyed casual sex with men, but Carlene was a little uncertain about this and wanted my advice.

As a psychiatrist, my role is not to give advice or to impose my own moral standards on my patients. My aim is help patients learn to think things through on their own so they can become more aware of the advantages and disadvantages of different options before they make a final decision. Then I encourage patients to learn from the consequences of their decision, which may be good or bad, so they can view a situation as an opportunity for personal growth. This relieves some of the pressure of having to be "right" and reduces the fear of doing the "wrong" thing, since you can often learn as much from a mistake as from a good decision. Expecting yourself to know the "right" thing to do in every situation is simply unrealistic.

I did feel that it was important for Carlene to take her own attitudes, feelings, and personal values into account as she made her decision. I knew that in the past, whenever Carlene had been rejected by someone she was interested in, she had a tendency to feel extremely hurt and inadequate and to become very self-critical. It often took her a couple of months to recover from the pain of a romantic rejection. Telling herself it was okay to have casual sex with Sam was not terribly realistic, because she was beginning to develop strong feelings for him, and what she really wanted was a meaningful relationship with someone who cared about her.

So the real question for Carlene was whether sex with Sam would be more likely to strengthen or to weaken their relationship. Since Carlene and I aren't fortune-tellers, we had to make an educated guess. It's important to keep in mind that Sam was pursuing Carlene at the same time he was going out with his steady girl friend. We can assume that the idea of having sex on the side was probably appealing to Sam. But it was quite possible that Sam might drop Carlene once he'd slept with her and completed his "conquest," or that he would continue to go out with both girls without making a commitment or being faithful to either one of them.

This aspect of male psychology is hard for many women to understand and accept. You may believe that if you act in a loving way and offer a man your entire heart, body, and soul, he should just naturally respond in the same way and give you an exclusive commitment. But it often doesn't work this way. Giving too much too soon is just as likely to scare a man away, and using sex to improve a shaky relationship will often have the opposite effect. Carlene may have to exert some discipline and wisdom in order to develop a more meaningful relationship with Sam.

One option would be to tell Sam that she's genuinely interested in him but that he needs to think about what he wants. Carlene could say that while their relationship is very exciting, it might be best for them to back off so he can explore his relationship with his steady girl friend without the distraction of Carlene. Carlene could tell him that if things don't work out with his girl friend, he could feel free to ask Carlene out.

This, of course, means being "old-fashioned," saying no to casual sex, and running the risk of losing Sam. It also means she will have to face the fact that she's in direct competition with Sam's other girl friend and that there's no guarantee what the outcome will be. And it means she may have to say no to Sam's sexual and romantic advances—and for many people, saying no can be very difficult. But the risk of losing Sam will always be there, and if Carlene doesn't hop into bed with Sam she may actually minimize this risk. People want what they can't have; the grass is always greener on the other side of the fence. Carlene is that green grass, and if she tells Sam that he can't come across the fence right now, he'll probably want to hop over all the more. But he's going to have to give up his other girl friend in order to get what he wants if Carlene doesn't give everything away for free.

Maybe to some readers this will sound overly crass and manipulative and not spontaneous or loving enough. I believe that human nature has a crass and manipulative side to it, and unless you take this into account realistically, you may be hurt and become bitter and ruin your chances for real love and caring. It's foolish to assume that other people will always look out for your self-interest, but if you protect yourself, then others will be more likely to respect you, and the self-esteem you feel will make it easier for you to give and to love.

When she talks this over with Sam it will be important not to sound needy, demanding or hostile. She'll want to come across in a friendly, self-esteeming way. If Sam agrees to think things over for a few weeks, whenever Carlene sees him she'll want to be upbeat and to make him feel good, but she should keep these interactions brief, so he won't feel he can have a relationship with Carlene until he makes up his mind about his girl friend.

There's one more tactic that may be important as a part of Carlene's overall game plan. Since Sam is playing the field, Carlene puts herself in a one-down position by getting exclusively fixated on him. It might be better for her to resist her fantasies of having a romantic, one-to-one relationship with Sam, and force herself to flirt with other men. Then she can play the field for a while as well. Carlene may not want to do this, since she's shy and it takes tremendous effort to flirt and be assertive with men, and the idea that Sam might be her one and only is a very tempting and seductive fantasy. But sometimes you can get what you want only by pursuing the opposite goal. Once Sam gets the idea she's going out with other guys, he may feel jealous and realize how much he wants her.

Here are the advantages of this approach:

1. Carlene won't make Sam feel trapped by insisting that he break up with his girl friend. By encouraging him to try to work things out with her, she gives Sam a maximum of freedom.

2. Sam will probably become more intrigued by Carlene because she'll be less available and more mysterious. She's given him the message that she respects herself, and that she won't let him use her. He'll know that while she cares about him, she's not afraid of losing him.

3. She won't risk getting into a situation where Sam gets to play Carlene off against his other girl friend or other women he might want to date.

4. She won't risk having sex with him and then being rejected and feeling used.

It's dangerous to rely on sex to create intimacy and

commitment. Sex can be the expression of your love, but it's no shortcut to love. Developing a sound relationship requires discipline, assertiveness, and a certain degree of risk. You have to be clear about what you want and willing to let go of a relationship if the other person doesn't have similar aims.

It's important not to buy into the idea that other people feel and function the same way you do. For many people, intercourse creates a certain degree of vulnerability and leads to greater feelings of love and trust. But some people use sex in other ways—as a tranquilizer against the stresses of school or job, as an escape from a troubled or dull relationship, or as a means of proving themselves through sexual conquest. If you have sex with someone who doesn't have intimacy in mind, you may end up feeling hurt and disillusioned. But if you find out where you stand first—and that requires hard work and saying no—then sex can become the expression of your love.

14

Temptations: The Dark Side of Single Life

Much of this book has focused on how to develop loving and sexually fulfilling relationships. Some single people are faced with a different problem: how to avoid unloving, destructive relationships.

Candy is a tall, thirty-six-year-old divorced professional woman who separated from her husband seven years ago. Since her separation she's had a string of unsatisfactory affairs with married men. Candy recently told me, "I keep striking out with these men. I'm zero for nine so far. One of the men I had an affair with several years ago died recently, and I couldn't even attend the funeral. It was almost as if I didn't exist in his life, and I didn't have a chance to grieve. . . . Overall, it's been a pretty lonely road, and I feel like I've been living in a vacuum."

What is motivating Candy? If these affairs aren't working out for her, why does she keep getting involved? She describes her experiences: "I'm a delightful partner for these men, but I represent the dark side of their lives. They just materialized at my door, and I have no idea what their lives are like apart from me. I sometimes wonder: What are their homes like? Their furniture?

"I'm a 'no strings' person, so they don't forget me. I bring pleasure to their lives. They call me on my birthday, but they can never come and spend the day with me. It's a hollow affection, because they never intend to stay friends indefinitely. I never pressure them or ask for anything in return.

"If I needed a couple thousand dollars or more clients for my business, these men would help me out in an instant. They'd do it out of guilt, but I never take advantage of them. Once I dated an executive of *Penthouse* magazine, and he even offered to set me up in a condominium and pay for my son's private school expenses. The attention made me feel special.

"But there's a price I pay. Now the holidays are coming up. Every Christmas I wonder if I'll be with someone who cares about me the next Christmas, someone I can share my life with. There've been eight Christmases in a row like this. I hate the holidays because they remind me that there's no one in the world who wants to be with me."

I was impressed with the fact that there was no bitterness or self-pity in Candy's voice. She recognized she was acting out a script of her own creation that wasn't leading anywhere. She wanted to understand why she was hooked on this pattern and what she could do to break out of it.

I asked Candy if she'd had any dates with single men since her divorce. She replied, "I avoid single men like the plague. I have a hard time even imagining what it would be like to go out with one. One of the things that bothers me about single men is . . . I fell head over heels in love with a doctor several years ago but after a while he left me. . . . It was *so* painful to me because I tried *so hard* to make that relationship work. And when it didn't, I tried hard to figure out why. I just couldn't get him out of my mind. For two years I thought about him constantly."

It sounded as if the fear of rejection was a strong motivating factor in Candy's life-style. I was curious why going out with married men would be any less stressful—after all, a married man would seem even *more* likely to reject her in the end. Candy explained, "With married men it was easier to accept the fact that they'd eventually leave me because of the ties in their lives. They had jobs, wives, children . . . and wealth. And reputations. Every man I went with has been Irish, Italian, or Catholic, and I've been their first long-term affair. I allow myself to be had, but I'm grabbing their nuts all the time and stirring up all that guilt. . . . These were real family men who talked about their kids and their homes. Their associates often thought of them as 'squares.' I'd snicker because I'd just spent the night with this conservative 'square.' '' Candy's frank disclosure suggested a second motivation for her affairs: revenge. Could it be that she enjoyed her role as seductress of these ''good'' men and liked to let them squirm with guilt?

She described a third motivation: The excitement of the affairs was a kind of ''high'' that allowed her to escape from the stress and pressure of her dual role as a professional woman and as a single mother for her learning-disabled son. ''I work *incredibly* hard to avoid any criticism at work. To get ahead as a woman, I've had to put out twice the energy, so I stay on the fast track of appearing charming, happy, successful, and strong. And I've made myself a martyr over helping my son—making sure he got the right counseling and the best school and enough of my time. The need to be a superwoman and a supermother is the source of my strength as well as my weakness, because it leads to my addiction to these affairs. They're like my cocaine. They keep me high and I don't have to take the risk of getting close.''

It appeared that many factors were contributing to Candy's habitual choice of married men as partners. These included fear of intimacy, fear of rejection, the desire for excitement and attention, and the business and professional advantages she enjoyed, as well as a certain intoxication with the power of her role as a temptress who could punish these men for their hypocrisy.

Candy's experience is a little atypical of many of the lonely women I've treated, because Candy doesn't fool herself about the nature of her relationships with these men. The usual scenario involves more self-deception. You may start to see a married man as a ''friend,'' and you both agree to keep things platonic and innocent. Soon you get sexually involved, but you make an agreement to keep things casual and not to get ''serious'' about the relationship. He does imply from time to time that he's unhappy with his wife, and this feeds your secret agenda—which you may not be aware of or willing to own up to at first—that you will save him from this unhappy marriage and prove that you can meet all the sexual and emotional needs that his wife neglects.

As the relationship evolves, your feelings for him begin to grow. Eventually you want more commitment and involvement, and you begin to fantasize about yourself as his wife. You become aware that you *are* falling in love with him in spite of your original agreement, and the logical question begins to nag at you: If his wife is so bad, why doesn't he just leave her? Coincidentally, just as you begin to feel this way, he starts to get more distant and evasive. This intensifies your longing for him, and you subtly pressure him to spend more time with you. He begins to feel resentful and trapped by you, just as he feels with his wife, and he backs off. This is the beginning of the end of the relationship, and when it's over, you feel bitter and betrayed.

It's important to realize that one of the reasons for choosing an inaccessible partner may be your lack of self-esteem. Having an affair with a married man allows you to keep the relationship of a fantasy level. You don't risk showing him what an imperfect human being you are. You also don't have to deal with him as he really is. You avoid the pain—and the pleasure—of developing a truly intimate relationship in which all your weaknesses may be revealed. It can be safer to pursue someone who doesn't really seem interested in you, because keeping him as a fantasy figure allows you to imagine that you're on the verge of having a wonderful, ideal relationship instead of confronting the insecurities and frustrations involved in developing a less than ideal real one.

The first step in breaking any habit involves developing the motivation to change. The need for sex and intimacy and the fear of being alone are powerful forces that can make it difficult to resist the impulse to have an affair, even with someone who seems to be using you. Telling yourself that it's "not right" to have affairs isn't likely to be a very powerful antidote to these urges, because these days many people's moral convictions are unclear at best. Furthermore, any loving relationship can seem very right when you're aching from loneliness and you have the desire to be close.

Step One: Rational Decision Making. The first step in dealing with romantic and sexual impulses that may be self-destructive is to make a rational decision about what's really in your best self-interest. I suggested that Candy make a list of the advantages and disadvantages of continuing to have affairs with married men. If you have a romantic habit you're trying to break—such as going out with a man who seems terribly attractive and exciting but who really doesn't respect you or treat you well—make a similar list. Try to be honest with yourself about the many payoffs of the way you're behaving. You can see from Candy's Cost-Benefit Analysis in Figure 14-1 that the advantages of her affairs included outstanding sex, friendship, freedom from anxiety, and good business contacts. Try to be equally realistic about the disadvantages of your behavior. Candy listed, among other things, the guilt and loss of self-esteem, the loneliness she felt on holidays, the distraction from her real goal of forming an intimate relationship, and the fear of discovery.

Once you've listed the advantages and disadvantages of the behavior you're trying to change, make a second list of the advantages and disadvantages of giving it up. Again, try to be realistic about the pros and cons. There are plenty of good reasons why you haven't changed yet. It can be difficult to say no to temptations because you may have to confront certain deeper fears and inhibitions. If you list every conceivable disadvantage of changing, you'll be in a much better position to make a decision you can stick with. You can see in Figure 14-1 that Candy's list of the advantages of dating single men included the chance to build a future. The disadvantages of dating single men included having to cope with conflicts about her career, as well as the hard work involved in finding eligible men to date. Many people look only at the advantages of change ("I'll be a new person and feel so much better about myself"), and they get temporarily psyched up by an illusory glow of excitement and become highly committed to change. But soon they get frustrated and disillusioned because they discover that change isn't easy, and they fall back into their old ways. Taking a hard look at the cost and benefits of changing can help you avoid this trap.

Figure 14-1
Rational Decision Making

Option A: Continuing to date married men

Advantages of Dating Married Men	Disadvantages of Dating Married Men
1. They'll treat me as "special"—gifts, trips, vacations, dinner shows, opera.	1. They're not available to me much of the time—holidays, birthdays. I can't call them at home when I want to talk.
2. No obsessing on my part—I don't have to worry about dating or getting rejected.	2. Their guilt and discomfort.
3. It's convenient and doesn't interfere with my daily routine.	3. I cannot make short- or long-range plans.
4. Passion—they are with me for sex, and the sex is superathletic and inventive.	4. No financial security or sharing.
5. Friendship—we have long phone conversations when they can't see me.	5. One man died, and I couldn't even attend the funeral.
6. Business—many of them are presidents of their companies. This provides valuable contacts with their firms and others.	6. Possibility of discovery by their wives or children.
	7. Loss of esteem in my son's eyes.
	8. Loss of self-esteem.
	9. I often fall in love and get hurt anyway.
(30)	(70)

Option B: Dating single men

Advantages of Dating Single Men	Disadvantages of Dating Single Men
1. Availability.	1. They seem skeptical and critical of my independence and feminism.
2. Chance to build a future.	2. I may fall back into old patterns from my marriage.
3. No other "allegiances" to wives.	3. They may expect me to cancel business trips for dates.
4. More time together.	4. If I get married before Erik is grown, he may rebel and follow my pattern of getting involved with drugs and sex.
5. A more "complete" love-companionship.	5. Where do I find these eligible men?
6. Better basis for trust and friendship.	6. If I get rejected, I have only me to blame.
7. A warm and energetic sex life—I hope! (*Note:* Does daily contact breed monotony for men?)	
(60)	(40)

Once you've listed the pros and cons of settling for the status quo versus changing, weigh the advantages against the disadvantages of each option. You can see from Figure 14-1 that Candy found that the disadvantages of having affairs outweighed the advantages by a 70:30 margin. In contrast, the advantages of dating single men outweighed the disadvantages by a 60:40 margin. This made it clear to her that her behavior was really not in her best self-interest.

Step Two: How to Resist Temptations. The Decision-Making Technique will help you develop a blueprint for change because you'll know what it is you're really aiming for, but this knowledge won't guarantee that you really will change. That's because temptations can become very strong at times, and when you feel lonely and you're faced with the chance to spend time with an exciting married man, you'll begin to think and feel differently. You'll start to talk yourself into giving in, and pretty soon you'll be hooked on the same old patterns again. The same thing happens to people with drinking problems who are trying to give up alcohol. When they wake up with a hangover, they feel determined never to take another drink again and it seems so clear and easy. A few days later, when they feel stressed about a personal problem or a business hassle, it becomes *awfully* tempting to have one little drink again. Sexual and romantic addictions work exactly the same way.

In fact, this is exactly what happened to Candy. Within several days of making her lists, one of her old lovers, a married man named Hal whom she'd seen on and off for several years, invited Candy to get together "just for close friendship and not for sex." Because she was feeling lonely and bored, she decided to get together with him. She thought the idea of a friendly intimate dinner sounded enjoyable, but she wasn't owning up to her desire for a real committed relationship. When he spent the evening talking about problems with his wife, Candy became furious and realized she'd fallen prey to her self-destructive patterns again.

One way to deal with this tendency is to write down the thoughts that make you feel tempted to give in. Then you can take a hard look at what you're telling yourself and develop ways of talking back to these thoughts so you can resist the temptations. The next time I saw Candy, I urged her to use the Daily Mood Log in this way. For the "Upsetting Event," she wrote down: "Hal calls and invites me to get together as 'friends.'" In the "Feelings'' section she indicated that she was feeling lonely and tempted, and then she wrote down her ''Automatic Thoughts'' and answered them, as illustrated in Figure 14-2.

Curiously enough, the automatic thoughts that tempt people to behave in a self-destructive manner contain many of the same distortions that are listed in Table 4-1 on page 51, but the distortions will be positive instead of negative. One common distortion is ''emotional reasoning''—Candy tells herself that if she *feels* strongly like seeing Hal, then it's probably a good thing to do. Another distortion is ''fortune-telling''—she predicts that seeing Hal will be wonderful and ignores the very real possibility that it may be quite upsetting to her. A third distortion is ''magnification'' and ''minimization''—she magnifies the positive aspects of seeing Hal and minimizes the problems that are likely to develop. This creates a very distorted view of the situation. Because Candy no longer visualizes the negative consequences of her self-destructive behavior, her actions begin to seem quite reasonable and logical.

The Devil's Advocate Technique is another powerful method you can use to combat destructive temptations. Imagine that you're very lonely and a friendly, exciting married man has indicated he'd like to get together for a drink just to talk and be friends. In your heart of hearts, you know that both of you have a little more in mind than just friendship. Now imagine that a clever, persuasive salesman is trying hard to convince you to go out with this man. See if you can refute the salesman's arguments. In my office, I acted out the Devil's Advocate procedure with Candy. You might have a friend who would enjoy acting it out with you. If not, you can write out a dialogue just like the one that follows. I play the role of the devil's advocate and I try my hardest to persuade Candy to accept a date with Hal:

DAVID (AS THE DEVIL'S ADVOCATE): Candy, you don't *really* want to give up these affairs with married men. You're not hurting anyone. Just think of how nice it would be to see Hal tonight!

FIGURE 14-2
The Daily Mood Log*

DESCRIBE THE UPSETTING EVENT—Hal calls and invites me to get together as "friends."

NEGATIVE FEELINGS—Record your emotions and rate each one on a scale from 0 (the least) to 100 (the most). Include feelings such as sad, anxious, angry, guilty, lonely, hopeless, frustrated, etc.

Emotion	Rating (0–100)	Emotion	Rating (0–100)	Emotion	Rating (0–100)
1. Lonely	90%	3.		5.	
2. Tempted	90%	4.		6.	

AUTOMATIC THOUGHTS Write down your negative thoughts and number them consecutively.	DISTORTION Identify the distortions in each "Automatic Thought."	RATIONAL RESPONSES Substitute more realistic and positive thoughts.
1. Gee, I really care about him and I want to see him.	1. Emotional reasoning.	1. Seeing Hal will be more of the same. Nothing ever really changes.
2. He needs to see me to make up his mind about leaving his wife. Things may change if I give our relationship a chance.	2. Fortune-telling.	2. He's been seeing me for four years, and he hasn't made up his mind about his wife yet! If I keep going out with him, he'll have no reason to leave his wife, since he'll be getting what he wants.

AUTOMATIC THOUGHTS	DISTORTIONS	RATIONAL RESPONSES
3. But I'm so lonely, and I *want* to see him.	3. Emotional reasoning.	3. I'm still lonely when I see him. In the long run, it only makes me feel worse.

OUTCOME—Review your "Rational Responses" and put a check in the box that describes how you now feel:
☐ not at all better; ☐ somewhat better; ☐ quite a bit better; ☑ a lot better.

*Copyright © 1984, David D. Burns, M.D., from *Intimate Connections* (New York: William Morrow & Company).

CANDY: Well, it would be nice to see Hal, but there are certain costs involved. I may be hurting myself.

DAVID (AS THE DEVIL'S ADVOCATE): Don't be so heavy! Lighten up a little. What costs are you referring to?

CANDY: Well, the guilt and discomfort.

DAVID (AS THE DEVIL'S ADVOCATE): You can deal with the guilt using the cognitive therapy techniques you learned from Dr. Burns. Guilt is just a needless emotion. You have no reason to feel guilty. You feel lonely, and what you're doing is your right, and besides—

CANDY: It may be my right to sleep with anyone I choose, but I'm not sure it's in my best interest to go out with married men. I may be lonely, but if I wait, maybe I can find someone I could really get close to.

DAVID (AS THE DEVIL'S ADVOCATE): Well, it's going to take a long time to find an eligible single man, so you won't lose a thing by seeing Hal tonight. Besides, you'll have a little fun, too. You deserve it! Give yourself a break!

CANDY: That's like telling an alcoholic that one drink won't hurt. One drink leads to another. What I'm concerned about is a pattern I'm trying to break. This is my chance to break that pattern, and I can do it by saying no to Hal tonight.

As the dialogue continued, I tried my hardest to persuade Candy to give in. I pointed out how bored and unfulfilled she felt, I emphasized how difficult it was to get into the dating scene, I suggested that maybe Hal would leave his wife and marry her, and so forth. When you write your own Devil's Advocate dialogue, you should also try your hardest to pressure yourself into giving in. This can help you resist temptations, because you'll become familiar with all the little tricks your mind plays on you when you feel tempted.

Men, of course, are not immune to temptation. Ernie is a divorced, thirty-five-year-old lawyer who first came for treatment because of feelings of shame about past sexual indiscretions. As a young man he'd been quite promiscuous and had several illegitimate children. Years later, he was still berating himself and suffering from spells of severe guilt and anxiety. One of his most shameful memories was having intercourse with the wife of a law-school buddy. Afterward Ernie felt humiliated and hated himself for betraying his friend, all the more so because his friend was insecure about his marriage and prone to bouts of depression. Ernie worried that his friend might end his life or that his friend's marriage would fail and that Ernie would be to blame. Shortly before Ernie came to me for treatment, his friend had died of a sudden heart attack. Ernie was grief-stricken but concerned that he might get sexually involved with his friend's wife again. She had a drug problem and was prone to bouts of depression; when she began to feel down she'd call Ernie and want to talk. He had no real love for her or any desire to strike up a serious relationship, and he sensed that giving in to his sexual impulses would be hurtful to both of them.

One evening she called and urged Ernie to drop by, so he brought his nine-year-old niece along as "protection just in case," to make sure things wouldn't get out of hand. While they were talking, Ernie started to feel sorely tempted and she invited him into the bedroom. They ended up kissing and caressing on her bed while Ernie's niece played in the living room. Ernie managed to tear himself away before their clothes were entirely off, and came to the next session feeling overwhelmed with panic and self-loathing. He was concerned that he would continue to succumb to the temptation and eventually have sex with her again.

I suggested that Ernie fantasize that he was visiting her apartment alone. I told him to imagine that she was wearing a seductive low-cut dress and talking to him in an erotic, inviting way. As Ernie visualized this scene, he began to feel sexually aroused. Then I asked him to write down his automatic thoughts on a Daily Mood Log, as illustrated in Figure 14-3. You can see how Ernie focuses on all the positive aspects of the scene—he thinks about her breasts and how exciting it would be to take her clothes off and make love to her—and he ignores or discounts the negative aspects—the guilt and shame he'll feel afterward, a possible worsening in her drug problem, the adverse effects on their family, and so on. Writing his automatic thoughts down and talking back to them helped him think things through a little more realistically and cooled his urges to have a sexual relationship with her.

Certainly Candy and Ernie—and the rest of us as well, I suspect!—will have to work at resisting a variety of temptations throughout our lives. Not only are there sexual temptations, but there are temptations to smoke, to drink excessively, to overeat, to cheat in business or in school. . . . Techniques such as Rational Decision-Making, the Devil's Advocate Technique, and the Daily Mood Log are exciting to me, not because they're likely to create a moral revolution, but because they provide a systematic way of understanding and dealing with these problems. I'm proposing that immoral and self-destructive behavior may in part result from cognitive distortions and from psychic blindness. But unlike depression, where we sell ourselves short and focus excessively on our shortcomings and mistakes, it may be that evil behavior results in part from the opposite tendency. We look only at the positive aspects of a situation and blind ourselves to the negative impact of our

FIGURE 14-3.
The Daily Mood Log*

DESCRIBE THE UPSETTING EVENT—Being alone with my deceased friend's wife.

NEGATIVE FEELINGS—Record your emotions and rate each one on a scale from 0 (the least) to 100 (the most). Include feelings such as sad, anxious, angry, guilty, lonely, hopeless, frustrated, etc.

Emotion	Rating (0–100)	Emotion	Rating (0–100)	Emotion	Rating (0–100)
1. Excited	99%	3.		5.	
2. Tempted	99%	5.		6.	

AUTOMATIC THOUGHTS Write down your negative thoughts and number them consecutively.	DISTORTIONS Identify the distortions in each "Automatic Thought."	RATIONAL RESPONSES Substitute more realistic and positive thoughts.
1. She's got a nice ass.	1. Mental filter.	1. So do other women.
2. She's good!	2. Mental filter; magnification.	2. So are a lot of other women I could date.
3. I'm getting turned on and I can't resist it.	3. Emotional reasoning.	3. I can resist it if I choose to.
4. I can worry about the guilt later.	4. Fortune-telling.	4. I felt guilty for years the last time I slept with her. It's not worth it.

AUTOMATIC THOUGHTS	DISTORTIONS	RATIONAL RESPONSES
5. It's going to be so sexually fulfilling.	5. Mental filter.	5. It might be fulfilling, but it might be a terrible experience.

OUTCOME—Review your "Rational Responses" and put a check in the box that describes how you now feel:
☐ not at all better; ☑ somewhat better; ☐ quite a bit better; ☐ a lot better.

*Copyright © 1984, David D. Burns. M.D., from *Intimate Connections* (New York: William Morrow & Company).

actions on ourselves and others. This would be a forgiving model of human nature in that "blindness" rather than "badness" would be seen as the source of the problem.

This is not to say that selfish motives and evil do not exist. However, the difficulty with these concepts is that they are emotionally colored and judgmental. Thinking of ourselves and others in these terms can make it difficult to acknowledge and accept personal shortcomings. In contrast, an understanding of the twisted, distorted thought processes that cause us to violate our own moral standards can take away some of the horror of confronting these negative aspects of our lives so we can have the courage to accept our weaknesses and grow.

APPENDICES

A

Selected Readings
for Single People*

Alberti, R. E., and M. L. Emmons. *Your Perfect Right: A Guide to Assertive Behavior*. San Luis Obispo, Ca.: Impact, 1978.

Baer, J. *How to be an Assertive (Not Aggressive) Woman*. New York: Signet, 1976.

Barbach, L. G. *For Yourself: The Fulfillment of Female Sexuality*. Garden City, N.Y.: Doubleday, 1975.

——, *For Each Other*. Garden City, N.Y.: Anchor Press, 1982.

Block, J. D. *Friendship: How to Give It, How To Get It*. New York: Collier Books, 1980.

Burns, D. *Feeling Good: The New Mood Therapy*. New York: Signet, 1981.

Creel, H. L. *Cooking for One is Fun*. New York: Quandrangle, 1976.

Dodson, B. *Liberating Masturbation: A Meditation of Self-Love*. New York: Bodysex Designs, 1974.

Downing, G. *The Massage Book*. New York: Random House, 1972.

Edwards, M. and Hoover, E. *The Challenge of Being Single*. New York: New American Library, 1974.

Ellis, A. *Sex Without Guilt*. North Hollywood, Ca.: Wilshire, 1977.

——. *Sex and the Liberated Man*. Secaucus, N.J.: Lyle Stuart, 1976.

---

*This list was adapted from one prepared by Dr. Susan Walen. She graciously permitted me to reproduce it here.

——. *The Intelligent Woman's Guide to Dating and Mating*. Secaucus, N.J.: Lyle Stuart, 1979.

Ellis, A., and R. Harper. *A New Guide to Rational Living*. Englewood Cliffs, N.J.: Prentice-Hall, 1975.

Halpern, H. M. *How to Break Your Addiction to a Person*. New York: Bantam Books, 1982.

Hauck, P. A. *Overcoming Jealousy and Possessiveness*. Philadelphia: Westminster Press, 1981.

Johnson, D. W. *Reaching Out: Interpersonal Effectiveness and Self-Actualization*. Englewood Cliffs, N.J.: Prentice-Hall, 1972.

Johnson, S. M. *First Person Singular*. New York: Signet, 1977.

Leefeldt, C., and E. Callenbach. *The Art of Friendship*. New York: Berkley Books, 1981.

Lindbergh, A. M. *Gift from the Sea*. New York: Random House, 1955.

Maslow, A. H. *Toward a Psychology of Being*, 2nd ed. New York: D. Van Nostrand, 1968.

May, R. *Man's Search for Himself*. New York: Norton, 1953.

Peele, S., and A. Brodsky. *Love and Addiction*. New York: Signet, 1976.

Russianoff, P. *Why Do I Think I Am Nothing Without a Man?* New York: Bantam Books, 1982.

Sarton, M. *Journal of a Solitude*. New York: Norton, 1973.

Smith, M. J. *When I Say No, I Feel Guilty*. New York: Bantam Books, 1975.

Thoreau, H. D. *Walden and Other Writings*, ed. by B. Atkinson, New York: Random House, 1937.

Zilbergeld, B. *Male Sexuality: A Guide to Sexual Fulfillment*. New York: Little, Brown, & Co., 1978.

Tapes

Burns, D. D. "Feeling Good About Yourself." This tape describes common self-defeating thought patterns and explains how to replace them with rational thinking to help boost self-esteem, increase joy in life, and combat bad feelings such as depression, anger, anxiety, and frustration. Available for $10.95 postpaid from *Psychol-*

ogy Today cassette series, Tape #20269, Dept. A0720, P.O. Box 278, Pratt Station, Brooklyn, N.Y. 11205.

Burns, D.D. "Nobody is Perfect." This tape helps you identify perfectionistic tendencies and shows how they work against you. It explains how to stop setting unrealistically high standards as a means to help increase productivity, creativity, and self-satisfaction. Available for $10.95 postpaid from *Psychology Today* cassette series, Tape #20268, Dept. A0720, P.O. Box 278, Pratt Station, Brooklyn, N.Y. 11205.

Burns, D. D. "Intimate Connections." This tape shows you how to identify and overcome feelings of loneliness and shyness so you can learn how to love and accept yourself and to develop better relationships with others. Available for $6.95 postpaid from Waldentapes, P.O. Box 1084, Stamford, Connecticut 06904.

For many additional references, see Peplau, L. A., and D. Perlman. "A Bibliography on Loneliness: 1932–1981," in *Loneliness: A Sourcebook of Current Theory, Research and Therapy*, ed. by L. A. Peplau and D. Perlman. New York: John Wiley & Sons, Inc., 1982. pp. 407–417.

B

Glossary of Self-help Forms

This appendix contains two copies each of five of the most useful self-help forms that are illustrated in the text, along with instructions in how to use each of them. For actual examples of how each form works, you can consult the following pages in *Intimate Connections:*

1. The Daily Mood Log: pp. 45, 76, 92, 144, 166, 177, 186, 207, 210, 214, 217, 234, 249, 255, 257, 260, 276, 280.
2. The Pleasure Predicting Sheet: p. 37.
3. The Cost-Benefit Analysis: pp. 56, 61, 63, 82, 97, 113, 169, 189.
4. Revise Your Communication Style: p. 125.
5. Qualities I'm Looking for in a Mate: p. 171.

1. The Daily Mood Log

Purpose. The purpose is to help you overcome painful emotions such as loneliness, depression, anger, shyness, guilt, frustration, worry, and fear.

Method. There are four basic steps:

1. Describe the Upsetting Event. At the top of the sheet, write a brief description of the situation or problem that's bothering you. It might involve coming home to an empty house after work, having an argument with a friend, or being rejected by someone you care about.

2. Identify Your Negative Feelings. Record your negative emotions and rate how intense they are between 0 (for the least upset) and 100 (for the most upset).

3. Change Your Thoughts. Tune in to the negative thoughts associated with your feelings and write them down, numbered consecutively, in the column labeled "Automatic Thoughts." Indicate how much you believe each of these thoughts between 0 (for the least) and 100 (for the most). In the middle column identify the distortions in these thoughts, using the "Checklist of Cognitive Distortions" on the back of the Daily Mood Log as a guide. In the column labeled "Rational Responses," substitute other thoughts that are more positive and realistic. Indicate how much you believe each of your "Rational Responses" between 0 and 100. Finally, evaluate how much you now believe each of your "Automatic Thoughts" between 0 and 100.

4. Outcome. Indicate how much better you now feel in the "Outcome" section at the bottom of the sheet.

Troubleshooting. If you are having difficulties breaking out of a bad mood when you use the Daily Mood Log, ask yourself these questions:

1. Do you really want to let go of the anger, guilt, or anxiety you feel? If you want to feel upset, it can be very difficult to eliminate your bad feelings. This is particularly true of people who feel angry, since they get consumed by bitterness and the desire for revenge and don't want to give up their negative feelings. If you feel confused about this, do a Cost-Benefit Analysis by listing the advantages and disadvantages of feeling the way you do. How will it help you to feel bad, and how will it hurt you? Sometimes negative feelings are healthy and appropriate. In this case, it might be better to work on ways of expressing them more effectively rather than trying to eliminate them with the Daily Mood Log.

2. Do not write descriptions of the upsetting situation or your negative feelings about it in the "Automatic Thoughts" column. Statements such as "John rejected me" or "I feel hurt" belong in the section for "Upsetting Events" and "Negative Feelings," not in the "Automatic Thoughts" column. Actual events and emotions are facts, so you cannot put the lie to them. You can put the lie only to the illogical thoughts that make you feel upset.

3. Have you identified the distortions in your "Atuomatic

The Daily Mood Log*

DESCRIBE THE UPSETTING EVENT—_____

_____

_____

_____

NEGATIVE FEELINGS—Record your emotions and rate each one on a scale from O (the least) to 10 (the most). Include feeling such as sad, anxious, angry, guilty, lonely hopeless, frustrated, etc.

Emotion	Rating (0–100)	Emotion	Rating (0–100)	Emotion	Rating (0–100)
1.		3.		5.	
2.		4.		6.	

AUTOMATIC THOUGHTS	DISTORTIONS	RATIONAL RESPONSE
Write down your negative thoughts and number them consecutiely.	Identify the distortions in each "Automatic Thought"	Substitute more realistic and positive thoughts.

*Copyright © 1984, David D. Burns, M.D., from *Intimate Connections* (New York: William Morrow & Company).

OUTCOME—Review your "Rational Responses" and put a check that describes how you now feel:
☐ not at all better; ☐ somewhat better; ☐ quite a bit better; ☐ a lot better.

CHECKLIST OF COGNITIVE DISTORTIONS*

1. All-or-nothing thinking: You look at things in absolute, black-and-white categories.

2. Overgeneralization: You view a negative event as a never-ending pattern of defeat.

3. Mental filter: You dwell on the negatives and ignore the positives.

4. Discounting the positives: You insist that your accomplishments or positive qualities "don't count."

5. Jumping to conclusions: (A) Mind reading—you assume that people are reacting negatively to you when there's no definite evidence for this; (B) Fortune-telling—you arbitrarily predict that things will turn out badly.

6. Magnification or minimization: You blow things way up out of proportion or you shrink their importance inappropriately.

7. Emotional reasoning: You reason from how you feel: "I *feel* like an idiot, so I really must be one." Or "I don't *feel* like doing this so I'll put it off."

8. "Should" statements: You criticize yourself or other people with "shoulds" or "shouldn'ts." "Musts," "oughts," and "have tos" are similar offenders.

9. Labeling: You identify with your shortcomings. Instead of saying "I made a mistake," you tell yourself, "I'm a jerk," or "a fool," or "a loser."

10. Personalization and blame: You blame yourself for something you weren't entirely responsible for, or you blame other people and overlook ways that your own attitudes and behavior might contribute to a problem.

---

*Copyright © 1980, David D. Burns, M.D. Adapted from *Feeling Good: The New Mood Therapy* (William Morrow & Company, 80; Signet, 1981).

The Daily Mood Log*

DESCRIBE THE UPSETTING EVENT—_____

_____

_____

_____

NEGATIVE FEELINGS—Record your emotions and rate each one on a scale from O (the least) to 10 (the most). Include feeling such as sad, anxious, angry, guilty, lonely hopeless, frustrated, etc.

Emotion	Rating (0–100)	Emotion	Rating (0–100)	Emotion	Rating (0–100)
1.		3.		5.	
2.		4.		6.	

AUTOMATIC THOUGHTS	DISTORTIONS	RATIONAL RESPONSE
Write down your negative thoughts and number them consecutiely.	Identify the distortions in each "Automatic Thought"	Substitute more realistic and positive thoughts.

*Copyright © 1984, David D. Burns, M.D., from *Intimate Connections* (New York: William Morrow & Company).

OUTCOME—Review your "Rational Responses" and put a check that describes how you now feel:

☐ not at all better; ☐ somewhat better; ☐ quite a bit better; ☐ a lot better.

CHECKLIST OF COGNITIVE DISTORTIONS*

1. All-or-nothing thinking: You look at things in absolute, black-and-white categories.
2. Overgeneralization: You view a negative event as a never-ending pattern of defeat.
3. Mental filter: You dwell on the negatives and ignore the positives.
4. Discounting the positives: You insist that your accomplishments or positive qualities "don't count."
5. Jumping to conclusions: (A) Mind reading—you assume that people are reacting negatively to you when there's no definite evidence for this; (B) Fortune-telling—you arbitrarily predict that things will turn out badly.
6. Magnification or minimization: You blow things way up out of proportion or you shrink their importance inappropriately.
7. Emotional reasoning: You reason from how you feel: "I *feel* like an idiot, so I really must be one." Or "I don't *feel* like doing this so I'll put it off."
8. "Should" statements: You criticize yourself or other people with "shoulds" or "shouldn'ts." "Musts," "oughts," and "have tos" are similar offenders.
9. Labeling: You identify with your shortcomings. Instead of saying "I made a mistake," you tell yourself, "I'm a jerk," or "a fool," or "a loser."
10. Personalization and blame: You blame yourself for something you weren't entirely responsible for, or you blame other people and overlook ways that your own attitudes and behavior might contribute to a problem.

---

*Copyright © 1980, David D. Burns, M.D. Adapted from *Feeling Good: The New Mood Therapy* (William Morrow & Company, 80; Signet, 1981).

Thoughts,'' using the ''Checklist of Cognitive Distortions'' as a guide?

4. Are your ''Rational Responses'' persuasive, valid statements that you really believe? Remember that rationalizations are not the same as ''Rational Responses.'' Rationalizations are phony, defensive statements that won't help you feel better because they don't reflect the truth. ''Rational Reponses'' are realistic, honest statements that can help you view a painful situation in a more compassionate and objective light.

5. Do your ''Rational Responses'' really put the lie to all your negative thoughts? You won't feel better until you find a convincing way to refute all of your ''Automatic Thoughts.'' As long as you still believe one or two of them, you may continue to feel bad. A therapist or friend can often help you talk back to automatic thoughts you have difficulty answering. Waiting a few days can sometimes help. Many patients tell me that when they go over their negative thoughts a week or two later, they are amazed to see how illogical they were, even though they seemed entirely valid at the time!

6. Are there other upsetting thoughts that you still haven't identified and written down on the Daily Mood Log? Sometimes there will be something that's bothering you that you haven't yet brought to conscious awareness. If you review the various activities you've been involved in and the people you've interacted with recently, you can often figure out what's upsetting you. Readers interested in learning more about this technique may wish to consult David D. Burns's *Feeling Good: The New Mood Therapy* (William Morrow & Company, 1980; New American Library, 1981).

2. The Pleasure Predicting Sheet

Purpose. One purpose of the Pleasure Predicting Sheet is to help you become more creatively and productively involved in potentially rewarding activities. A second purpose is to help you develop greater independence and self-reliance by testing beliefs such as: ''I'm bound to feel miserable when I'm alone'' or ''The only true happiness comes from being with others.''

Method. In the "Activity" column you schedule activities with the potential for satisfaction, learning, self-improvement, or personal growth. If you feel depressed and can't think of anything that seems rewarding or worthwhile, you can schedule activities that used to be enjoyable even if you don't think they'll be very satisfying anymore. Include activities you can do by yourself (such as jogging or reading) and others you can do with friends. Indicate who you plan to do each activity with in the "Companion" column. Do not put the word "alone" in this column. Instead, use the word "self" to describe your companion when you're scheduling an activity with yourself. This will remind you that you never really need to feel alone if you regard yourself as a companion and friend.

In the third column, which is labeled "Predicted Satisfaction," predict how satisfying each activity will be on a scale between 0 (for the least possible satisfaction) and 100 (for the most). You must make these written predictions before you do each activity. Finally, record how satisfying the various activities turn out to be after you've completed them, using the same 0 to 100 rating system in the last column ("Actual Satisfaction").

After you've used the sheet for several days, you can examine the "Actual Satisfaction" column and learn how pleasurable and rewarding the various activities turned out to be. This will help you learn what gives you the most and the least satisfaction. You may find that many of the things you usually do, such as watching TV or overeating, turn out to be rather unrewarding, whereas certain things you might ordinarily avoid, such as cleaning out your desk or exercising, will turn out to be far more rewarding than you anticipated. By the same token, you may find that certain activities you think will be wonderful—going on a date or being with friends or family—sometimes turn out to be considerably less enjoyable than you thought they'd be.

Discovering that you can often be as happy when you're alone as when you're with friends or lovers can be a tremendous source of self-confidence and help you overcome the belief that happiness always comes from loving relationships with other people. Paradoxically, the self-esteem you feel when you realize that you don't really

PLEASURE PREDICTING SHEET*

Activity Schedule Activities With a Potential for Pleasure or Personal growth	Companion (If Alone, Specify Self)	Satisfaction	
		Predicted (0–100) (Record This *Before* Each Activity)	Actual (0–100) (Record This *After* Each Activity)

*Copyright © 1984, David D. Burns, M.D., from *Intimate Connections* (New York: William Morrow & Company).

PLEASURE PREDICTING SHEET*

Activity Schedule Activities With a Potential for Pleasure or Personal growth	Companion (If Alone, Specify Self)	Satisfaction	
		Predicted (0–100) (Record This *Before* Each Activity)	Actual (0–100) (Record This *After* Each Activity)

*Copyright © 1984, David D. Burns, M.D., from *Intimate Connections* (New York: William Morrow & Company).

"need" others to feel good about yourself will usually lead to improved relationships with people, because you'll have more to offer them and you won't be so desperate and afraid of rejection.

3. The Cost-Benefit Analysis

Purpose. The purpose is to help you change a self-defeating attitude, emotion, or behavior by balancing its advantages against its disadvantages.

1. Changing a Self-Defeating Attitude

List the attitude you wish to change at the top of the sheet. The types of attitudes you might want to modify could include:

• I can't feel happy and worthwhile until I have a partner who loves me.

• It's abnormal to be alone.

• Being alone means there's something wrong with me.

• If someone isn't perfect (or very exciting to me), there's no point in going out with him or her.

• I'm basically inferior to people who are more intelligent (or popular, attractive, talented, wealthy, etc.)

Then list the advantages and disadvantages of that attitude. Ask yourself, "How will it help me to believe this? And how will it hurt me?" The advantages of believing that "I can't feel happy and worthwhile until I have a partner who loves me" might include the fact that you'll work extremely hard to find someone and when you do you'll feel worthwhile. The disadvantages would include the facts that when you're alone or rejected you'll feel miserable and that other people will control your self-esteem. Remember to list the advantages and disadvantages of believing you *need* a lover before you can feel happy and worthwhile, not the advantages and disadvantages of having a partner or a lover. It would not be appropriate to put "I'll have someone to love" in the "Advantages" column, since believing that you need a partner won't magically give you someone to love. In fact, the truth may be the opposite. Believing that you can't find happiness until you have a lover may make it *harder* to find someone to love.

Cost-Benefit Analysis*

The attitude or belief I want to change:_____

_____

Advantages of Believing This	Disadvantages of Believing This

*Revised Attitude:*_____

_____

_____

*Copyright © 1984, David D. Burns, M.D., from *Intimate Connections* (New York: William Morrow & Company).

Cost-Benefit Analysis*

The attitude or belief I want to change:_____
_____

Advantages of Believing This	Disadvantages of Believing This

_Revised Attitude:_____
_____
_____

*Copyright © 1984, David D. Burns, M.D., from *Intimate Connections* (New York: William Morrow & Company).

After completing your list of the advantages and disadvantages of a particular belief or attitude, weigh them against each other on a 100-point scale. Put your ratings in the circles at the bottom of the sheet. If the advantages of the belief are considerably greater, you might put 70:30 in these circles. If the disadvantages are slightly greater, you might put 40:60 in them. If the disadvantages of an attitude outweigh the advantages, it means that it isn't very helpful for you to think this way. Try to revise your attitude so it will be more realistic and helpful to you, and write your revised version at the bottom of the sheet. A "Revised Attitude" might be "It's okay to *want* someone to love and a partner could enrich my life, but I don't *need* a partner to feel happy and worthwhile."

2. Changing a Self-Defeating Emotion

The types of feelings you might want to modify could include loneliness, anger, resentment, sadness, depression, guilt, shame, bitterness, worry, fear, envy, and frustration. Describe the emotion you wish to change at the top of the sheet. Then list the advantages and disadvantages of feeling this way. If you're worrying about an upcoming date or a test you have to take, ask yourself how it will help you to worry about it. Then ask yourself how the worrying will hurt you. Some people think that if they worry they'll try harder and do a better job. On the other hand, you may be worrying so much that you won't do as well as when you feel more relaxed.

After you've listed the advantages and disadvantages of a particular emotion, balance them against each other on a 100-point scale, as described earlier. If the disadvantages are greater, use the Daily Mood Log to change your feelings. If the advantages are greater, then your negative feelings may be healthy and appropriate. In this case, you might want to think about ways of expressing them more productively and effectively.

3. Changing a Self-Defeating Behavior

Describe the behavior you want to change at the top of the sheet. The types of behavior you might want to modify could include going to bed with someone who uses you or

Cost-Benefit Analysis*

The attitude or belief I want to change:_____

_____

_____

Advantages of Feeling This Way	Disadvantages of Feeling This Way

*Copyright © 1984, David D. Burns, M.D., from *Intimate Connections* (New York: William Morrow & Company).

Cost-Benefit Analysis*

The attitude or belief I want to change:_____
_____
_____

Advantages of Feeling This Way	Disadvantages of Feeling This Way

*Copyright © 1984, David D. Burns, M.D., from *Intimate Connections* (New York: William Morrow & Company).

Cost-Benefit Analysis*

The behavior I wish to change:_____

_____

Advantages of This Behavior	Disadvantages of This Behavior

Alternative Behavior:_____

_____

_____

*Copyright © 1984, David D. Burns, M.D., from *Intimate Connections* (New York: William Morrow & Company).

Cost-Benefit Analysis*

The behavior I wish to change:_____

_____

_____

Advantages of This Behavior	Disadvantages of This Behavior

*Alternative Behavior:*_____

_____

_____

*Copyright © 1984, David D. Burns, M.D., from *Intimate Connections* (New York: William Morrow & Company).

accepting a date with someone who perpetually calls you at the last minute; having an affair with a married man; avoiding asking someone out because you feel shy and insecure; overeating or drinking excessively when you feel lonely; or giving in to a self-destructive sexual impulse.

List the advantages and disadvantages of this behavior in the appropriate columns. Ask yourself, "How will it help me to behave like this, and how will it hurt me?" Think of the positive and negative effects on you as well as on other people. Remember to consider short-term effects of your actions, as well as the long-term effects. Try to be thorough and honest with yourself. Take subjective feelings and objective facts into account.

It can also be helpful to list the advantages and disadvantages of an alternative action or behavior. For example, you could do a Cost-Benefit Analysis of dating married men versus dating single men. Sometimes it helps to look at the consequences of several possible options.

Once you've listed the advantages and disadvantages of various behaviors, balance them against each other on the 100-point scale, as described earlier.

4. Revise Your Communication Style

Purpose. The purpose is to help you develop new ways of communicating with people in situations that are difficult or upsetting to you. Typical problem areas include flirting, dealing with criticism, or being more assertive and open and about how you feel.

Method. Write down what the other person said in the first column, marked "S/he Says." It might be something that someone who was flirting with you said, or it could be a sharp remark that upset you.

In the middle column, put down what you said to them. You might have become silent and pouty, made a lame comment, gotten defensive or argued. Try to point out why your response wasn't particularly effective. For example, if you argued or defended yourself, it might have led to fight or a frustrating argument. If you're unsure why your response wasn't effective, ask a friend or a counselor for suggestions.

Next, write down a more effective response in the "Re-

Table B-1
Six Principles of Effective Communication*

LISTENING SKILLS		SELF-EXPRESSION SKILLS	
1. Empathy	You listen attentively to what the other person is saying and feeling and reflect this back to them in a sympathetic, nonjudgmental way.	1. Stroking	You express positive regard, even in the heat of battle. You show respect for the other person's thoughts, feelings, and ideas.
2. The Disarming Technique	You find the grain of truth in what the other person is saying, even if it seems illogical, distorted, or unfair.	2. Tactful Presentation	You express your own thinking and feelings in an objective, constructive manner. You avoid coercive, inflammatory language or put-downs.
3. Inquiry	You use questions to learn more about the other person's thoughts and feelings. You transform vague criticisms and objections into concrete issues that can be dealt with effectively.	3. Problem-Solving	You resolve any "real" problems through brainstorming and compromise *after* the air is cleared by using the preceding techniques.

*Adapted from David D. Burns, M.D., "Persuasion: The all-hits-no-misses way to get what you want," *Self* (April 1981), pp. 67–71. For more information, see also David D. Burns, M.D., "Verbal Judo: How to Talk Back Under the Fire of Criticism," Chapter Six of *Feeling Good: The New Mood Therapy* (New York: William Morrow & Co., 1980; Signet, 1981).

Revise Your Communication Style*

S/HE SAYS	I ORDINARILY SAY	REVISED VERSION
In this column record something your partner typically says that you find upsetting.	In this column record what you usually say. Point out why your statement is self-defeating.	Substitute a more effective statement.

*Copyright © 1984, David D. Burns, M.D., from *Intimate Connections* (New York: William Morrow & Company).

Revise Your Communication Style*

S/HE SAYS	I ORDINARILY SAY	REVISED VERSION
In this column record something your partner typically says that you find upsetting.	In this column record what you usually say. Point out why your statement is self-defeating.	Substitute a more effective statement.

*Copyright © 1984, David D. Burns, M.D., from *Intimate Connections* (New York: William Morrow & Company).

vised Version'' column. Think of ways you might have handled the situation differently. Often, the more effective responses in the right-hand column will include the ''Six Principles of Effective Communication'' listed in Table B-1. If you have trouble thinking of better responses to write down in the ''Revised Version'' column, wait a few days or ask a friend you respect what they might have said or done. Modeling your responses on someone more experienced can be an excellent way of learning.

Comment. Often, when you've having trouble communicating effectively, it will be because you feel upset. Feelings such as anger, guilt, shyness, or nervousness can make it extremely difficult to communicate effectively. When you feel upset, use the Daily Mood Log and/or the Cost Benefit Analysis to reduce your negative feelings. Once you feel more relaxed and self-confident, it becomes far easier to communicate effectively.

5. Qualities I'm Looking for in a Mate

Purpose. The purpose of this form is to get you to evaluate people you're interested in more realistically so you can avoid two traps. The first trap is dwelling on someone's best qualities and overlooking his or her shortcomings, so that you start to fantasize that the person is totally wonderful in all respects. The second trap is when you become obsessed with one or two negative qualities someone has and you conclude that she or he is a total loser.

Method. In the column marked ''Qualities,'' list twenty characteristics you're looking for in a partner. You might include attractiveness, faithfulness, a sense of humor, availability, the appropriate age and race, openness, intelligence, ''good chemistry,'' a common value system, and similar interests. You can list these qualities in any particular order.

After completing your list of twenty qualities, write down the names of several people you've known or dated at the top of the sheet. Rate them in each of the twenty categories on a scale between 0 (this is the lowest possible rating for any quality or characteristic) to 5 (this is the highest possible rating for any quality). If you aren't entirely sure about how to rate someone for a particular quality because you don't know him or her well enough yet, put your best guess. You can revise your ratings later on when you get to know the person better.

Add up all twenty ratings for each person you listed. Since each of the ratings is between 0 and 5, each person's total score will range between 0 (if she or he rated 0 in all of the twenty categories) and 100 (if he or she rated 5 in all of the twenty categories).

Now ask yourself these questions:

1. How high would someone's ratings have to be, between 0 and 100, for me to have one date with him or her? _____ [Put your answer here]

2. How high would a person's ratings have to be for me to go out with him or her more than once? _____

3. How high would someone's ratings have to be for me to go out with him or her regularly or exclusively? _____

4. How high would someone's ratings have to be for me to want to marry him or her? _____

5. How high would someone's ratings have to be for me to feel happy and worthwhile and for us to have a rewarding, satisfying relationship? _____

The first four questions were serious ones that can provide useful guides for you. Knowing what you're looking for in a partner can help you evaluate people more objectively. Once you know how high a person's ratings are, you can decide if you'd want to date that person never, once, or regularly. The fifth question was a trick question, and I hope you had trouble answering it. It's probably not to your advantage to link your self-esteem or your capacity for happiness to your partner's ratings. Many people with rather "ordinary" partners feel very happy and fulfilled, while many others with partners who seem fabulous are miserably unhappy and dissatisfied. Ultimately, your self-esteem and your potential for intimacy will depend more on the effort you're willing to put into your relationship and your commitment to your partner. Given these essential ingredients, you'll be well on the way to a successful and satisfying relationship.

Qualities I'm Looking for in a Mate*

People I've Met or Dated

Qualities	1. David	2. Bob	3. John
1. Wants and willing to work on a committed relationship	0	0	
2. wants children	0	0	5
3. supportive	3	3	3
4. makes me laugh	4	3	4
5. make at least 30,000 year	5	5	4
6. likes to do things hikes, go to plays	1	5	4
7. spiritual	1	1	5
8. weighs more than me	5	5	5
9. between 38-42	5	5	0
10. enthusiastic about life	1	3	3
11. ambitious	1	3	3
12. responsible	5	4	4
13. self-confident	4	4	2
14. caring & Affectionate out not over	1	1	2
15. interested in world affairs moderate	4	4	2
16. like to to liberal philosophy	1	3	2
17. fun to be with	4	4	4
18. good lover	1	4	4
19. Acceptive of Princess	5	1	2
20. easy to be with calls and gets together with me often 2x's per week	0	0	4
TOTALS	51	58	

---

*Copyright © 1984, David D. Burns, M.D., from *Intimate Connections* (New York: William Morrow & Company).

Qualities I'm Looking for in a Mate*

People I've Met or Dated

Qualities	1.	2.	3.
1.	5		
2.	0		
3.	3		
4.	4		
5.	5		
6.	5		
7.	5		
8.	5.		
9.	0		
10.	3		
11.	3		
12.	5		
13.	1		
14.	4.		
15.	3.		
16.	3.		
17.	4.		
18.	4.		
19.	4		
20.	5		
TOTALS	70		

*Copyright © 1984, David D. Burns, M.D., from *Intimate Connections* (New York: William Morrow & Company).

C

How to Overcome an Inferiority Complex

This appendix illustrates how cognitive therapy techniques can be applied to problems such as loneliness, inferiority, and low self-esteem. I have included considerable actual dialogue, which was excerpted from tapes of therapy sessions, so that professional readers and interested nonprofessionals can get a feel for how the therapeutic process evolves with a real patient. Keep in mind that every therapist's style is different. Mine happens to try to be unique, and it would not be desirable for other therapists to try to mimic it. It's preferable to apply the cognitive techniques in a natural way that you feel comfortable with. Keep in mind that good therapy requires two necessary ingredients: technique and caring. The best results occur when you combine specific problem-solving methods with empathy and rapport. Too much emphasis on problem-solving techniques will make the therapy seem mechanical and superficial. Too much emphasis on empathy and the sharing of painful feelings can make the therapy overly slow-moving, and the patient may begin to feel worse and worse. A skillful balance of technique and caring will result in the most rapid therapeutic gains.

Janice is a twenty-six-year-old single woman who was doing administrative work for a social service agency in New York at the time she sought therapy. She complained of painful feelings of loneliness and inferiority which had plagued her since childhood. Janice was convinced she was a second-rate human being. Here's how she described her feelings the first day we met: "I feel like I'm shrouded in a gray cloud. . . . I can't seem to get back into the sunshine. . . . I've cried myself to sleep for the past ten or fifteen years. I feel that people don't like me. I think I'm awkward and klutzy. At social gatherings I blank out. I feel like I *should* be witty but I can't think of anything to say. I'm vague, uncommitted, indecisive, and inadequate; in short, I'm just plain mediocre."

Janice often saw in others what she felt she lacked in herself. As she walked down the street on the way to work, she would notice well-dressed professionals and executives and tell herself, "They're the Beautiful People. They have what counts. There's nothing really special or unique about me."

Janice's discouraging habit of comparing herself to other people and ending up on the short end of the stick is common among depressed and lonely people. They often notice everyone else's positive qualities but find little about themselves to feel proud of. They're often convinced that since they're not especially intelligent, witty, talented, successful, or sexually endowed, they're just *average*, unexciting, and dull.

As I got to know Janice, I was impressed with the savageness of her self-critical thoughts. Regardless of what she was doing, an inner voice always commented. "That's not good enough. Someone else could have done better." This made her feel frustrated and inferior. She recognized that she had these upsetting thoughts all day long, but she argued that they were realistic because she was convinced that the people around her were in fact brighter and more talented, attractive, and socially polished. Because she saw herself as "only average," she concluded she was inferior and that it was foolish to hope that her feelings could ever really change. She believed she was essentially and irreversibly a second-rate human being.

As a way of showing Janice how unreasonably hard she was being on herself, I suggested that we play a game in which I would be an "average" psychiatrist in private practice who did not measure up to the outstanding talents of his associate, Dr. X, who was a superior therapist and scholar. I instructed Janice to be my critical inner voice.

She was to try to make me feel inferior because I was only "average." I used this unusual therapeutic maneuver to try to show Janice how to defend her self-esteem against all her relentless self-criticism. The session may be of some historical interest to professional readers, since it illustrates the first time I used a new technique I had developed called the "externalization of voices." This powerful method allows therapists to use dramatic techniques to modify patients' self-critical thoughts, often in a remarkably short period of time. The approach has become quite popular with therapists around the country and seems to generate considerable enthusiasm when I demonstrate it in lectures and workshops.

I would like to emphasize that in the following dialogue Janice and I are portraying the two parts of her mind. This is not "assertiveness training," in which you learn to defend yourself against another human being who's giving you a hard time. The "externalization of voices" method shows patients how to defend against a far crueler enemy: the critic that lurks in their own minds.

JANICE (PLAYING THE ROLE OF THE INNER CRITICAL VOICE): Compared to Dr. X., you don't measure up.

DAVID (PLAYING THE ROLE OF THE SELF-DEFENSE): In what ways do I not measure up?

JANICE (AS INNER CRITIC): He's a more skillful and effective therapist, and his academic contributions in the literature are more highly respected. Doesn't that make you feel bad?

DAVID (AS SELF-DEFENSE): No, it makes me feel good, because it means I have plenty of room to grow. When I was a medical student, I could only help thirty to forty percent of the patients I worked with. I hardly knew what I was doing. I've been improving continually since then, and there's no reason for me to stop learning now.

JANICE (AS INNER CRITIC): I could understand your point if Dr. X were significantly older. Say, if he had thirty years on you, it would not be reasonable to compare yourself with him. But you are both the same age. He's obviously brighter, and he's achieved so much more.

DAVID (AS SELF-DEFENSE): He probably *is* more intelligent, and he seems to be an unusually talented therapist. But are you saying that makes him a better *person?* Does that make me an inferior human being?

JANICE (AS INNER CRITIC): Well, face the facts! He's got what counts! You don't!

DAVID (AS SELF-DEFENSE): What he's got *does* count. Are you saying he's got everything that counts, and I've got nothing?

JANICE: It's just that what you have doesn't count much. You're just average at best.

DAVID: Are you saying my work with my patients isn't satisfactory?

JANICE: You know you can't settle for just being an *average* or *satisfactory* psychiatrist. After all, a lot of people depend on you! You can't just piddle along like you were a garbage truck driver.

DAVID: I'm not sure I know what's so terrible about being a garbage truck driver. But what I'm doing required substantial training and effort, and I do help many patients.

JANICE: Well, you may help some patients because they don't have any basis for comparison. But if your patients were transferred over to Dr. X, they'd say, "Oh, now I see what a loser Dr. Burns is. Here I am moving so much faster with Dr. X."

DAVID: But most of my patients do seem satisfied. They usually achieve their goals and they don't seem concerned about whether I'm the greatest therapist in the world. They seem more concerned with whether I care about them and I can help them. They're looking for personal results, not a "world champion therapist."

JANICE: Well, that may be, but they don't know any better. I'm just emphasizing the objective fact that *you're not as brilliant, effective, accomplished, or worthwhile as Dr. X!*

DAVID: Well, I certainly agree with you that I'm not always as effective, and that's one of the brightest thoughts in my life. The fact is, that gives me a little room to improve. Learning is one of my greatest sources of satisfaction. Just think of all I can still learn! It's very exciting to think about that!

JANICE: Yes, but doesn't it bother you that your professional peers don't respect you? You may always find somebody who will love you or some darn fool who will lick your hand. But who will really respect you?

DAVID: Who doesn't respect me, aside from you?

As the dialogue evolved, it became clear that Janice was afraid of being "average." She seemed to expect that she had to be number one in order to respect herself. My strategy was to show her that it's okay to be "average" in one or more areas of your life. Really, why is being average so terrible? Does it mean that you won't be able to find satisfying work or interesting activities or that no one will love or respect you? If so, we're all out of luck, because every human being and every object in this universe is "average" in most respects. Take the sun, for example. On the one hand, it is huge and has poured out enormous masses of energy for thousands of years. Yet it is only an "average" star. Imagine the sun complaining, "That Betelgeuse in Orion is sixteen hundred times as bright as I am! And twenty-seven million times as great in volume! What's the use of shining anymore! I'm so inferior!"

Janice felt that if she wasn't outstanding, people would be disappointed in her:

JANICE (AS SELF): The record that is always playing in the back of my mind is that I have to live with the expectations of other people. You're just not good enough unless you get an A. It's just expected you've got to be that way. Everything else is inconsequential.

DAVID: Who taught you that?

JANICE: Well, I guess—I don't know. I don't think anybody ever *said* it. It was just a reality when I was growing up. Everybody was very successful. My grandmother was a famous biologist and my mother is a hospital administrator. My brother is a very successful surgeon.

DAVID: Was she the grandmother that raised you?

JANICE: Granny, the one who raised me, was nothing in particular, but she was very, very, very anxious that we succeed, that we get into the best schools, et cetera.

DAVID: Okay.

JANICE: The message was that you just don't get the strokes from people unless you are doing something exceptional.

I suspect that's where Janice picked up this belief she was "inferior." Many people who are prone to depression and low self-esteem were raised with the idea that they have to succeed in order to be acceptable and worthwhile. They feel they're not going to be loved for themselves, but that they'll have to *earn* love. The game is to succeed, then you get a little stroke, and then you succeed some more and you get another stroke. It's a game you can win for a while by constantly achieving. The strokes make you feel good, but it's like becoming a heroin addict because you've got to get that A or earn that promotion to feel high. So you keep shooting up all the time, trying to achieve. Meanwhile, you don't develop the capacity to experience yourself as having any inherent worthwhileness. You treat yourself like a commodity, and your feelings of self-esteem are never really secure, because there's always the risk of failing or not measuring up to everyone's expectations.

The attitude that you have to earn your self-esteem and *prove* yourself all the time puts terrific pressure on you. In contrast, if you decide that you can love and accept yourself regardless of how successful you are, then you won't have to be measuring or doubting yourself anymore. You'll be free of the constant burden of your self-criticism.

Janice wasn't going to buy these ideas too readily. She kept insisting that there wasn't *anything* special enough about her that would make her desirable and lovable. She was certain she had no basis for loving and accepting herself, as the following dialogue illustrates.

JANICE: I feel there's nothing about me that's *unusually* good. I mean I'm a nice—a vaguely nice person. I'm not physically deformed. I can walk two or three miles. You know, I can do very average things, but I'm not the kind of person that would cause somebody to say, "I really like to be with her." And I haven't seen any evidence that I'm worthwhile.

DAVID: No, there is no evidence. No matter what your achievements are, you can always say, "It's not good enough," or, "I'm not desirable." Let's go back to the psychiatrist example. Even if I were ninety percent effective, you could still label me as inferior and put me down because I wasn't ninety-nine percent. Just how good do you have to be in order to feel happy with yourself and to love and respect yourself? And why should you even have to earn your self-esteem in this way? Why not simply make a declaration of self-esteem and decide to accept yourself regardless of how smart and successful you are? Ultimately, you're responsible for this decision.

JANICE: I was thinking—I was just searching my life to see when I've ever been encouraged or when I've ever encouraged myself. No matter how well I do, I always seem to feel I've fallen short. But how do you know that you are good if you don't rely on other people's opinions?

DAVID: People can judge the validity or value of something you do or say, but that's not the same as giving them the right to judge how worthwhile you are as a person. Do you want to put your self-esteem at the mercy of other people? The issue is not whether you're "good" or "no good." You see, that's polarized thinking. The issue is whether you're willing to love and accept yourself. It might help to make a list of the advantages and disadvantages of believing "I must be truly outstanding at everything I do in order to be lovable and worthwhile." You could also list the advantages and disadvantages of telling yourself, "I must have everyone else's approval to be a worthwhile person." Ask yourself, "How will it help me to believe these things, and how will it hurt me?"

I wanted Janice to understand that her feelings of inferiority were based not on *reality* but on her bad habit of always saying, "I'n not quite good enough." One form of distorted thinking that causes this problem is all-or-nothing thinking. Janice reasoned, "What I do has to be outstanding or it's no good." Since her performance rarely measured up to her impossible standards, she was constantly berating herself. I suggested a way she could work on overcoming this tendency at home.

DAVID: I want you to do an exercise between now and next session. I want you to think of every quality you can think of: maleness, femaleness, intelligence, beauty, blueness of the sky, or anything you want to think of. Now, ask yourself if people or objects in this universe can be neatly defined with all-or-nothing categories. For example, are some people "perfectly smart" while others are "totally stupid"? Is the sky "perfectly blue" one day and "perfectly gray" on another? Would you say these walls in my office are perfectly white and clean or completely dirty?

JANICE: Dirty white.

DAVID: So they are not *all* clean? The fact that they are not *all* clean—does that make them totally dirty?

JANICE: No, but the dirt really detracts from them. . . . Okay, I see what you are saying.

DAVID: Well, the amount of detraction is a *relative thing*. It doesn't detract at all for me, since they were freshly painted three weeks ago. So how dirty can they be? Do you see what I mean? It's arbitrary whether or not you're going to get distracted by miniscule amounts of dirt on a wall. You've got to learn to live with your imperfections, because everything and every person in this universe is imperfect in every respect. There's no perfection in this world. And it's your insistence that you must always be perfect or outstanding that makes you think you're always a loser.

JANICE: Yes.

DAVID: If you are obsessive enough, you can take a wall from a surgery room that's been scrubbed and find some crack or speck of dirt and sit and sob about it. But it's pretty arbitrary. You see?

JANICE: Yes.

DAVID: If you should conclude after doing this exercise that there is very little, if anything, that breaks down into all-or-nothing categories, then you may realize that most things are relative. For example, you may decide that there's no such things as an "intelligent" or "stupid" human being unless you arbitrarily draw a cutoff point at some I.Q. level. But this would be absurd. Where do you put the cutoff point that divides the "intelligent" from the "stupid" people? The same reasoning applies to looks, talent, et cetera. And if there is no meaningful cutoff point, it follows there is no such thing as an "inferior" human being. Work on this between now and the next session, and then we'll see how you can talk back to that critical voice in your head.

JANICE: Yes, I understand. The session has been very exciting. I feel like there's a chance the problem is caused by my way of looking at things. I'm beginning to understand where this sense of inferiority comes from.

DAVID: Okay. Now tell me why that is exciting to you.

JANICE: It's like a boulder in my life, and I'm actually pushing against it now, whereas before I just saw it dimly in the distance and avoided it.

DAVID: I see. So you are beginning to define a problem in your life, and that problem seems to you like a boulder that you're pressing against. Why is that exciting?

JANICE: The exciting thing is first of all that we have actually found the boulder, and there's a really hopeful feeling that we can do something about it.

DAVID: You've done a great deal already. You know, it may be that you're going on to learn how to crack this particular boulder open.

JANICE: Yeah. And it's encouraging to me to know that this is something that I didn't see at all before.

DAVID: Right. It's exciting to find out that you have a blind spot, because that means you can learn some new ways of looking at things so you won't bump your head so often.

The next time Janice came in for a session she reported that her mood had improved considerably. Her depression and feelings of inferiority had actually vanished. She explained that this was the result of discovering that the world cannot be described in all-or-nothing categories.

JANICE: I found that there are mitigating features in everything.

DAVID: Can you give me some examples of that?

JANICE: Well, suppose I feel blue because I tell myself that I'm disorganized. Then I ask myself: Am I always disorganized? What did I do yesterday that was organized? Suddenly the blue mood disappears.

DAVID: Right!

JANICE: Am I always organized? No, but I don't have to be.

DAVID: Okay. Look at yourself today. Are you organized or disorganized?

JANICE: Well, I'm organized.

DAVID: Right. Your clothing is organized, your posture is organized, your speech is organized, your hair is organized. Look at my hair—it's been disorganized by the wind today.

JANICE: But I'm not completely organized because . . .

DAVID: Nor would you want to be.

JANICE: Because I left my attaché case spread open on the floor.

DAVID: I'm not perfectly organized, either. I can't find this crucial memo that I was working on. My secretary was slaving over it for days and I apparently misplaced it. You see?

JANICE: Yeah.

DAVID: So then you decided that you are partially organized and not totally organized. What do you conclude? Why does this help your mood?

JANICE: It feels pretty good. I'm partially organized, and that's good enough. I don't have to be perfect.

DAVID: Right. So what other qualities did you look at in your homework assignment?

JANICE: Whether I was liked, whether I had been having a good time. Various things like that.

DAVID: And what was the outcome of these?

JANICE: Virtually the same. I am liked by *some* people but not all. I can have a good time *part* of the time, but it doesn't have to be always.

DAVID: What effect did that have on your feelings?

JANICE: Made them very positive, as you see from the fact that my depression finally disappeared after twenty or so years.

DAVID: Let's assume that at some future time you again begin to feel temporarily depressed, thinking you are inferior. What could you tell yourself? What have you learned that you would like to remember for the rest of your life? If you had to condense this new understanding into a sentence or a paragraph, just what would you say?

JANICE: Well, I can scan back over a period of time and find that things are not all one way or the other. I can remind myself I've had experiences which have been positive, effective, useful, creative, whatever.

DAVID: You're saying that things are not all one way or the other way, but somewhere in between. Now, why is that important information? You could say, "Well, therefore I'm mediocre. I'm always in between." Do you see what I mean? Why is it helpful to learn that things in this world are not all one way or the other way?

JANICE: It is unnecessary and unrealistic to think of things or people as totally negative or as totally positive. Neither assessment is a solid basis for action.

Because Janice had experienced a rapid transformation in her outlook and in her mood, I decided to utilize the "externalization of voices" technique to see if she was really sure of herself. I told her we'd turn the tables around from the previous session when she got to attack me as an "average" psychiatrist. I explained that I would take the role of *her* former self-critical thoughts and attack her as ruthlessly as I could to see if she could really defend her new feelings of self-esteem. I was curious to see if she would crumble when I criticized her. This would show me whether she had integrated these insights into an effective and powerful new philosophy at the gut level, or whether she was just involved in sterile intellectualizations.

DAVID (PLAYING THE ROLE OF JANICE'S INNER CRITICAL VOICE): So you're always in between. Doesn't that mean you're basically a mediocre, inferior human being?

JANICE (AS SELF-DEFENSE): No. Everything and everyone in the world is a mixed bag. Positives and negatives.

DAVID (AS CRITICAL VOICE): Well, isn't that a good reason to feel miserable—that we are living in a universe of mixed bags? It seems you would get astronomically depressed to think that the whole universe is made up of mixed bags.

JANICE (AS SELF-DEFENSE): It's a source of variety and stimulation. If we were all walking around as black or white squares, it would be quite boring. There would be no shades of gray.

DAVID (AS CRITICAL VOICE): All right. But consider your own grayness—you say you're average in most respects, and you say you are only a little above average in intelligence. Doesn't that mean that you're inferior to all these really bright people?

JANICE (AS SELF-DEFENSE): Ah . . . maybe. Maybe it means that I am not as intelligent as they, in some respect, but I have stronger qualities in other areas.

DAVID (AS CRITICAL VOICE): Such as what? Which strong qualities do you have?

JANICE (AS SELF-DEFENSE): I'm not sure.

DAVID (AS CRITICAL VOICE): There, you see, you have no strong qualities! You really arc inferior!

JANICE: Umm . . . okay. I think I'm perceptive and sensitive to other people. These are qualities that a lot of people don't have.

DAVID: But a lot of people are more perceptive and sensitive than you!

JANICE Yes, but it seems to be that the people who are intelligent are not necessarily perceptive and sensitive, and vice versa.

DAVID: But there are a lot of bright people who are also very perceptive and sensitive, and you are inferior to them!

JANICE: I have other fine qualities.

DAVID: Such as what?

JANICE: I'm artistic, a good cook, a good analyzer of problems.

DAVID: But whatever quality or ability you name, there are people who are much better at it than you are. Think of the famous chefs in Paris. Think of the brilliant analysts at Princeton!

JANICE: Yes, there are plenty of people who are better in each of those areas. So what?

DAVID: And there are undoubtedly people who are better in *all* of those areas than you.

JANICE: Undoubtedly there are, so what?

DAVID: Well, just think about it. There's probably some great cook in Paris who is also an artist and has a 150 I.Q. and is sensitive. He's way ahead of you, and you'll ncver catch up.

JANICE: But I don't *want* to be that person. I don't *need* to be that person to be happy.

DAVID: Ah . . . now, that's a very interesting claim. But what I've been telling you is that if you are inferior to people in so many ways, then you are bound to feel mediocre and unhappy. But what you're telling me is that you can let other people be more intelligent or finer cooks and you can still be happy? How can you do that? I don't understand how you can be happy and—

JANICE: I was thinking about this, this morning. I think it's a matter of setting a standard for myself that I know pleases me and holding to that. I don't need to be a *cordon bleu* chef to be happy.

DAVID: Why not?

JANICE: Well, I'm not into that kind of food for every day. I just have to be able to cook the kind of food that pleases me!

DAVID: Whenever you walk downtown you're going to see people in fancy suits and beautiful clothing. They are the "Beautiful People," and you are going to know that you aren't one of them. That's going to remind you how inferior and inadequate you are. How can you live with that? You're going to settle for being a lowly snail?

JANICE: Well, first of all, I'm probably inferring a lot about them. Somebody that I see from fifty feet away isn't necessarily . . . I really don't know their exact I.Q. and their personality, and I don't know where they're hurting, either.

DAVID: You may not know, but you know darn well that a lot of those men are a-hundred-and-fifty-thousand-dollar-a-year executives, and you know some of the women you see are charming, appealing, effective, highly paid, highly charged human beings. You know that's true for quite a number of them. They go to the Riviera and they probably jet-set around the world, going to conferences and—

JANICE: That's true.

DAVID: So doesn't that kind of leave you behind? How can you be happy knowing what a failure you are in comparison to people like that?

JANICE: Well, I have always thought that one of my strengths has to do with my adaptability and flexibility. Because of my training and experience in anthropology I can cover a very wide range of places, from intensive high-level planning sessions at the United Nations to grass-roots work with the small Apache tribes in the mountains of Arizona. I think that there are probably few of those people who can do the same thing.

DAVID: But there are people who are much better anthropologists and conference organizers than you.

JANICE: That's true.

DAVID: So how can you be happy when there are people who will publish books in anthropology? Why, I have an associate who has published several books in anthropology, and he created a whole new theory. He's way ahead of you!

JANICE: Yes, but it's just a matter of deciding what my standard would be for myself in each of these respects. Now I think I can assess what it is, and make sure that I don't compare myself with anything beyond that.

DAVID: Well, now you're just like an ostrich. You're going to put your head in a hole in the sand and ignore all these important things. You're going to find your happiness by ignoring reality?

JANICE: Ignoring whose reality?

DAVID: The reality of the universe, that there are people who are better anthropologists and wear fancier clothes and have higher salaries and do more traveling than you.

JANICE: That's true, they do, but that doesn't mean that I necessarily have to be unhappy.

DAVID: Why? How can you be happy when all of these high-powered people are doing all these fabulous things? You're just basically an inadequate, inferior human being. I suppose you can have your own inadequate little puddle of happiness. You can have your own inferior package of dull joy, but you're never going to have the kind of ecstasy that those "Beautiful People" have.

JANICE: I'm not so sure about that. Perhaps they have some flaws, too.

DAVID: Aw . . . you're just trying to put them down, and that shows how inadequate and envious you are.

JANICE: You know, I think that I don't need to cut them down anymore. I have more than enough skill and redeeming qualities to make myself a happy life, and it really doesn't make much difference whether you're soaring off on comets, or what you're doing. *If I'm happy doing what I'm doing, that's what's important!*

DAVID: Say that again?

JANICE: *If I'm happy doing what I'm doing, that's what's important!*

At this point in the session I gave up attacking Janice. It was clear that she was no longer being dominated by other people's excessive expectations and she was no longer intimidated by the ruthless self-criticism that had always made her feel inadequate and short-changed. Instead of comparing herself to others, she was tuning in on her own uniqueness. Instead of disqualifying everything she did, she began to appreciate and enjoy herself. We stopped role-playing at this point and explored her new feelings about herself.

DAVID: How have you found happiness in doing what you're doing? How did you accomplish that?

JANICE: Well, I've been pretty effective in my current work. Could you believe that the last couple of weeks I've been organizing meetings and working out intricate agendas? And that really pleases me. When I look at what I am doing, I'm no longer saying, "It isn't good enough." Instead, I take delight in it. Life can be pretty delicious, if you don't go around putting yourself down all the time.

DAVID: You mentioned some of your experiences earlier— the work that you did in Asia and the work that you did in Arizona.

JANICE: A lot of those experiences were effective because they involved working with people, not with paper. I developed very warm relationships with the people there. They were stimulating experiences for me in ways that I hadn't expected.

DAVID: You have had a very unusual career, haven't you?

JANICE: Very varied. Yeah.

DAVID: In a way you have been like your own comet. Just that you have been ignoring your own shine.

JANICE: I don't know if it's a comet or a clover leaf. You know, it doesn't make any difference. Who knows what it looks like from the outside? Nobody else can really tell me what it looks like.

DAVID: I've been trying hard to play the role of your own internal critical voice. Have I been doing a good job of

that—saying the kinds of things that you used to say to
yourself? I was doing my hardest to tear you down. And
you just sat there calmly, kind of brushing the insults
away like so many flies on a sunny summer day. Right?

JANICE: Yes.

DAVID: So how does it feel to be able to do that?

JANICE: It feels like I'm in control. Essentially you're
teaching me to challenge any negative thought and to
examine it. I am learning to evaluate what I say to
myself. It never occurred to me before. It's been very
exciting!

As Janice learned to talk back to her internal critical
voice, she experienced a surge of self-esteem. Her sense of
inferiority was based not on *reality*, but on her constant
nagging thought: "No matter what I do, it's not good
enough and therefore I'm not desirable." She had been
trapped by impossible standards that were making her
miserable. As she put her own strengths and weaknesses
into a more realistic perspective, she realized that she
didn't need to be extraordinary in order to feel satisfied
and happy. She discovered that there is no such thing as an
"inferior" human being, and that what she had was suffi-
cient for inner peace and self-esteem.

Many people who feel inferior believe that unless they
are truly outstanding in at least one respect, they can't feel
truly happy and worthwhile. *Nuts!* Being outstanding at
something is no guarantee of happiness. Many of the
world's greatest artists, musicians, businesspeople, and
scientists have had personal lives tormented by depression
and suffering. In contrast, there are millions of people
whose lives are only "ordinary" who experience life as a
wonderful and joyous adventure.

How can this be? You can be just "average" at something and derive enormous satisfaction from it. I have
always felt exhilarated by a good game of table tennis, but
I don't have to win to enjoy it. In fact, I enjoy the game
most when I just barely lose, because a better opponent has
challenged me to my limits and given me the chance to
improve. The thrill of rallying is far more exhilarating to
me than the ultimate victory or defeat.

If you doubt this, you can perform a simple experiment

and find out. In the next few days, schedule a series of activities with a potential for satisfaction, pleasure, or personal growth. These might include such things as reading a book, straightening up your desk, jogging, doing some needed repair around the house, having sex, going out for an ice-cream cone, or just walking through the woods with a friend. As you are doing each activity, ask yourself two questions: (1) How much satisfaction am I actually experiencing between 0 percent (none at all) and 100 percent (the most possible)? (2) Am I one of the world's top experts at this activity, or am I just "average" at it? I think this will make you aware that you don't need to be especially "outstanding" in order to enjoy life's activities to the hilt. So why worry about how superior or inferior you are?

You may feel you have to impress people with your intelligence, personality, and achievements in order to get them to like or love you. This is a myth. Relating to people successfully depends more on loving yourself and others, being genuine and open with your feelings, and expressing a sincere interest in people. Instead of worrying about whether you're good enough, let them know you care about them and think *they're* "the best." This is the secret of a rewarding relationship.

Summary

The main points of this appendix are:

1. Feelings of inferiority are never based on reality. They always result from your self-critical, illogical thoughts. These negative thoughts contain such distortions as:

• All-or-nothing thinking: You tell yourself that everything you do has to be the very best or it isn't any good at all.

• Magnification and minimization: You constantly compare yourself to other people, exaggerating the importance of their best qualities and ignoring your own.

• Mental filtering: You focus on all your shortcomings and imperfections.

• Disqualifying the positive: You insist that your accomplishments, talents, and good points aren't worthwhile.

2. Happiness and self-esteem don't come from how "outstanding" you are, but from your willingness to love yourself and to think about yourself objectively—including a fair assessment of your strengths and weaknesses—without making global judgments about how "worthwhile" or "inferior" you are *as a human being*. Your cooking skills or abilities to play tennis may be inferior to someone else's, but this doesn't make you an inferior human being. You may be less successful or intelligent than millions of people, but this doesn't make you less worthwhile. You may not have as good a figure or as fancy a home as a movie star living in Beverly Hills, but this doesn't make you one iota less special or lovable. There is, in fact, *no such thing* as an inferior human being. Therefore, you couldn't possibly be one!

3. Lovability and desirability have more to do with your own self-esteem and your capacity to *give* love and to make other people feel special than with your ability to impress people with how attractive or successful you are.

4. Pleasure and satisfaction come from the process of being active and getting creatively involved in life, regardless of the level of skill or talent you bring to an activity. You can enjoy a jog or a friendly game of volleyball or cards with friends just as much as or more than people who are world champions in these areas.

5. Most people are pretty "average" in most respects. Since nobody is truly "perfect" in even *one* respect, it follows that we're all "defective" in *all* aspects. No one has a perfect face, a perfect figure, or a perfect mind. These defects and imperfections don't make us "inferior"; they just make us "human." Feelings of inferiority don't prove that you're any less worthwhile than anyone else— they simply show that you haven't learned how to love and accept yourself yet!

Follow-up

Since Janice's "transformation" was extremely rapid— the therapy consisted of fewer than a dozen sessions over about a month—many therapists will be dubious about the long-term effects. Janice moved to California shortly after the sessions excerpted here, so I called her several years later out of curiosity to see how she was doing. Her life had included many positive and negative experiences, including the loss of her job because of funding problems and a broken love affair, but she hadn't forgotten how to dispute her negative thoughts, and as a result she hadn't succumbed to bouts of inferiority or depression. Her ability to maintain her self-esteem in the face of several significant disappointments was quite impressive.

That "externalization of voices" method that was so helpful to Janice has considerable potential in the treatment of inferiority and low self-esteem. Therapists who use this method should apply it with sensitivity. Remember to reverse roles whenever your patient becomes upset and has trouble talking back to the negative thoughts. This will allow you to provide support and model effective responses. Then, when the patient sees how you talk back to the self-critical thoughts, you can again reverse roles and let the patient try the role of self-defense again.

Certainly I don't mean to create the impression that all patients are as easy to treat or as cooperative and bright as Janice, and even when rapid improvement occurs, there can be setbacks requiring periodic "tune-ups" after the completion of therapy. The purpose of the therapy is not to show patients how to be happy all the time, but to teach them that there are things they can do to learn to understand and overcome their painful moods and encourage them to apply these skills whenever they need them throughout their lives.

Psychiatrists, psychologists, and other counselors who are interested in learning more about cognitive behavioral therapy for patients suffering from loneliness and low self-esteem may wish to consult:

1. Primakoff, L. "One's Company; Two's a Crowd. Skills in Living Alone Groups," Chapter 12 in *Cognitive Therapy for Couples and Groups*, (A. Freedman, ed.) New York: Plenum Press, 1983, pp. 261–301.

2. Rook, K. S., and L. A. Peplau. "Perspectives on Helping the Lonely," Chapter 21 in *Loneliness: A Sourcebook of Current Theory, Research and Therapy*, L. A. Peplau and D. Perlman, eds. New York: John Wiley & Sons, 1982, pp. 351–78.

3. Young, J. E. "Loneliness, Depression and Cognitive Therapy," Chapter 22 in *Loneliness: A Sourcebook of Current Theory, Research and Therapy*. pp. 374–405.

4. Burns, D. D. *Feeling Good: The New Mood Therapy*. New York: William Morrow & Company, 1980; Signet, 1981.

About the Author

David D. Burns, M.D., is the president of the Behavioral Sciences Research Foundation and director of the Institute for Cognitive and Behavioral Therapies at the Presbyterian-University of Pennsylvania Medical Center. He is a graduate of Amherst College and received his M.D. from Stanford University School of Medicine. Among the many awards and fellowships he has received is the A. E. Bennett Award for his research on the chemistry of moods from the Society of Biological Psychiatry. Dr. Burns is the author of the best-selling book *Feeling Good: The New Mood Therapy*, which describes cognitive behavior therapy, a new approach to treating depression, anxiety, and personal relationship problems by addressing their roots in the way we think. *Feeling Good* was published in 1980 and was named one of the top ten behavioral-science books of the year by *Behavioral Medicine*. Dr. Burns has contributed his research findings in numerous scientific papers and chapters in professional books. He is a frequent lecturer to civic and professional groups around the country. He and his wife, Melanie, have two children and reside in Gladwyne, Pennsylvania.

Index

Ⓢ **SIGNET**   Ⓜ **MENTOR**

ROLES PEOPLE PLAY

(0451)

☐ **THE NEW MALE-FEMALE RELATIONSHIP by Herb Goldberg.** The best news since liberation: men and women *can* love each other! This thoughtful book reveals how men and women can enjoy relationships that are fulfilling, joyous, and challenging, where conflicts lead to growth and intimacy, where lovers can be best friends. "Excellent, valuable, informative."—*Kirkus Reviews*   (148401—$4.95)

☐ **THE HAZARDS OF BEING MALE: Surviving the Myth of Masculine Privilege by Herb Goldberg.** This breakthrough book about how American men are conditioned by society to play a role whose impossible demands psychically cripple and eventually kill them, does for men what women's lib is doing for women ... "A must!"—*Houston Chronicle*   (152174— $3.95)*

☐ **THE NEW MALE by Herb Goldberg.** The most important voice in male liberation today probes the inner workings of the macho mystique and provides a clear vision of how men can free themselves from hurtful stereotypes ... "Fascinating ... highly readable ... will find a wide and understanding audience!"—*Library Journal*   (093399—$2.95)

☐ **THE MYTH OF WOMEN'S MASOCHISM by Paula J. Caplan, Ph.D.** Is the victim to blame? In this groundbreaking book, a noted psychologist brilliantly refutes the false notion that women enjoy pain and demonstrates the real reasons why women remain in unhappy relationships. "Definative! Successfully debunks one of Freud's most damaging assertions."—*Ms. Magazine*   (147383—$3.95)

*Prices slightly higher in Canada

Buy them at your local

bookstore or use coupon

on next page for ordering.

Ⓞ **SIGNET**

FOR LOVERS ONLY

☐ **LOVE AND ADDICTION by Stanton Peele with Archie Brodsky.** This provocative book focuses on interpersonal relationships to explore what addiction really is—psychologically, socially, and culturally. "A rare book."—*Psychology Today*   (148606—$4.50)

☐ **MAKING LOVE: A MAN'S GUIDE by Whit Barry.** What a woman really wants ... and what makes it even better. The total guide for men to every stage of the lovemaking experience—and to a richer, more satisfying sexual life: Including new rules to turn the most intimate moments into the most arousing for her. Plus many more tips that every man should know to please a woman.   (153839—$3.95)

☐ **MAKING LOVE: A WOMAN'S GUIDE by Judith Davis.** What does a man *really* want, anyway? You'll find all the answers in this one book that tells you how to turn your man on, including 20 sure-fire turn-ons to seduce him so he stays seduced; scores of gloriously imaginative ideas in the art of making love memorable; the well-known secret that kindles the steamiest sensual thrills; plus much, much more. (149831—$3.95)

☐ **HOW TO LIVE WITH A MAN: Everything a Woman Needs to Know by Judith Davis.** Loving a man is not the same as living with one, and this warm, supportive no-nonsense guide shows you how to avoid the mistakes and solve the problems that can devastate your relationship, and how to deepen your joys and fulfillment.   (131762—$2.95)

☐ **WOMEN MEN LOVE/WOMEN MEN LEAVE: WHAT MAKES MEN WANT TO COMMIT by Dr. Connell Cowan and Dr. Melvyn Kinder.** From the best-selling authors of *Smart Women, Foolish Choices* comes this indispensible guide to the puzzling patterns of a man's needs, fears, expectations and—yes!—commitment. Learn how to be a woman a man loves—and stays with—forever.   (153065—$4.95)

Prices slightly higher in Canada

Buy them at your local bookstore or use this convenient coupon for ordering.

NEW AMERICAN LIBRARY
P.O. Box 999, Bergenfield, New Jersey 07621

Please send me the books I have checked above. I am enclosing $_____
(please add $1.00 to this order to cover postage and handling). Send check or money order—no cash or C.O.D.'s. Prices and numbers are subject to change without notice.

Name_____

Address_____

City _____ State _____ Zip Code _____
Allow 4-6 weeks for delivery.
This offer is subject to withdrawal without notice.